TWO WORLDS AND THEIR WAYS

TWO WORLDS
AND THEIR WAYS

by

I. COMPTON-BURNETT

LONDON
VICTOR GOLLANCZ LIMITED
1979

Copyright © 1949 by I. Compton-Burnett

ISBN 0 575 02610 3

First published 1949
Reissued 1952
Second reissue 1964
Third reissue 1979

Printed in Great Britain at
The Camelot Press Ltd, Southampton

CHAPTER I

"My dear, good wife!" said Sir Roderick Shelley.

The former replied without raising her head.

"The money subscribed divided by the number of subscribers gives you the average subscription. Twenty-four pounds, ten shillings and sixpence, divided by thirty-five. Would you do a sum like that in your head, Roderick? Or could you not do it at all?"

The latter expressed no opinion, indeed had none.

"Come, my pretty," he said.

"Fourteen shillings," said Maria Shelley, looking at him over her pencil. "Of course I am neglecting the pence."

Her husband repeated his words, neglecting the pounds and shillings also.

Maria gave him a smile and extended a hand in his direction, or gave the smile to herself and put a hand into space. He tapped a spoon on a saucer with more acquiescence than impatience, and rested his eyes on the scene beyond the window. His most satisfying vision was the flat, green land about his fading walls, and his only music the wind in his native trees sighing over the ground where he would lie. To be without it would be to be without a grave.

"Meals are such a waste of time," said his wife.

"Any congenial way of spending it tends to be called that."

"I wish we could do without them, or without so many."

"The wish is often fulfilled in your case."

"I only eat to keep up my energy."

"You attain your object. I am a person of a wider range."

"You are always boasting, Roderick."

"That may be as true of yourself."

5

"People who do not know us, might think we were disagreeing."

"So they might," said Sir Roderick, smiling. "And what kind of person would it take to know we were not?"

Maria's hand encountered the coffee-pot and closed on it. Her husband pushed a cup beneath it and pursued the uncertain stream, and as he withdrew it, tilted the spout to a safe angle. She gave him a glance at the suggested waste of energy, and filled her own cup before she put the pot down.

"Thank you, my pretty," he said, and stirred his cup.

Maria opened a letter and ignored her own. With her broad, massive frame, her crumpled, weatherbeaten face, her prominent, greenish eyes and the signs of fifty-three years, she was no one's pretty but Sir Roderick's; while the latter, with his unshapely figure, his slits of blue eyes, his fleshy features and a chin and neck more undefined than is usual at sixty-eight, was no one's pretty at all. He saw his wife as she was when he married her, sixteen years before, or at about that time had ceased to see her. She saw him as he was, and saw an engaging quality in him, that she believed was apparent to no one but herself, though it was the first thing that strangers noticed. He was aware of it himself, as he saw its effects, but was protected by his natural ease.

"Are you having no breakfast this morning, Maria?" he said, holding a spoon above a dish.

"I wonder why we still call them your sisters-in-law. Though I don't know what word we are to use. And we give enough advice to ourselves, or at any rate, I do."

"And have some over for other people. There does seem to be a fair supply."

"The most trying part of being a second wife is the existence of the first wife's family. I did not ask for their opinions, or if I did———"

"You did not mean you wanted them. Advice suggests that we ought to change, and why should we tolerate that?"

"I do not think I have ever followed their advice."

"It was necessary to increase the dose. And in its present strength it seems to be having some effect."

"You think you put things neatly, don't you, Roderick?"

"Yes," said the latter, with a smile.

"One would not think you would be able to express them at all."

"No," said Sir Roderick, as if seeing the truth of this.

"How did you come to have one sister-in-law who keeps a school, and another married to a man who keeps another? It does not seem to fit with you."

"I married into a different stock. I am a clod, a squire, a turnip, anything you please. Or nothing you please, I daresay."

"You are a very self-satisfied person."

"I have no great wish to improve. Perhaps that is what it means. But I have not much opinion of myself."

"I wonder if I have," said Maria, with an air of turning her eyes on herself, but actually turning them on her husband. "I wonder why two women wanted to marry you, Roderick."

"You must answer for one," said the latter, who knew the number was larger than this, and found it caused him no wonderment.

"She was much better-looking than I have ever been," said Maria, glancing at a protrait. "Would you call me plain?"

Sir Roderick looked at the face before him, and realised it was years since he had called it anything.

"You are yourself, my pretty. To me your face is your own."

"I wonder if a second wife often wishes she had known the first. I feel I should like to have a talk with her. But I am rather unlike other people."

"You are yourself," repeated her husband, not disputing this.

"I am glad my boy is a younger son. I want him to have

7

a life of personal effort. It is what I should choose for him."

"I hope he will like it as well as you do, as he will not have any choice."

"I never grudge Oliver's mother the place she left her son. I believe Sefton will go further."

"He probably will, and fare worse. If I had ten sons, I should like them to be elder sons. I have liked being one myself."

"Mary!" said Maria, in a meditative manner. "Mary Shelley. How familiar the name must have been to you! It is strange that she and I should have different forms of the same name, when we were to be different forms of the same thing; your wife, Roderick."

"It is a common name," said the latter, and said no more.

Maria gave him a look in which sympathy predominated.

"I can never bear to think of those years between your marriages. I cannot imagine what you did."

"My dear, good wife!" said Sir Roderick, not referring to his earlier marriage and only romance.

"You do not often look at her portrait. I suppose you can look at the one in your mind."

Sir Roderick was silent, finding he had looked at neither so often of late. He had ceased to speak of his first wife, not because her death had broken his heart, though it once had done so, but because the heart had mended.

"My dear, the past has its own life and its own death."

"It is said that it never does. But I suppose it gets old like everything else. Miss Petticott will miss the children, if we take this advice and send them to school."

"We can easily make up to her."

"We can impose demands on her time and patience. That is what they do. It will be harder to make up to ourselves. I wonder if they all know they are to have breakfast down here today."

"Has anyone told them?"

"They must know that workmen are repairing the wall of the schoolroom. The damp was coming through. Do

8

not be slow, my dear. Did Mary treat Oliver as I treat my children?"

"No. It was different."

"Was she fonder of him?"

"It was not quite that. She did not want to improve him."

"Perhaps there was less room for improvement when he was a child. How I talk like the ordinary stepmother! But it has been good of me to have her father in my house for all these years. Of course these letters are really addressed to you."

"Why 'of course', when you have read them?"

"The advice is meant for us both. I wish I could regard myself as exempt from it. I always read the letters and give you the gist of them. You will not read the writing."

"What is the good of writing that cannot be read? And why make the characters in Greek when you are writing in English?"

"I can read any writing as if it were print."

"People are proud of such trivial things," said Sir Roderick, interpreting the tone. "And the gift may have its danger."

"You and I have no secrets from each other. Indeed I have none from anyone. Have you any secrets, Roderick?"

"No," said the latter, after the pause of a man who, if he had secrets, would have them remain so.

"They think we are failing in our duty to our children. The curate at two about the charity sale. I wonder what makes me think of that."

"The sight of an envelope prompted you to make a note on the back."

"Well, remind me that the note is there. I shall be keeping the envelopes."

"Why should I remember what you will not, when it is your affair, not mine?"

"I have a great many things on my mind."

"And so have I. And their all going wrong does not make them any fewer," said Sir Roderick, frowning over

9

the problems of his estate, in which he could not command success.

Maria smiled over her own problems, in which she found she could.

"Well, how about these schools and the children?" she said, putting her pencil in the middle of an envelope, as though in observance of a correct course.

"I was never the better for education."

"You might have been, if you had had more of it. I daresay that is what the schoolkeepers think. And you do not know what you would have been without it."

"What I am now, as long as I had learned to read and write."

"What more did you learn?" said Maria. "They feel the children should go further. And you need not say 'and fare worse', as there is no likelihood of it."

"They want them in their schools for their own purposes. We want them in our home for ours. And as our stake is the larger, we have the right to decide."

"We must use it fairly. And I doubt if you have it, Roderick. You gave up your rights during your first marriage, and such things do not come back. But we will leave the matter for the moment. It may all look different presently."

"It will look the same to me. I never understand the effect of a different time on other people."

"Good morning, Sir Roderick; good morning, Lady Shelley. I suppose I should put the names in the other order. I am always impressing on Sefton the doctrine of 'ladies first', and then I fail myself on the first opportunity. Well, I suppose few of us practise what we preach."

"Good morning, Miss Petticoat," said Sir Roderick, with a movement of rising, that he did not complete.

The newcomer looked at the table, as though uncertain of her claims to what it afforded.

"I understood we were to have breakfast down here, Lady Shelley."

Maria gave a smile and gesture with her eyes down.

"Sit down, Miss Petticoat, sit down," said Sir Roderick, with a note of putting someone at ease, who might not be so. "Sit down and give us your opinion on a matter that concerns you as much as ourselves. The question is arising again of the children's leaving their home for school. Our connections cannot let it rest, and we are forced to the point of considering it. What help can you be to us?"

"Well, really, Sir Roderick, I had not thought of the matter. And perhaps I am hardly the person to be consulted. It might be thought to involve me too closely. Not that I should not despise myself, if I could not give an honest opinion. And I do see there is much to be said on both sides."

"Come, Miss Petticoat, you will not leave us. You are one of ourselves. My wife could not make a list or go to a meeting without you. And the children will always be having holidays, or being ill or expelled. We had no thought of a parting. Maria is upset at the bare idea."

"I have never had the idea, so that is not quite true," said the latter, putting down the letters. "Will you have a hot roll, Miss Petticott? They ought to be finished today—that is why my husband and I are struggling with them."

"Thank you, Lady Shelley; they make a nice change from toast. Not that that is not the best thing for every day. I say to the children, when they tire of it—" Miss Petticott broke off as Maria's attention failed.

"My dear, Miss Petticoat has no coffee."

Maria almost raised her eyes.

"My dear, Miss Petticoat has no coffee," said her husband in the same tone, as though a first appeal hardly qualified for success.

"Do you know you always pronounce Miss Petticott's name 'Petticoat'?"

"I pronounce it as it is said. Of course I know the name. What does Miss Petticoat say herself?"

"Oh, do not worry about it, Sir Roderick. It has quite a

nice, little, homely sound. I should quite miss my pet name," said Miss Petticott, hurrying past these words. "Not that it is meant in that way, of course; that is only my way of putting it. But I should quite miss the variation in the name, as you pronounce it. And I believe the derivation is not very different. The name is derived—" Miss Petticott again broke off, finding that inattentiveness, which she had encountered in her pupils, was a family characteristic.

"I shall take matters into my own hands, Miss Petticoat. I am not going to let you be neglected for another moment."

"Thank you, Sir Roderick. I do not know why I should be spoilt like this," said Miss Petticott, taking a rather full view of conventional attention. "I cannot say why the children are so late. I cannot explain it."

"They are puzzled by finding no breakfast in the school-room," said Maria. "If you would ring the bell in the hall, it will suggest that we are downstairs. They do little thinking for themselves."

"Allow me, allow me, Miss Petticoat," said Sir Roderick, keeping his eyes averted from Miss Petticott's progress to the door. "I do not know why our duties should devolve upon you."

The latter returned with the brisk steps of relief of mind. She saw every reason why duties should fall to her share, or saw the one reason, that they gave her her foothold in the house. She was a buxom, cheerful woman of forty-six, with cheeks of unvarying red, hair turning grey, bright, full, brown eyes, and features of the shapeless kind that involves so many shapes. She had the fewest wishes of any person in the house, indeed, had one wish, that she would have enough money for her old age; and this was eased by the hope that, if she remained long enough with the Shelleys, they would provide it.

Voices sounded on the stairs and Maria raised her eyes.

"The children are talking to Aldom again. I do not know how to prevent it."

"Neither do I, Lady Shelley, as you do not wish it to be forbidden."

"I can hardly wish that. There is nothing against their talking to him. But they talk to nobody else. I suppose they do need more companionship."

"I do my best for them, Lady Shelley."

"You do too much, Miss Petticoat. Do not give them another thought," said Sir Roderick. "The little ruffians prefer the servants' company. It is more on their own ground. They are all equally uneducated. I mean, you have not had time to get them up to your level. We hope they may reach it in the end."

A girl and boy entered and advanced to embrace their parents. They came to their father first, but he motioned them to pass him and give Maria the first greeting. They took no notice of Miss Petticott, an omission that neither she nor they nor anyone else observed. Sir Roderick's face lit up with affection and pride, Maria's with affection and pride and eager hope, Miss Petticott's with reflected light.

Both children resembled both their parents, but they showed less likeness to each other. Clemence looked her father's child, but her build was shapely and her own, and her features had a sharper mould. Sefton, still in a childish stage, already showed his mother's massiveness. His features seemed to be Maria's before life had changed them. They both had their mother's grey-green eyes, Sefton's the wider and more simply expressive. His sister's seemed a veiled and deeper edition of them, but when the veil was lifted, held their own light. There was something uncertain and wary about them, and while they hardly saw Miss Petticott, they saw their father often, and their mother whenever her eyes fell upon them or attracted theirs.

"Aldom says the walls of the house are rotten," said Sefton, in clear, conscious tones.

"I expect he said that the wall of the schoolroom had

13

some rot in it," said Maria. "Now is not that what he said?"

"Yes, I think it was."

"We must quote people correctly another time. That is only fair to them, isn't it? We must not give a wrong impression. Would you have waited upstairs until someone came to fetch you?"

"We thought the breakfast might come up. It is sometimes late."

"Not as late as this. You are a very dependent pair. Would you like to go somewhere where you would learn to rely more on yourselves?"

"No," said Sefton, his eyes changing.

"Go where?" said Clemence.

"Maria, say what you mean," said Sir Roderick. "Children do not need to have things made puzzling for them."

"Do they know what I mean?" said Maria, smiling.

"Oliver's aunts have written again," said Clemence, looking at the letters.

"They hardly need things to be made so easy," said Maria. "And what have Oliver's aunts to say, Clemence?"

"They want us to go to their schools."

"Well, they think it would be better for you."

"Then they ought to want it."

The parents laughed, Maria with an exultant note, and Clemence smiled and avoided their eyes. Miss Petticott saw their amusement and showed some herself.

"I think they feel a real concern," said Maria. "Indeed they show that they do. It is kind of them to take an interest in you."

"We don't want them to take it," said Sefton. "Wouldn't they be paid, if we went to their schools? Then it would be a good thing for them as well as for us."

"We do not talk about that side of things," said his mother.

"If you talk about one side of a thing and not the other, you only talk about half of it," said Clemence. "Would

14

they be paid as much for us as for children that were not related?"

"The same," said her father. "You need have no doubt on that score."

"Might it be better to go to people who were nothing to do with us?"

"You think that things would be less likely to be brought home, in more than one sense?"

"Well, that is what you think."

"What could Miss Petticott do, if we went?" said Sefton.

"How do you mean? Do?" said Maria.

"She would do less, and that might be good for her," said Sir Roderick.

"She would not leave us, would she? I mean, she would be here when we came home?"

"Now do you think we could spare her?" said Maria.

"No. That is why I wanted to know."

"We should want her in the holidays," said Clemence, feeling the need of one adult who made for ease.

"And we want her all the time," said Maria. "You are not the only people whom she is glad to help."

"They did not think they were," said Sir Roderick. "They were afraid of her having the feeling in too wide a sense."

"Well, you go and tell Miss Petticott how much you feel for her, and how glad you are that you can still depend on her," said Maria. "Come, that is not too much to do for someone who has done so much for you."

It was more than the children saw as within their power. Their code was rigid and immutable, and admitted of no breach. No word of sentiment, no gesture of affection escaped them. On the occasion of Miss Petticott's holiday they had recourse to manifold ruses to avoid what threatened to be an annual embrace. She accepted a position whose nature forbade change, and on this occasion rose to it. She got up and brought a hand down on a shoulder of each.

"Oh, we understand each other. We should not do any better for putting it all into words."

"But we ought to be able to express our feelings sometimes," said Maria. "A reluctance to do so really comes from thinking of ourselves."

"It would be hard to put an end to everything of which that may be said, Lady Shelley."

"Is it all settled then?" said Sefton, looking at his mother.

"No, no, my dear. We are only talking about it. But you are a boy, and Clemence is getting older. It seems that a change will have to come before long."

"You would not like always to be at home, would you?" said Sir Roderick.

"Yes," said Sefton, looking him in the eyes.

"My little son!" said Maria.

"Why isn't it a good thing always to be at home?" said Clemence with equal innocence.

"My little daughter!" said Maria.

A manservant, who had followed the children into the room, winked at them from behind the table. He was a small, insignificant man about thirty, with a sallow, crooked face, small, supple features that seemed to vary their form, and an oddly boyish look that suggested it would never leave him. His eyes watched the doings at the table from lowered lids, while his ears were always alive. He was the companion of Clemence and Sefton to an extent known only to Miss Petticott, who observed silence on matters beyond her control. He accorded her the easy respect that he saw as her due, but did not disguise his knowledge of his power. Some of it he used, and some he might not have known he possessed, as his sense of his obligations was not less, that he would not have acknowledged it.

"Where have you been, Aldom?" said Maria.

"Well, my lady, the workmen may not be any the worse for an eye upon them."

"Did they do any better?" said her husband.

"Well, Sir Roderick, they might have made more confusion than was the case."

"And did you help to make things right?"

"The moment was hardly ripe, Sir Roderick, some things having to get worse before they are better."

"You might as well have been down here," said Maria.

"Yes, my lady, though the day's routine may be none the worse for the exchange of a word," said Aldom, with a momentary exposure of eyes as blue as his master's.

"Well, you can attend to your work now."

Aldom carried a dish from the room, and Maria waited for the door to close.

"You should not exchange glances with Aldom, my dears. It is not a thing that is done by people who know how to behave. And to do it with a servant before your parents! Aldom himself would not think any more of you for it. And Miss Petticott must have been quite ashamed after the trouble she has taken with you. Do you think it is fair to her to do her so little credit?"

"I am glad I did not see it, Lady Shelley," said Miss Petticott, who was expert at avoiding such sights, and had not done much more than feel it. "I should have been as ashamed as you say."

"Well, we will not think any more about it, except to be sure it will not happen again. Go on with your breakfast, my dears. Do not hurry because there has been a mistake, that will soon pass from our minds."

Aldom returned and felt Maria's eyes, knew what had passed, and continued his duties with an air of being unconscious of it.

"My boy, attend to Miss Petticoat," said Sir Roderick to his son. "Keep your eye on her, and see she has what she needs. We shall think you do not look after her upstairs."

Sefton had seen the obligation as reversed, and passed Miss Petticott something in an unaccustomed manner, and found it received in a similar one.

"My little son!" said Maria, leaning forward to take his hands and look into his face.

Sir Roderick looked at Clemence, as though he might do the same to her, but went no further. Sefton remained with his eyes and smile fixed, until his mother released him and looked round the table.

"How nice it would be, if this were our family! I forget how different my life is from other women's."

"Why do you suddenly remember it?" said her husband. "You know I do not forget. It is not the least thing you have done for me."

"It has been a hard thing in my life," said Maria, who found little difficulty in revealing herself. "And it is not like something that is over and behind. It goes through the past and future. What do you think of it, Miss Petticott?"

"That it is so well done, Lady Shelley, that I did not know it went against the grain."

"I ought not to betray it. What is the good of undertaking a thing and then failing in it? And what a way to talk before the children! Not that there is anything that Clemence does not know."

"I knew you did not want Oliver and Grandpa here, when I was a child."

"And when was that?" said Sir Roderick, who had no aspirations for himself.

Maria made a warning gesture, and the subjects of the discussion entered the room, two large, dark men with heavy, aquiline faces, dark, heavy-lidded eyes, thick, white, noticeable hands, and such a likeness between them, that the discrepancy in years might have been the only difference. It was not a negligible one, as the dividing years were forty-eight.

Oliver Firebrace and his grandson, Oliver Shelley, were the former father-in-law and the elder son of Sir Roderick, the thorns in Maria's flesh, and the half-brother and adopted grandfather of Clemence and Sefton. Sir Roderick

18

had waited many years between his marriages, and his first wife's father had so long made his home in his house, that Maria, in the exaltation of her own romance, had suggested his retaining the place. He had accepted the offer and hardly modified his life; presumed on his knowledge of the past; given all his feeling to his grandson, and done no more for Maria's children than accept their adoption of their brother's name for him. Maria regretted her generosity, but enjoyed her husband's appreciation of it. Sir Roderick had a pitying tenderness for such creatures as aged men and children and women, and shrank from breaking his tie and, as it seemed to him, his faith with his earlier mate. He had no beliefs remaining, but could not rid himself of a feeling that she could observe him from some vantage-ground and approve or condemn his course.

Her son was the less to him, that he bore no deep resemblance to her. He was the less to Maria, that he bore none to his father, and had acquired a feeling that he meant rather little in his home. He was scarcely fifteen years younger than Maria, had dropped any filial mode of address, treated her as a friend, and on the whole found her such. She had a vein of humility that subdued her personal claims, and he had one of self-confidence that saved him from mistrust of himself. Maria had also a vein of justice, and though she regretted his existence and his grandfather's, never questioned their right to it.

Her life was dominated by her love for her children, and her desire for them to advance and impress their father rose to a passion and held its threat. Sir Roderick had no great feeling for personal success, but Maria had no suspicion that they did not see things through the same eyes. That her children should excel their brother in his sight was the ambition of her life and of her heart.

"So my governesses have written again," said Mr. Firebrace, looking at her letters. "I remember those envelopes in Oliver's youth. They wrote at the same time and never knew it. Laid their plans together and forgot to plan ahead.

A pair of simple women. You had the best of the three, Roderick."

"I was never in any doubt of it."

"They are anxious for Clemence and Sefton to go to their schools," said Maria, with a suggestion that the relations of the first wife had claims to make on the second.

"Peddling their wares! You would think they would have more opinion of themselves, when they hold their heads so high."

"One of the letters is from Oliver's uncle," said Sefton.

"An upright person and a worthy governess."

"He is a man and a schoolmaster, Grandpa."

"Well, that may be part of the truth."

"Miss Petticott is a governess."

"Good morning, Miss Petticott. I did not know you were here. It is your habit to be elsewhere. What does the boy mean by what he says of you?"

"He means that Miss Petticott is like anyone else," said Clemence. "And you seemed to think a governess was different."

"I was talking of the male of the species."

"The masculine of governess would be governor," said Sefton.

"There is no such thing, as Miss Petticott will tell you. Not that you do not show she has told you many things."

"I see what you mean, Mr. Firebrace. And you are right in a sense."

"Yes, yes. You are a sensible girl, my dear. And now what causes your pupils to mock at me?"

"They are amused by your calling me a girl, Mr. Firebrace."

"And you are not to them. Well, no doubt you would have them remember it."

"You went to your uncle's school, Oliver. I forgot that," said Maria. "Of course that was in its early days. But what would you say of it?"

"That I gave it nothing, and took what it had to give. I liked that, or I like looking back on it."

"Your uncle was a young man then," said Sir Roderick, "though he did not seem so to you."

"I despised him for his youth."

"He was over thirty," said Maria. "How do you feel about him now when he is sixty-two?"

"I pity his age."

"The prime of life is short according to your view."

"According to anyone's."

"Well, what did the school give you?" said Maria.

"It taught me to trust no one and to expect nothing," said her stepson, in his deep, smooth, rapid tones. "To keep everything from everyone, especially from my nearest friends. That familiarity breeds contempt, and ought to breed it. It is through familiarity that we get to know each other."

"I dislike that sort of easy cynicism."

"So do I, but because it is not easy. It is necessary, and necessity is the mother of invention. The hard mother of a sad and sorry thing."

"I wonder if you know what you mean. I certainly do not. Can you tell me plainly if you were happy at the school?"

"I learned to suffer, and that is the basis of happiness. It teaches the difference, which is the deepest of all lessons."

"I cannot think how you can be your father's son."

"I am my mother's son, and the nephew of her sisters, and her father's grandson. You see how I can be those."

"You are a family I do not understand. Do you understand them, Roderick?"

"Well, we are used to each other. And probably no one fully understands anyone else."

"My father spoke there," said Oliver. "I do sometimes hear his voice. It is partial understanding that carries danger. It suggests more than the truth."

"Which of your aunts do you like the better?" said Maria.

"I should like to prefer Aunt Lesbia, because of her esteem for herself. Most of us despise ourselves because we have such good reason, and admire other people because they cannot be as bad as we are. To admire oneself is a great sign of quality. But I find that Aunt Juliet is more to me."

"Do you admire yourself?"

"Be careful, Maria; I might dare to tell the truth."

"On which side?" said Sir Roderick.

"On either side. There my father spoke again."

"I do not admire myself so much," said Maria.

"Do not dare too far," said her stepson. "Beware of revealing what you do not admire. Other people might not admire it either."

"I do not see why they should."

"And neither would they. Be in no doubt about it."

"I am not in any doubt."

"You are in more than you know. Or have any right to be. We think our little failings have their own charm. And they have not. And they are great failings."

"I wish I knew whether to trust Sefton to your aunt and uncle."

"You cannot do that. You can put him into their charge."

"It does not seem a fair thing to do."

"It is not. The system is part of a great wrong."

"Are boys happier at home?"

"Well, I would not say that."

"Were you happier here?"

"Well, I had no mother. I was left to servants, and that is the best of all fates. I took everything from them and gave them nothing. It seems I have a habit of doing that."

"Were you happier after your mother died?"

"I ceased to give anything, and that was a burden lifted. But I have never got over it. No one has taken her place."

"You mean that I have not."

"That is what I mean."

"You would like her to be here instead of me and my children?"

"Well, I remember how I did like it."

"And you think your father would like it too?"

"I had not thought about him. My thoughts run on myself. And most people cannot relive the years. Only gifted people with empty lives can do so."

"And that is how you would describe yourself?"

"Well, you often talk of my empty hours. And my gifts are fluency, perception, music, an exotic charm."

"You mean that you think so?"

"No. That is what you mean."

"Well, should not they help to fill the hours?"

"They do fill them. They are only empty in a sense that does not count. Though I know that you count it. And now the little unspoken things are out between us. They might just as well not have been unspoken. And we shall have a better relationship, which is a pity, as we have had an easy one. I should hate things to go deeper between us."

"They are only out on your side."

"Maria, you sail under false colours. You are as dangerous as anyone else. Well, let that be our safeguard. Let those hidden things lie between us and keep us apart. It would be so awkward to come closer."

"The boy talks in his own way," said Mr. Firebrace.

"I never know what the two of you talk about upstairs," said Maria.

"If you did, the talk would not be upstairs," said Clemence, causing her parents to exchange a smile, or causing her mother to turn one on her father.

"We do not know either," said Oliver. "If we did, we should not talk. We should tell each other of matters, which would be quite different."

" 'Sefton' is a nice name, isn't it?" said Maria, on a sudden note of content, induced by the sight of her son.

23

"Is it a name?" said her husband. "I forget why we thought it was."

"It is the surname of my father."

"Had he no baptismal name to serve your purpose?" said Mr. Firebrace.

"It was Peter, and I do not like names of disciples."

"That does put a dozen out of court."

"Don't you like the name, 'Sefton,' Roderick?"

"It has come to suggest the boy to me. It has settled into its place."

"Who gave me my name?" said Clemence.

"I did," said her mother. "I named you both. It is a common name in my family. Your father could only suggest the name of 'Anne.' "

"It was my mother's name," said Sir Roderick, as if he supported the suggestion. " 'Clemence' has a flavour of your puritan background, or had before it took on its own meaning."

"Well, that is not a thing to be ashamed of."

"Father can hardly agree," said Oliver. "Disadvantages do not count in the woman he makes his wife, but they remain disadvantages. How otherwise can he arrange for them not to count?"

"I did not come to you empty-handed," said Maria. "The sober background prevented that. I do not see why we should not talk of money, if we can use it."

"If we could not, we could use nothing else," said Mr. Firebrace. "The position is not our choice."

"You would have to have a great deal of money, never to talk about it," said Clemence. "And I daresay none at all, never to think of it."

Maria sought her husband's eyes.

"Money is said to be power," said Miss Petticott. "But it seems to me a superficial view. And such power is often misused."

"Well, it is used," said Sir Roderick. "And we prefer that that should not be the case."

24

"So much of my money has gone into the place," said his wife. "Anything that the land takes, it never seems to return. I wonder if we should have been happier without it."

Sir Roderick gave her a dumb look and turned his eyes to the window. That he had put her on his land seemed to him the thing he had done for her. Her yielding it her money had been the fair return. As he asked himself what he had done, he knew he did not wish it undone.

"Ah, your life calls for gratitude as well as mine," said Mr. Firebrace. "And we neither of us give it. We should be more grateful to have no reason for it."

"We cannot have everything as we should choose," said Maria.

"No, that is so. I do not take another view."

"I do not have it myself."

"No, no. I know I am here, my dear."

"You are very ill-mannered, Grandpa. Speaking the truth from your heart," said Oliver. "You should speak half-truths with your lips like any other man."

"I do not know it was much more than half, my boy."

Sir Roderick gave a covert glance at his elder son, the only person to earn from him so uncharacteristic a thing. He knew he had suffered from his second marriage, had been superseded in his heart. He knew that his own compunction severed them further, that he had found himself wishing that Sefton was his heir. His homage to the past was the homage of the living to the dead.

"Are you looking back a score or two years, my boy?" said Mr. Firebrace, who liked to detect Sir Roderick in doing this.

"Well, not so much less than that. I was thinking of my Naboth's vineyard. That piece of land that I sold from the heart of the place," said Sir Roderick, whose thoughts reverted so readily to this, that he hardly had a sense of violating truth. "That farm where Aldom has his home. I was hoping that Oliver might buy it back one day."

"Or wishing that Sefton could," said Mr. Firebrace.

"Wishing he could himself," said Oliver. "Hoping that Maria would. I hardly know where the farm lies, or where to look for it. And I don't think I knew that the place had a heart."

"Oh, you are not my son," said Sir Roderick, saying the last thing he would have had himself say.

"That has been so since Sefton was born," said Mr. Firebrace. "But no one need be a thing twice over, and he has been mine."

"Aldom's mother wants to sell the farm," said Sir Roderick. "Or so Aldom tells me; I have never seen the woman. She wants to have a shop in the village. I live in fear that someone will buy it and put it from my reach."

"Why did you sell it?" said Oliver.

"Come, my boy, you can guess as much as that," said Mr. Firebrace.

"I wonder what it is like to lead a simple life with only one marriage involved in it," said Maria. "It is odd to think that most people have it."

"Your qualities would be wasted, if there was no demand on them," said her husband.

"I suppose they were wasted in Mary's case, if she had them. Well, it is no good to go on for ever."

"None at all," said Mr. Firebrace.

"Why did Father marry twice?" said Sefton.

"He got very fond of someone twice," said Maria.

"It is a good thing it did not happen with both at the same time," said Clemence.

"Shouldn't we be here, if the first wife had not died?" said Sefton.

"Of course not. Things are like that with second marriages. Anything that happens brings a lot of other things with it. And marriages do it especially."

"Thirteen and three-quarters," said Maria in a low tone. putting her finger-tips together and looking into space.

"Then is Father sorry we are here, glad that she is dead?"

"No, no, my little son," said Maria. "Having you makes up to him for what he lost."

"If you are sure of that, you are sure of all you need to be," said Mr. Firebrace.

"That is true," said Maria, meeting his eyes. "Now Lesbia and Juliet want to come on a visit next week. I must write and say they will be welcome."

"And not the other governess?"

"Lucius will come with Juliet, if that is what you mean."

"Then we shall have four with Miss Petticott. And only one genuine example among them."

"I hope I am that one, Mr. Firebrace?" said Miss Petticott, almost with archness.

"Yes, yes, that is so. I never mind the real thing."

"You children may run upstairs now," said Maria, willing for a withdrawal that included Miss Petticott. "We have had two pairs of eyes fixed on us long enough. And what has been happening to two pairs of ears, I do not dare to think."

Miss Petticott rose and clapped her hands to marshal her pupils, and withdrew the third pair of eyes and ears with deliberation and ease. She allowed a group to gather on a landing without appearing to notice it. It consisted of her pupils, their nurse and Aldom, who had left the dining-room with an air of sudden purpose. The four voices, full and clear and with an undeniably similar note, followed her to the schoolroom, but she had learned when eyes and ears should cease to function.

"So school is in the wind again," said Aldom. "I am glad I cannot be sent to right and left at other people's will. I belong to myself."

"And to Sir Roderick and her ladyship, while you are in this house," said Adela. "And you can be sent where they like, as far as I can see. And you will soon be sent for to the dining-room. What do you think you are?"

"A prince in disguise," said Aldom.

"Well, the disguise goes deep enough."

"And are you a princess, Adela?" said Sefton.

"No. Servants are as good as anyone else," said Adela, disposing of any need for the flight of fancy.

"Well, no one seems to know it," said Aldom.

"Well, you would not expect them to act up to it, if you have noticed anything."

Adela was a lively, healthy-looking woman of thirty-five, with interested, busy eyes, a confident cast of feature, and an independent mien that could be decorous. She was one person with the children, another with their parents, with Miss Petticott a third, and with Aldom herself, though through all the characters went something of the same essence.

Aldom had two characters, of which one was his own. Whether or no he was a prince in disguise downstairs, he was someone in disguise.

"I expect we can do as we like about going to school," said Clemence, swinging her feet from a window-seat.

Sefton looked at her in question.

"Then you will stay at home," said Adela. "So we shall see if that is the truth."

"One begins to look at the matter all round. There is more than one side to everything."

"She has come on since I first knew her," said Adela, looking at Aldom.

"As is natural, as that was thirteen years ago," said Clemence.

"He is still a little boy," said Adela, putting her arm round Sefton.

"Oh, look at the love," said Aldom.

"It seems a shame to send a child like him away from his home."

Sefton proved his agreement by showing some emotion.

"There, there, perhaps it won't happen. I don't feel as if it would," said Adela, successfully checking it.

"You won't say anything to Mother or Father to make them send us," he said to Clemence.

"No, I shall just let matters take their course."

"He is going to school at eleven. I left school then," said Aldom. "It was nearly twenty years ago, in the year eighteen hundred and seventy-five. I had gone as far as was required."

"Oh, you!" said Adela, not accepting any parallel.

"And how far had you gone?"

"We left in the end, wherever we were," said Adela, leaving anything incidental to be inferred. "I never could see that schoolbooks led to anything. They are nothing to do with life, and it is life we are concerned with, not the records of what it used to be. And why send the two at the same time, when one of them is three years older?"

"Clemence is a girl," said Aldom.

"You should really call me 'Miss Clemence.'"

"Oh, the grandeur!" said Adela. "Not that you shouldn't, Aldom. I wonder how you think of yourself."

"I told you as a prince in disguise."

"You would not say 'Clemence,' if Mother or Father were here."

"Well, we shouldn't, any of us, be quite the same then," said Adela. "I daresay you are not the same in the dining-room as you are up here. What would you say, Aldom?"

"Well, you might not say that I was the same then either."

"The prince is even more disguised," said Clemence. "I expect we shall get to be more the same, if we go to school."

Sefton looked at her with trouble in his eyes at her acceptance of the threat to their lives.

"So you are going to leave us behind, are you?" said Adela.

"Well, of course, our position is different."

"The person whose position I should not like, is Miss Petticott," said Adela. "I would rather be one thing or the other, and know where I stood."

29

"I don't find knowing it such an advantage," said Aldom. "I would not mind its being a little less to the fore."

"I wish we could always go on in the life we know," said Sefton. "We have not learned what to do in any other."

"It may be time you did," said Aldom. "Changes must come. I may get to be known for what I am."

"I should think that is taking place," said Adela. "If it has not already done so."

"Are you really something we don't know?" said Sefton.

"I am the general man, called by courtesy the butler. And not always so much courtesy either."

"Oh, Father and Mother are much better than most people," said Clemence.

"And quite right that she should think so," said Adela, looking into Aldom's eyes. "And I am not saying it is not the case."

"Well, I mightn't be better than they are, in their position."

"Are you better now?" said Sefton.

"Well, I am a useful person, ready to soil my hands."

"So that is what he thinks of himself," said Adela.

"Trial by ordeal," said Clemence.

"What is that?" said Adela. "And where have you got hold of it?"

"Oh, one hears all sorts of things between daybreak and dusk."

"It is my belief that most of what she says, comes out of her own head."

"It is talking to Mr. Oliver," said Aldom. "That gives her an opportunity. But it may be better for her to go where there are more and different."

"And what do you know about what is better for her? Children do not need to get old before their time. And what does she want with common knowledge? She is not in the position of Miss Petticott. It would only reduce her level."

A step sounded on the stairs, and a change took place in the atmosphere that was almost tangible.

"No, Miss Clemence, this is a different sort of wall. No damp could come in here," said Aldom, in an instructive tone. "You see, the bricks are not just painted. They are covered with cement."

"Do you understand now, Master Sefton?" said Adela, in an almost severe manner.

"Yes," said Sefton, in a tone of just coming to this point.

"A lesson in building?" said Maria, smiling as she reached them. "But what about the other lessons that are waiting? And Miss Petticott waiting too! This is not the way to prepare for school."

"Poor little things! To have that thrown at them, whatever they do or say!" said Adela, looking after them. "When I was their age, I was welcome under my father's roof."

"I don't know that I was," said Aldom. "My father did not do much for me."

The children certainly had a feeling of hardly being this, as the day wore on, and the idea of exile sank into their minds. The feeling was heightened by the necessity of having meals where their presence seemed superfluous, if not unsuitable. Tea at an earlier than their usual hour enhanced the position, especially as Maria appeared reluctant to assume the duties involved. She stood in the hall with a list in her hand, and her mind distracted by something that eluded it.

"Is her ladyship coming to make the tea, Aldom?"

"I cannot say, Sir Roderick," said Aldom, glancing through the door, and then applying a light to the lamp under the kettle, a duty that Maria saw as her own. "She is within sight and hearing."

"And might be a thousand miles away."

"Not as far as that," said his wife, coming suddenly into the room, and at once going to the lamp to reverse the arrangements. "The kettle here and the lamp underneath it, Aldom. Not here and here, so that half the heat is wasted. I have explained that before."

"Yes, my lady."

"There would be nothing else except expenses and enough refreshments to prevent any feeling," said Maria, letting go her pencil and holding out her hand for Aldom to restore it, and bringing her eyes to rest on Miss Petticott as the likely source of attention.

"I do not know who is to have that," said Sir Roderick, "but we do not appear to be among them."

"You do not have things always going on in your head."

"And I do not wish to. A free mind makes an alert, attentive person."

"Would you describe yourself as that?"

"I have done so."

Maria took up the teapot and smiled at the faces round her.

"One, two, three, four, five, six cups to be filled before I reach my own! And though I may not be an attentive person, I happen to be a thirsty one. What would you all do without me?"

"We should fill the cups," said her husband. "And what is to happen with us with you, I do not know."

"Do not lose your sense of proportion. Tea is not such an important thing."

"It is the need of all of us at the moment. Your own as well."

"Pray, let me pour out the tea for you, Lady Shelley," said Miss Petticott.

"No, I must not shirk the duties of my place."

"That is the feeling of us all," said Sir Roderick.

"Of course not, Lady Shelley. I did not mean to usurp those. Indeed, it would not be possible. I only thought I might save you trouble."

Maria smiled and handed her her cup.

"Now, why should I come first, Lady Shelley? I refuse to drink my tea until you have had yours."

Maria filled the other cups, supplied her own and sat in disregard of it, and incidentally in disregard of Miss Petticott. Sir Roderick drank with relief and without compunction, and looked towards the teapot.

"Some more tea, Roderick?"

"Thank you, my pretty."

Miss Petticott indicated Maria's cup.

"Some more tea, Miss Petticott?"

"Lady Shelley!" said the latter, still pointing.

Maria moved a hand towards her cup, but allowed it to waver and receive her stepson's, and Miss Petticott sat back in her chair.

"Aldom," said Maria, "what do you think we should want at this stage, being the number of people that we are?"

"Fresh tea, my lady?"

"Then might you not bring it to us?"

Aldom left the room.

"Now, Miss Petticott," said Maria, when the tea was brought.

Miss Petticott handed her cup in simple resignation.

"You are incorrigible, Lady Shelley."

"Now, my girl and boy. Now Roderick again and Oliver."

"And now Lady Shelley," said Miss Petticott. "We have earned it. Do not play us false."

Maria drained her cup, replenished it and drained it again.

"Suppose I were to desert you all," she said, looking over it. "What would you do?"

"Why do people say such things?" said Oliver. "At the moment we should be doing what we are now."

"I cannot help imagining it sometimes," said Maria, with a sigh for the picture evoked.

"We are not ungrateful, my pretty."

"Why does Father call Mother that?" said Sefton.

"He got into the way of it when they were younger," said Miss Petticott, in a low, explanatory tone. "And he has never given it up. There are often little habits like that between happily married people."

"Then isn't she pretty any longer?"

"That is not for me to say. No doubt she is pretty to him," said Miss Petticott, looking nowhere in particular with distending eyes.

"Then you don't think she is pretty?"

"She has not asked me what I think."

"But the boy has," said Mr. Firebrace, with enjoyment.

"I cannot answer him. He is old enough to know that."

"What do you think yourself, Mother?" said Clemence.

"I am pleasant to look at. I was never any more."

"Thank you, my dear," said Sir Roderick, extending his cup.

"And now, Miss Petticott," said Maria.

"No, thank you, Lady Shelley, no more," said Miss Petticott, with a sense of retaliating for personal discomfiture.

"Come, change your mind, Miss Petticoat," said Sir Roderick. "Do not leave me drinking alone."

"Well, in that case, Sir Roderick."

"I suppose the children are not going to school this time any more than at any other?" said Mr. Firebrace.

"This time seems to be different," said Maria. "I suppose the day must come."

"I used to suppose it until I perceived it was not the truth."

"Do you want to be rid of them?"

"I have no feeling on the matter. The idea did not come from me. The question is whether you do."

"It is whether it is best for them. Your daughters think it is."

"I should pay them no heed. They have to gain their bread."

"What do you think, Miss Petticott?" said Oliver.

"That does not bear on the matter either, Mr. Shelley, and so has no point in being thought, if I may express it as

34

the children would. And I do agree that Sefton is a boy, and that Clemence is getting older."

"Well, yes, so do I," said Oliver.

"It may sound an obvious thing to say, but it has its own truth as obvious things so often have."

"I should have thought it had only ordinary truth."

"Well, truth of any kind should be enough for us, Mr. Shelley."

"Oh, who has taken the last jam tart?" said Maria in rallying reproach.

Sefton restored the tart to the dish.

"But what can we do with it now that those grubby hands have been over it?"

Sefton resumed possession of the tart.

"Did you ask Miss Petticott if she would like it?"

Sefton looked uncertain whether to proffer it at this stage.

"I could not eat any more, Lady Shelley."

"But conventions should be observed. Sefton must remember another time."

The latter began to eat the tart, uncertain what other course to take.

"It is nice?" said his mother, with the same touch of reproach.

"Yes."

"You do not sound very sure about it?"

This was natural, as Sefton was eating the tart without tasting it, in his desire to be rid of it and be at ease.

"So it has gone," said Maria, in the same manner. "It did not take long, did it?"

"No."

"My dear, the boy must have his tea," said Sir Roderick. "And surely the morsel has played its part."

"'The evil that things do, lives after them,'" said Clemence.

"How many tarts were there in the dish?" said Maria. "Did you happen to notice, Miss Petticott?"

"Well, I actually did, Lady Shelley. They were arranged in a pattern. Five pairs and one in the middle."

"Very good taste," said Oliver.

"Did you have one, Roderick?"

"No, they did not come my way."

"Did you, Miss Petticott?"

"No, Lady Shelley. But I had quite enough without them. I could not have managed any more."

"I had two," said Oliver, "and so did Clemence."

"Then Sefton had seven. Really, Sefton, you should pass things to other people, and not just sit in front of them and despatch them yourself."

Clemence and Sefton laughed at the phrase, and Maria looked faintly gratified.

"Where is the boy to sit, if not at the table?" said Sir Roderick.

"He should remember there are other people there. I am afraid he does not get much discipline upstairs."

"He behaves very nicely, Lady Shelley," said Miss Petticott. "He always does as he is told."

"He waits to be told. I suppose that is it."

"He did not think of passing the things on this table," said Clemence. "He thought they were nothing to do with him. He is not used to being down here."

"Is that it, my little son? Come and give your mother a kiss," said Maria, holding out her arms.

Sefton went and stood within them. Sir Roderick beckoned to Clemence and accommodated her in the same way. Mr. Firebrace and Oliver rose one accord, linked their arms and danced to the door, keeping in step with each other. Miss Petticott's were the only eyes that followed them.

"A queer household, Miss Petticoat?"

"Well, it is individual, like all households, Sir Roderick. We should not like them without their little idosyncrasies. It would take from the variety and zest of life. The world would be a poorer place."

The children remained in their parents' embrace, uneasy in it, willing to escape, but feeling its safety in view of the menaced future. When release came, Sefton went at once to the door.

"Go after him and comfort him, Clemence," said Maria. "He is upset by being convicted of greediness."

"By being accused of it," said Sir Roderick. "What would you have a boy do with the food in front of him?"

"I do not want him to be a copy of other boys. But no doubt they will make him so. He will be spoiled; both of them will. But I suppose it cannot be helped."

"Of course it can," said her husband, his eyes following his daughter. "There is no need for them to leave their home."

Maria saw his look and knew she had given him the first thing in his life, knew too that she had never held the place. She gave a sigh, honest, discouraged, resigned, and Sir Roderick heard it and bowed to fate.

"I will go and attend to my flock, Lady Shelley," said Miss Petticott. "I have a feeling that they are in need of their shepherdess."

"Yes, go and make things comfortable for them, Miss Petticoat," said Sir Roderick.

Miss Petticott mounted to the schoolroom, now restored to its normal use. Sefton was standing by the table with emotion on his face. Clemence regarded him with easy sympathy, and Adela, sunk in the armchair on the hearth, with question.

"I hope we are not to have supper downstairs," he said.

"It would be the most dangerous of all the meals," said his sister. "It would be dinner, and we should be particularly unworthy of it."

"Well, I expect you will have it up here," said Miss Petticott, taking a chair with a glance at the one in use. "And our manners may be the better for a touch of polish. Perhaps we are sinking too much into our own groove."

Adela indicated her lap to Sefton, but as it was not

37

accepted, had no choice but to rise and yield the seat.

"Thank you, Adela," said Miss Petticott, taking it as something that was due.

"Children are better in their own quarters, ma'am."

"That does seem to be so. But they must learn to be happy and easy anywhere. Miss Clemence is getting older."

"I wonder why people are so struck by that in my case. It must be a common thing."

"To hark at her!" said Adela. "She does not need to be hurried forward. And she will never have to fend for herself."

"She will have to do other things. And going to school may be the right beginning."

"It is the beginning of the end," said Clemence.

"Now what do you mean by that?" said Adela.

"What I may."

"I don't think she needs so much school to help her."

"We shall have to be brave, you and I, Adela, and put ourselves in the background. What is best for the children is best for us. That is how we must see it."

"There are places I like better than a background, ma'am. And I am not so sure about its being best. It may not amount to that."

Sefton took a book and leaned back and crossed his legs. Adela spoke to Clemence with an elaborate movement of her lips, and enough sound coming from them to render the pantomime meaningless.

"Did anything go wrong downstairs?"

"Something about a plate of tarts. Nothing that meant anything."

"Well, I should hope he is allowed to help himself at the table in his own home!"

"I had seven," said Sefton, looking up to throw light on the matter.

"To think of him! Doing that of his own accord! And everyone's eyes on him! And him not downstairs above once or twice a year!"

"It was Mother's eyes that were on me," said Sefton, with a hint of a smile.

"And they are not coming on fast enough at home."

"Come and sit here, Sefton, and have a luxurious hour," said Miss Petticott, rising from her chair. "I am going to my room for a time."

Miss Petticott had hardly closed the door, when it opened to the sound of Maria's voice.

"Oh, who has taken the best armchair for himself?"

There was scarcely a pause before Adela spoke.

"And who shows he doesn't dare to meet the governess? That doesn't suggest the character that is intended."

Sefton drew a breath, and Clemence sprang on to the table and swung her legs as though from a rash height.

"Aldom, do the scene at the inn, when you fetched your father from the supper," said Sefton.

"And not too many of the words, with Miss Clemence here," said Adela. "She won't have to get used to what you had to."

"*Miss* Clemence all of a sudden!"

"And time you said it, being what you are, a man and not of any age."

The children stood, absorbed in the scene. Adela sat with her mouth open in mingled interest and lack of it. It held its own until it seemed to sustain a sudden shock. A change seemed to shiver through it. The innkeeper spoke with another voice, lived and moved as another man. Clemence and Sefton glanced at each other and the door.

"A scene from the village school?" said Maria. "What a life-like master!"

"Yes, my lady," said Aldom, with a sheepishness that involved acting equal to any he had shown.

"And what put that into your heads?"

"They have heard some talk about school, my lady," said Adela, in bustling explanation. "And that set their thoughts running on the line. And Aldom is something of a mimic and was a character when he was at school."

Maria did not question the account, being unaware of the duration of this period.

"It was something of Master Sefton's, my lady, that I was mending for him. And my memory having played me false, I have come up without it," said Aldom, naturally looking rather distraught, as his memory was doing him even less service than he said.

"I think some people need a good deal of amusing," said Maria, with her reproachful note, and no thought that in this case her children might hardly be provided for. "And I think we must all go about our duties. Aldom can bring the toy another time. It was kind of him to mend it, but he will be late in setting the dinner."

"Not beyond what a little haste will obviate, my lady, it being possible to put out an effort even at the end of the day."

"Where is Miss Petticott?" said Maria, seeming not to hear.

"She went to her room for something," said Clemence, giving the impression of a transitory errand.

"And has found the something and brought it down with her, and here it is!" said Miss Petticott, holding up an atlas in the doorway, her ear having caught Maria's step on the stairs. "And now a gap in our life can be filled, and a hiatus can disappear, and all those things can happen that I have been desiring for some time. I am a happy and contented woman."

"Can you come downstairs and help me with these envelopes, Miss Petticott? I seem to have got behind. It is so difficult to keep up with everything."

"Certainly, Lady Shelley. I am always glad of a little occupation at the end of the day, when the real work is done," said Miss Petticott, holding her hands as if their idleness were a source of discomfort to her.

"I hope we give you enough time to yourself," said Maria, feeling that the expression of the hope was a substitute for its fulfilment, and finding it so accepted.

"Aldom in the schoolroom! I suppose we cannot do anything. I hope it does not often happen."

"No, not too often, Lady Shelley. And only in the most casual way. Just a man's line of interest or a piece of instruction that I cannot give. I am a woman and Sefton is a boy, and it is surprising how early the difference asserts itself."

"Clemence is a girl; that is our problem," said Maria, accepting a gulf between Miss Petticott and her son. "I suppose the change will have to come, though it breaks my heart."

"Indeed, Lady Shelley, it almost breaks mine. I shall find myself living for the holidays, when my work will begin."

"We shall find some for you at the other times. Never fear."

"Then I will not, Lady Shelley. I will depend on you. I know you are a person to be trusted."

Adela and the children confronted the fact that danger had approached and passed.

"Mother might have heard the drunken talk," said Sefton, in an awed tone.

"Well, she did not; so we need not build up on that."

"She might have asked what the toy was."

"Well, she knew what no one else did, that it was a toy. She did not need to ask so much."

"And Aldom could have told her, though we could not," said Clemence. "And the Petticoat is a great support. When she cannot help things, she shuts her eyes to them. And she might do worse."

"The Petticoat! So that is the latest."

"We often called her that, when we were young."

"Oh, did you? Then it is your proper nickname for her," said Adela, in a serious tone.

"We even said it to her face," said Sefton.

"Most children nickname the governess," said Clemence.

"And I should like to know how much you know about most children."

"What we hear and what we read, and what we know by the light of nature, and our own light."

Adela's silence did not challenge this account.

"Oh, is that the way we talk about Miss Petticott, who has been so kind to us?" said Maria's voice. "Now suppose we tell her about all we feel for her."

"Now that is enough," said Adela. "There must be an end to cleverness when it is all of one kind."

"Go on with the talk at the inn, Aldom," said Sefton, who reacted swiftly from emotion that was past.

"Mother and the Petticoat will be closeted together for some time," said Clemence.

"Yes, that is the newest thing," said Adela, "and they are supposed to have done it all the time."

"Well, so they have, off and on."

"Clemence told you, Adela," said Sefton.

"Poor old Petticoat!" said Clemence.

"So it has come to stay," said Adela, "whether it was here before or not."

"Are we expected to go down to dinner?" said Clemence.

"Hark at her! Expected to go! So they can't do without them all of a sudden."

"No, your supper will be brought up here," said Aldom. "What is wrong with the room now?"

"Then go on with the scene, Aldom," said Sefton. "There is time before Miss Petticott comes back."

"The Petticoat, if you please," said Adela. "Pray let us have it right, if we have it at all."

The children resumed their survey of the scene, became involved in it, and finally relieved Aldom of two of the parts. Adela sat between them and the door in the combined capacity of sentinel and spectator. As the excitement waxed, precautions waned; Adela allowed one character to supersede the other; the open door did its work. Maria stood on the threshold with Miss Petticott behind, the latter's relief that she had not been in charge, the only enviable feeling on the occasion.

"Well, what a commotion for two small people to make!" said Maria.

The children felt a shock they did not define. Was the protagonist to be passed over? Was their behaviour beyond the pale of words? Was he himself struck dumb, petrified, dissolved by shock? The last appeared to be the case; Aldom was no more; and advantage might be taken of it before the long grief supervened and held its course. And Adela's voice was her own.

"They get excited, my lady. They were acting a scene. It is what they learn with Miss Petticott that puts it into their heads. I got quite lost in it, sitting and watching them."

"They had the door wide open," said Maria, taking this safeguard of guilt as a proof of innocence. "We heard the noise and could not think what it was. I suppose it is a sort of play. Go on from where you were, my dears; and if it is good enough, I will bring Father up to see it."

The children cast about in their minds for words—of Aldom's, of Shakespeare's, of Miss Petticott's—to meet the need; took a step towards Maria and uttered some sounds, and looked at Miss Petticott with their hearts in their faces.

"Oh, come, Lady Shelley, you do not know how sensitive we are about our artistic efforts. I am afraid self-conscious is the word, but that is no help, as we cannot get away from ourselves. We must accept the artistic temperament and take what it has to give us in its own good time. It is a tax on patience, but we do not make such demands on you in vain."

"Well, I will be patient, though I do not think the noise I heard, quite bears out that view. Thank you for all your help, Miss Petticott. Good-night, my little shy actor and actress."

The children received the caress with as much consciousness as could have resulted from any dramatic gift. Miss Petticott followed Maria to the staircase and engaged her in talk, bringing her pencil down at intervals on some papers in her hand. Her eyes remained on the papers as she retraced her steps, so that a figure that flashed from behind the sofa to the stairs, escaped her notice.

"Well, you are a nice pair," she said to her pupils. "Keeping your artistic efforts for when I am away, instead of giving me the benefit of them! I shall not expect such scurvy treatment another time. I feel I have deserved better at your hands." The pupils had something of the same feeling. "And I should not act any more tonight. Miss Clemence is flushed, Adela, and Sefton is pale, and you are rather pale yourself. I recommend a rest to you all, before you go to bed. And I expect my advice to be followed."

CHAPTER II

"I HAVE COME to offer you myself," said Lesbia Firebrace, as she mounted the Shelleys' steps. "Because I have nothing else to offer. When people say that, they are content with their offering and expect other people to be."

"This is, indeed, a pleasure, Lesbia," said Sir Roderick, with a simple air of welcome.

"It is good of you to find it so, Roderick," said Miss Firebrace, her simplicity so well-matched as almost to suggest something else.

"My dear, you are welcome, welcome," said Mr. Firebrace, pressing forward and displacing the host, indeed seeming to assume the character. "You are in your father's home again. I wish it were that to you, but things must be as they are. I have been looking to this day; I can do that under any roof."

Miss Firebrace's filial greeting seemed hardly to accord with her grey head and experienced face. She was a small, odd-looking woman of sixty, with small, clear, grey eyes contrasting with a sallow skin, features that, like the rest of her, seemed to conform to some standard of her own, and sparse, iron-grey hair worn short at a time when the fashion carried some meaning. In her case it was an outcome of illness, that she had not troubled to rectify, but she accepted any significance read into it as an enhancement to her personality. This was a thing to which she gave attention, though she had not created it, merely rendered it its due.

Her sister was a plainer, feminine counterpart of her father and nephew. She followed with the air of the secondary character, that she clearly fulfilled in her family and in her father's sight. He greeted her with equal affection, but without any touch of deference, a distinction that had become established. She had an air of being clever, complacent and dissatisfied, and was all these things and would have denied none. Her complacence, like all her qualities, was real, and as deeply rooted in her as in the rest of her family. Oliver's mother had been between the two sisters in age, and had been the dearest to her father, or been rendered so by death, a state less grudging of advantages than of the opportunity to enjoy them. Her sisters accepted this view of her life, seeing it as mild compensation for losing it.

Juliet's husband followed her, tall and upright and a person apart, and also evincing the slight humility of mien. He had a Grecian profile, thin, silver hair, and ice-blue eyes so honest that they seemed to hold some menace. His name of Cassidy seemed to have arisen out of himself.

Mr. Firebrace gathered them about him, put his arms about the women, marshalled his grandson to the front of the group, and fulfilled his part as a patriarch ordering his family. The pathos of his life was clear at the moment of its passing.

"I feel I am a guest in my own house at these times," said Maria to her husband.

"Well, they are guests in other people's, and that is not so good. And it is the old man's moment. He was once in this house in a different place."

"It must bring it all back to you, Roderick. I can see you are living in the past."

"I live in the past and in the present, as all reasonable people must. The past is in us, and the present with us," said Sir Roderick, with his not infrequent sense of surprise at himself.

"If you are not the host, you are nothing in your own home."

"Well, that is easy, and I am equal to it. We should all be able to be nothing there. More is asked of people who are something anywhere else."

"Here is scope for you, Maria," said Oliver. "It is a

46

great position. You can show all the deep and subtle qualities that generally escape notice. I wish I had such an opportunity."

"You might make use of it, and so miss it," said Lesbia.

"Perhaps I should. It is that touch of the actor about me."

"We cannot have passed over our hostess in making our greetings," said Lesbia, coming towards Maria. "That is not a possible thing, and it is fortunate that it is not."

"Maria gives you a real welcome," said Sir Roderick.

"Lesbia, Juliet, Lucius, Mr. Firebrace, Roderick, Oliver," said Maria, handing the teacups as she filled them.

"We are too many," said Lesbia. "It neutralises the inconvenience of a large party, for someone to say they are too many."

"I am not at my ease," said her sister, "shocking thing though that is. It is not that I cannot take kindness; I am rather fond of taking it. But I have not the grace that can accept. Neither has Lucius, but people assume that he has. I appear to take everything for granted."

"I hope you do so in this house," said Sir Roderick.

"But I do not. I am trembling with gratitude and a sense of presuming on the past."

"I always feel that my family and I ought not to be here at these times," said Maria.

"Well, neither ought you," said Lesbia, in her soft, almost mysterious tones. "It was all complete without you, even to the blank caused by death. You have added to the finished picture, which is known to be a mistake. But the addition is always worth while in itself."

"That is why the temptation to make it is never resisted," said Oliver.

"I was not a conscious artist in the matter," said Maria.

"Well, art is instinctive," said Lesbia.

"The impulse in matters of this kind commonly is," said Mr. Firebrace to his grandson.

"Father seems to have forgotten how to speak to anyone but Oliver," said Juliet.

"Well, that is no wonder, my dear. My memory in the matter has not had an easy time."

"My children must feel superfluous in their own home," said Maria.

"What harm does that do?" said her stepson. "Whatever it is, I have always suffered it."

"We had your letters about them, Lesbia," said Sir Roderick.

"I have no doubt you did. People always have letters. They never really go astray. But I was not thinking of your children at the moment; I was thinking of myself, improper though it is."

"I am sure you meant the advice for the best," said Sir Roderick, not concealing the tendency of his own thought.

"Yes, Roderick, we did," said Lesbia, in a sudden, impressive tone. "We were thinking of the children's welfare. And who is more qualified to do that? Children's welfare is the object of our lives."

"My children's welfare has that place in mine. It is simply a more concentrated feeling."

"Clemence has had no experience outside her own home. This house is the bound of her universe."

"And long may it be so," said the father.

"Of course we are not asking for pupils," said Juliet. "It is not conceivable, and that is a good thing. People might form the conception."

"Are you thinking of yourself or of Clemence, Roderick?" said Lesbia, in a neutral manner.

"Of myself, improper though it is," said Sir Roderick, with triumph in his tone. "I like to have my girl at home; I like her to think of me and not of other people; I like to keep her feeling and not share it. In other words, I have the only kind of affection for her that is worth having or worth giving."

"To be with Roderick must be a liberal education," said Juliet.

Maria's eyes rested on her husband, as though questioning if this could be the case.

"Is there not a good deal of simple selfishness in the feeling?" said Lesbia, in a tone of taking a purely theoretic view.

"Of course there is, or it would not be the kind worth giving," said Sir Roderick. "How do you separate a personal feeling from yourself?"

"I believe it is the only kind," said Juliet. "When people love other people better than themselves, it means that they are prepared to give them up, or not to see them for their own sakes, or do something else that shows indifference."

"A good definition of sending people to school," said Sir Roderick.

"I am arguing against my own advantage. No wonder Lucius is looking at me. I am almost on his plane."

"Might it not be better for them to go to schools kept by strangers?"

"Yes, Roderick, that might be better," said Lesbia, in a quiet tone, that yet had a faintly scolding note. "It would be necessary to look at the matter from all its sides."

"What difference would it make to them to go to connections?" said Maria. "If one thing is better than the other, there must be some difference."

"Well, we should have to be careful to show them no favour," said Juliet. "And to let no sign of interest or affection escape us. And awkward things might reach home, that would otherwise escape notice. And their companions would see them as the relations—no, of course, the connections—of people who earned their living by service to themselves; and I believe they might see them as relations. And they would get a good deal of knowledge of life."

"Yes. Yes. It would have that side. It would have that educational point," said Lesbia. "And we are not related to them, you know."

"It seems that you ought to be," said Oliver.

49

"Yes, Oliver, it does seem so."

"Would you advise us to send Sefton to you, Lucius?" said Sir Roderick.

"Well, well, I am the last person to give the advice. I might be prejudiced in favour of my own methods. It might be so, as I have given my life to them. I would rather hold aloof."

"It was I who wrote the letter," said Juliet. "And that was because I could not disobey Lesbia. Lucius only gets pupils in spite of himself. That is why he has so many. People like their boys to go where they are not wanted."

"Why?" said Sir Roderick.

"They think they will get so much. If they were only to get a little, they would be wanted."

"Lesbia, would you advise us to send Clemence to you?" said Maria, in a definite tone.

"I would, Maria, and for the reason that Lucius gave for not advising the same thing, that I am prejudiced in favour of my own methods, as I have given my life to them."

"Well, I suppose the matter is settled," said Maria, with a sigh.

"The two kinds of advice seem to lead along the same way," said Sir Roderick.

"Settled need not be the word as yet," said Lesbia, looking at the window, "though it is a good thing to have the lines of the matter clear. Questions will arise and will not be gainsaid, and among them is the matter of a vacancy. I do not generally allow such problems to follow me into the country."

"Is there a vacancy or not?" said Sir Roderick.

"Letters arrive by every post," said Lesbia, stooping to adjust her shoe. "When I have the data, the matter can be settled."

"You are rash, Aunt Lesbia," said Oliver. "Suppose letters do not arrive at such intervals?"

"Then I must say that they have not been forwarded," said his aunt with a laugh. "They are waiting for me at home."

"Why should other pupils have preference over Clemence?" said Sir Roderick.

"They may make a definite application," said Lesbia, in an incidental tone.

"I did not think about vacancies," said Juliet. "I am so undignified. And I do not know about them. Perhaps mere space does not attract my attention. Or I may be used to it."

"We have plenty of room," said her husband. "We are not running the school at full numbers."

"Lucius, you have even less dignity than I have. And it is not true that people have nothing to fear, if they speak the truth. They have everything to fear. That is the reason of falsehood. And now we fear that they will not send Sefton to us. Why should they when there is a vacancy?"

"A school may not be any better for being so full," said Sir Roderick.

"But when it is better, I suppose it is full," said Juliet.

"It seems that my line was the right one," said Lesbia, with a smile.

"So Clemence can go to you, if we wish to send her?" said Sir Roderick.

"No, seriously, Roderick, that question must wait."

"Aunt Lesbia spoke, as she said, seriously," said Oliver.

"What made you decide to be a schoolmaster, Lucius?" said Sir Roderick, keeping his tone neutral.

"I thought the work was of use and interest, and perhaps I had not much choice."

"What a beautiful answer!" said his wife. "So open and uncringing. Simple, too, which is always creditable."

"Yes, simplicity is to the good," said Lesbia, half to herself, "if there is no reason to dispense with it."

"We do not often avoid it," said Oliver. "Complexity is so much more difficult."

"That is what I should have thought," said Juliet, "if I dared to think it. But I am never sure of myself."

"Is no one going to ask me why I chose the profession?" said Lesbia.

51

"No, my dear," said Mr. Firebrace. "A woman is a governess or nothing. But it is natural to ask to man."

"Oliver, must you play the piano just while we are talking?" said Maria.

"Yes, I must, Maria. The need is upon me. And you have been talking more easily for my subdued and sensitive accompaniment."

"I wish I had your services for a term," said Lucius. "My music master is to have a rest, and it is difficult to get a substitute."

"Well, why not make the boy a governess with the rest of you?" said Mr. Firebrace. "Why should we have exceptions in the family?"

"I should like to be one for a term," said Oliver. "I should like to see the world of school from a different angle and know why it is called a world. And to know if schoolmasters do what they are supposed to; destroy each other in imagination, and treat boys with hysterical cruelty, and ruin them by romantic devotion, and lose heart and hope and become machines. Because it does not sound so very like machines. And I should like Grandpa to learn what it is to be without me. Some little thing that he takes for granted might return to him and loom larger than any great one. And Father would learn that he does not really want to be without his elder son. Maria would learn nothing, as she does want to be without me."

"A governess is born, not made," said Mr. Firebrace.

"Well, may we regard it as settled?" said Lucius.

"Yes, sir. I must call you that now, instead of 'Uncle Lucius', or the masters would laugh at me. Or is it only the boys? There is so much I want to know."

"Is this all nonsense, or is it serious?" said Maria.

"It is serious on my side," said Lucius.

"It is both one thing and the other," said Mr. Firebrace, looking from Lucius to his grandson. "But I think it is to be carried out."

"Well, perhaps it would be good for Sefton to have a

grown-up brother at the school," said Maria. "It might give him a background."

"You are given a real reason for your going, Oliver," said Sir Roderick.

"It would make no difference," said Lucius, "or anyhow would be no advantage. Their paths would not cross, and the boys would think no more of Sefton. They have little respect for labour held to be worthy of its hire."

"Of course boys are the most conventional of creatures," said Juliet, "though I never quite know how it was discovered. They do not eschew breaches of convention. When any trouble arises, it is generally about those."

"I suppose some breaches of convention are conventional," said Sir Roderick.

"So, my boy, they are making a governess of you between them," said Mr. Firebrace.

"Yes, I should have thought someone else would have supposed that," said Lesbia.

"Shall we send for the children, and ask them what they think?" said Maria.

"We will tell them what has been decided," said her husband. "We will not ask them for opinions that are to be disregarded, about their own future."

"Yes, you are right, Roderick," said Lesbia. "To have one's fate in the hands of other people is one of the hard features of childhood and merits sympathy. I find that is one of the demands of my life, to give sympathy of the right kind and degree; and I hope the power has grown with exercise. And they have not tried the new conditions. We should wait for their judgement until they have."

"They may as well come down," said Maria. "We should all like to see them, or anyhow Roderick and I would."

"There is only one thing for us to say, and so, of course, it goes without saying," said Lesbia.

"It is fortunate that things that go without saying, are such harmless things," said Juliet. "If they were not, we should live in danger, as they always seem to be said."

"Aldom, ask Miss Clemence and Master Sefton to come downstairs," said Maria.

"Yes, my lady. Is Miss Petticott to come too?"

"We need hardly trespass on Miss Petticoat's time," said Sir Roderick, with a hint of preferring his own choice of phrase.

"Now I should like to see Miss Petticott," said Lesbia. "I am interested in all forms of education, and hers is different from mine. And I should like the present question to be discussed before her. It is what I should choose in her place, and in such matters we are safe in judging other people by ourselves."

"Miss Petticott too, my lady? Yes, my lady," said Aldom, looking at Maria and going to the door.

"I think Aldom takes the conventional view of the teaching profession," said Lesbia with a laugh.

"He may see the different position of someone who teaches in the house," said Sir Roderick.

"Now why is it different?" said Lesbia. "I fail to see any difference. I recognise none. I see the same aims, the same interests, the same hopes in both that branch of the calling and mine."

"He may see a different income and a different degree of independence."

"I hope he does not see our income," said Juliet. "I never turn my eyes on it. It is shocking to get so much out of the charge and training and food—yes, food—of helpless boys. We can hardly look for people's respect. And nothing ought to have respect, that has so much besides."

"You have not the same reason for discomfort, Lesbia?" said Sir Roderick.

"No, I can hold my head high. And I think on the whole I prefer it in that way. On the basis of a simple and fair return for what it is in my power to give. I give it and ask but the means to live, and I think that makes for true content."

"My content is the other kind, and I do like it better," said her sister. "But I have the grace to feel ashamed."

"Why do you call it grace?" said Oliver. "Things that are mixed up with shame ought to have some other name, and really have it."

"How do you do, Miss Petticott?" said Lesbia, rising at the opening of the door, on which she had kept her eyes. "I am looking forward to my talk with you. You and I are to have something in common——" She broke off as she encountered the children and realised one difference in Miss Petticott's branch of the calling, a vagueness in the matter of precedence.

"How do you do, Miss Petticott?" she said again, sending her eyes past the children as a relief to the check. "I have been looking forward to my talk with you. You and I are to have something in common, a pupil, in addition to the other things common to us both. You hold the superior position with regard to her; you have laid the foundations; my task is to add the superstructure, a humbler part. I hope you will give me your help, a generous office, as I have given you none."

"Indeed, Miss Firebrace, you put things very kindly. I will do anything I can. I am sorry to lose Clemence, but glad for her to have any advantages that should be hers. And I shall have her in the holidays. I must think of that."

"Yes, yes, the holidays," said Lesbia, in her soft tones. "They have their significance in the educational round. I often wish I had more to do with the holidays. They are not the least of the formative influences. They admit the use of initiative, of free will. They cannot be."

"Does not Miss Petticott have any?" said Oliver.

"Well, Mr. Shelley, holidays are short when the life involves the sharing of a home. And I shall soon have a change of work, and that is known to be a rest."

"It is a good thing it is known," said Juliet. "Or how should we find it out?"

"A change of work!" said Lesbia. "That too will have

its effect on the guidance when it comes into force again. The wider the experience, the wider the survey. That is why I keep my holidays for my own interests. I feel I am not the narrower for them."

"Anything seems to do for education," said Juliet. "It seems rather pointless to keep a school for the purpose."

"Do you teach in your school, Juliet?" said Sir Roderick.

"No, not now. I used to, but it was not a success."

"I should have thought the boys would like you."

"They did. They liked me too much. And I could not bear to lose their affection. That was the whole thing."

"Could you not teach them without losing it?"

"No, I could not be harsh with them."

"Can nothing be done without harshness?"

"No, everything is done by it."

"Are there no other methods?"

"Yes, I believe so, but no successful ones."

"I thought it was not allowed in these days."

"It is always the things that are not allowed, that achieve results. No notice is taken of things that do nothing."

"I suppose it creeps in in spite of the theories. And small doses have more effect."

"Well, they have some effect," said Juliet.

"How do you do, Clemence? How do you do, Sefton?" said Lesbia, turning as if on a second thought. "I hope you can forgive this invasion of your home."

"I did not greet them, as you did not," said Juliet, "I thought it might be making advances to possible pupils. But I am glad you have done it. I was wondering how things were to be."

"I had forgotten the problematic future relation at the moment," said Lesbia, with a smile. "If I have lost my dignity, I must do my best to recover it."

"If you had greeted them when they came in, you would have kept it," said Oliver.

Sir Roderick gave a glance almost of approval at his son.

"What do you think of the relative claims of home and

school?" said Juliet to the children. "Well, somebody has to say it. And I am used to taking the thankless part. It leaves Lucius aloof for the good of the school. I suppose we should be ruined if he said that sort of thing."

"I think the first things would always come first," said Clemence.

"There does not seem much good in a home, if you have to leave it," said her brother.

"I suppose there is no help for it, for a boy," said Lesbia, resting her eyes on them in acceptance of their point of view. "In Clemence's case there may be more freedom of choice. She can depend upon Miss Petticott in solitude, if it is preferred. And if Miss Petticott will accept the responsibility."

"She would be lonely by herself," said Maria.

"The trap was right in your path," said her husband.

"No, Roderick, I do not set traps," said Lesbia. "Maria presumably meant what she said, and there is truth in it. Or do you say there is not?"

"I want both my children in their home. Sefton can go on with his tutor until his time for a public school. They have a right to each other's companionship, and a girl has a right to her father's roof."

"Well, that is one side of things," said Lesbia, on a more cordial note. "So let us leave it at that. And I shall be interested in the result of the experiment. For that it must be said to be. Everything is grist to my mill, as I have said, in the sphere of preparation for life."

"Did you know that your brother was to be a governess with the rest of them?" said Mr. Firebrace to the children.

"You do not address the children of your own accord more than twice a year," said Maria.

"Perhaps that would be about the number of times."

"How do you mean, Grandpa?" said Clemence.

"Music mistress at his uncle's school."

"Music master," said Sefton.

"No, I meant what I said, my boy."

"Then will he be there when I am there?"

"Yes, I thought you would be glad to hear that," said Maria. "It will make a background for you. There will be someone to appeal to, if anything goes wrong."

"Then he will have to acknowledge the relationship," said Oliver.

"And why should he not do that?"

"Well, I shall have to play the piano for the hymn at prayers."

"How did you know?" said Juliet. "I am so relieved. I was wondering if Lucius would dare to tell you, or if it would devolve upon me."

"Why should I mind his playing?" said Sefton. "He plays at home."

"There is no reason to mind," said Maria.

"You little know what you say," said her stepson.

"I do not suppose he will give me any reasons when he comes home."

"No, I do not suppose he will."

"What is all this mystery?" said Maria, in an exasperated manner. "Why should not school be an open and natural life, like any other?"

"Like what other?" said Mr. Firebrace.

"Do not try to be suggestive, Grandpa. It is not a thing you can do. I could give Maria some reasons, and I shall know some more when I return. And some of the life is natural. Perhaps that is why it cannot be open. It could not be both."

"I hate to feel there is so much that does not go into words," said his stepmother.

"It does throw a shadow. And it must remain dark, sinister and hovering. And it is over innocent lives. But there is no need for Grandpa to hint that it is over lives like our own. As if they were innocent."

"Well, what about this question of school, Roderick?" said Maria, in a weary tone. "Shall we put it to the vote? To go or not to go? Hands up, those in favour!"

No hand was raised and Maria looked round in doubt.

"No, no, I am aloof," said Lesbia, shaking her head. "I have given my opinion. It must be taken for what it is worth. I do not give it a second time."

"Of course Lucius and I cannot vote for having an extra boy," said Juliet. "And Lucius is never in favour of anything. He cannot let his personality go to pieces."

"I am in your position, Miss Firebrace. I am aloof," said Miss Petticott. "Our minds do seem to work on the same lines."

"I am against their going," said Sir Roderick. "I do not mind giving the opinion a second and a third time."

"I vote in favour of it," said Oliver. "The results may afford me some amusement. I expect it will have some results."

"I give the casting vote, also in favour," said Mr. Firebrace. "When I have a family of governesses, it is not for me to stand in their light."

"Then the ayes have it," said Maria. "I have not voted myself, but no one has noticed that."

"A note of dignified sadness," said Oliver. "When Sefton goes wrong at school, it will come to his mind. There must be something to do that."

"It has been settled all the time," said his father. "And I ask that we shall not continue to assume it is not. And I hope they will not stay long."

"I should not think they will. The results of their going are to amuse me; and if they stay long, I do not see how they could."

"Well, I am tired of the riddles and mysteries," said Maria. "They give such a shallow touch to everything."

"That is a hard saying and meant to be one," said Oliver. "I thought they gave a subtle touch, and I still think it."

"What do the people who are most concerned, think of its being settled?" said Lesbia, in a quiet tone.

"I knew it was," said Clemence.

"Why did we think it was not?" said Sefton.

"That I cannot tell you," said his father.

"I do not know that it is settled now," said Lesbia, laughing. "I shall be prepared for either event. And it will not make so much difference, as long as we know in time."

"It will make a good deal of difference to us," said Clemence.

"I should not be so half-hearted, if I ran a school," said Maria.

"Well, your methods would be more direct," said her husband.

"Which kind of method do you think best?" said Oliver to Clemence, noticing her look.

"There does not seem to be much difference. All methods are direct really. It is not as if we could not see the indirect ones working."

The parents suppressed amusement, or seemed to do so, and Maria put her arms about her children and guided them to the door, as though they had been sufficiently stimulated by adult company. Lesbia kept her eyes on Clemence as long as the latter was in hearing.

"Clemence has no social intercourse except with older people," she said, as if she could deduce this.

"The two children are very good friends," said Miss Petticott.

"Yes, but her brother's companionship cannot lead her beyond a certain point," said Lesbia, turning fully to the speaker and continuing under the protection. "Not beyond considering the effect of her words, and speaking with a sense of being listened to. It leaves her helpless there." She dropped her voice and seemed to speak to herself. "And helplessness merits help."

"She is not at all behind her age, Miss Firebrace."

"No, the growth has been normal, but with the gaps resulting from the lack in the environment."

"I always think the gaps are the best part of education," said Sir Roderick, who thought this, or thought of it, for the first time.

"Well, I daresay we could all show plenty of them," said Lesbia. "We will not make the lists."

"I thought it was a mistake to do so," said Oliver.

"Lucius has more gaps than anyone," said Juliet. "Some people might think he was almost wholly a gap. But it is dangerous to copy him."

"It is always a mistake to copy the peculiarities of a work of art," said Oliver. "And that is what people do. But as they cannot copy the merits, what is their choice?"

"And gaps would be particularly easy to copy," said Juliet.

"Well, I think I will go upstairs," said Maria, "and visit the victims of a mistaken upbringing."

Lesbia rose at the same time, so unobtrusively that the action escaped notice, and as she met Maria's eyes, spoke with sudden firmness.

"It will help me, Maria. So I will not risk having permission denied."

The two women mounted the staircase, and Sir Roderick rose as an afterthought and followed. No sound came from the schoolroom, and Lesbia's expression registered the evidence of lack of life. Maria entered with a defiant look, as though prepared to defend what she saw.

This caused her to pause and glance at her companion, as if to make sure of her position at her side. Her smile hovered for a moment, and steadied as it was supported by her husband's mirth. Lesbia's voice was the first to be heard.

"So I have lost no time in implanting an impression of my personality. Something about me has not delayed to do its work. To whom are we indebted for the recognisable presentation? For I think we must accord it the merit of being that."

Miss Petticott, her pupils and Adela sat at attention before a masquerading figure. The trappings of the latter sorted themselves out to the eye. The stuffing of Adela's armchair supplied the short grey hair; a scarf of Miss

Petticott's the grey and shadowy garment; a strap, with some scissors depending, the belt with its silver attachment, at sight of which Lesbia restrained a movement of her hand towards her waist. Here sources of supply had failed, and Aldon's nether garments provided the basis of the whole. His small, supple figure and pliable, sallow face were a possible substitute for the model's lineaments.

He began to divest himself of his disguise, as though unconscious of what he did. Lesbia looked on with modderate interest, Sir Roderick with more, Maria with some disappointment that no achievement was to be accredited to her children.

"Well, if simple ingenuity is of any use to us, they will have that help," said Lesbia, looking at the accoutrements, as they were discarded, and then going into easy mirth. "It does not often fall to anyone to witness her own dissolution."

"Had you nothing else to do with your time, Aldom?" said Sir Roderick, in a tone that seemed to be neutral, because he could not decide on its expression.

"Well, Sir Roderick, I have acted at school before, as is known to her ladyship, it not being the custom to work from morning till night. And this time it seemed to fit the occasion, as it was an imminent experience."

"And it has its educational value, Miss Petticott?" said Lesbia, in a tone that just held a question. "As all work and play should have."

"Well, really I do not know, Miss Firebrace. I did not know what the scene was to be. I was quite taken aback when it began. I had not any idea of it."

"I do not suppose you had. I am not so conceited as to suppose that this particular thing would occur to you. And no doubt you trusted your pupils. Trust should exist in all relations; and if it is to be on one side, it must be on the other. And I believe in self-government, in things that admit of it. And amusements are surely to be reckoned amongst those."

"I will go now, my lady," said Aldom, and did as he said.

"Well, if Clemence is not prepared for her new life, it is not Aldom's fault," said Lesbia, in another tone. "I hope the light thrown upon her path will illumine it. It would be a pity if all that thought and contrivance were wasted. I might feel quite flattered by being the instigator of it."

"Aldom had only about half an hour between waiting at tea and coming up here," said Maria, as if this feeling might occur in too great a degree.

"Yes, it was the most concentrated effort."

Sir Roderick laughed.

"What are you laughing at, Roderick?" said Maria.

Her husband continued to laugh, and began to do so to excess, looking at Lesbia, at Miss Petticott, at his children, as he made up the arrears of his emotion.

Lesbia smiled on him with indulgence.

"You are still young in heart and mind, Roderick. Childish things are not of those that you have put away."

Sir Roderick was checked by this interpretation of his mood, but not to the point of overcoming it, and continued to be subject to outbreaks, as the talk went on.

"Really, Roderick, I am ashamed of you," said Maria. "Indeed I do not know how far to be ashamed of all of you."

"Oh, that is too much of a feeling, surely," said Lesbia, as though some easy condemnation would meet the case. "People cannot always present themselves in the most becoming light. We all have our more ordinary moments."

"What may be your jest?" said Mr. Firebrace, leading his family into the room.

"A merry one," said his daughter. "We came up and caught Aldom in the act of impersonating me in my professional character. And very realistic it all was. Observed and plausible and failing in none of the stock humours. Whether or no it was worth doing, it was done quite well."

"And you put off being amused by it until Aldom had left you. Well, we see your reasons."

Sir Roderick, who had put off some of his amusement for longer than this, now allowed it to escape him.

"Why, my boy, I have not seen you laugh like that for thirty-two years," said Mr. Firebrace, choosing to mention the time that had passed since his daughter's death.

"You are wonderful, Roderick," said Juliet. "A vow never to smile again is hardly ever kept so long."

Sir Roderick's vow, if he had made one, was once more broken.

"I love to see Father happy," said Oliver.

Lesbia went into mirth, as though here were really cause.

"I do not know why I am laughing so much," said Sir Roderick.

"I can tell you, Roderick," said Lesbia, gently. "Your emotion at losing your children is finding its outlet; the more so that I, the cause of the loss, am also the cause of the laughter."

"Is that really so?" said Sir Roderick.

"Aunt Lesbia, you have quenched the light in Father's eyes," said Oliver. "I should think that is probably one of the greatest of wrongs."

"Lesbia has become Clemence's headmistress," said Lucius. "Being mimicked and mocked is a symptom of the state."

"I did not think you knew that," said Juliet. "I suppose you are really a person whom nothing escapes."

"Yes, yes. It is a thing that does happen to a certain degree," said Lesbia, in a considering, open tone. "To a certain degree, and in the spirit prompted by the object of the mimicry. We want a word more sympathetic to both sides."

"I fear we all do not," said Lucius.

"Well, the atmosphere of different schools must have its difference."

"And girls may be different from boys," said Sir Roderick.

"Yes, that is quite true, Roderick," said Lesbia, in cordial agreement.

"I thought that girls were more subtle and cruel in their methods," said Juliet.

"Now did you really think so?" said her sister. "Or are you just repeating what you have heard?"

"I think I thought that was thinking so. I believe it generally is. When people think about a thing, they do say what they have heard. If they had heard nothing, they would not think about it."

"You have full opportunity of observing boys. That may help you to draw some conclusions."

"I try not to use it, in case it may lead to that. And the boys would hardly let it be a full one. And conclusions would come between me and the parents, who seem to have no idea of them. I do not think they ever form them."

"I suppose you know you are contradicting yourself?"

"I must be one of those ordinary women who do not pretend to be consistent. Why do they not pretend to be? We all pretend to be honest and kind and intelligent, and surely it is not so much more to add consistence. People are so conceited; they only pretend to be the higher things."

"Girls are themselves," said Lesbia, in a quiet, even voice. "Individual, variable, understanding and loyal in their own way"—she gave a faint smile, as though such things as mimicry did occur to her—"in need of supervision and training to bring out their best; and the best may be very good."

"You can keep a girls' school without any sense of guilt. But the best in anyone is good. How would you manage about the other things in them, if they came to the fore? We do not know what would be our problems, if we dared to face them."

"The deduction may be simply that girls are more suited to school than boys. They are more responsive and receptive, more open to influence. Boys may sometimes be better at home; I have often thought it."

"But do not strike at the foundations of our livelihood."

"What do you think, Lucius?" said Maria.

"I am no advocate of sending young boys from home. I see it as unnatural and sometimes harmful. But we have to do our best with the system. It is established."

"It must be," said his wife. "One cannot help wondering how it came about."

"It is no good to go back and consider the matter from the beginning," said Maria.

"None," said Oliver. "If it were, it would have been of good by now."

"We are doing as Lucius said, my dear," said Sir Roderick. "Making the best of the prevailing system. We are agreed that it is a bad one, even Lesbia in the case of boys."

"I am surprised that Lesbia should aim at our establishment, and spare her own," said Juliet.

"Grandpa looks as if he were thinking something," said Oliver.

"I think that parents should do their own duty."

"Why did you not say that before?" said Maria, with a note of despair.

"It was not such a strange thing to think, that people should need to be informed of it."

"It would have made no difference, my dear," said Sir Roderick. "It is what we thought ourselves, and it made none."

"But I wish people would not keep their opinions until after a decision, and then air them."

"They may not know them until then. Juliet was right in her account of the way they form them."

"What is it, that you say of me?" said Mr. Firebrace.

Maria put her hands to her head.

"Come, my pretty, let us go downstairs. We have done our best, and must leave it. No one can do more."

"We have done nothing," said Maria.

"Well, that is usually people's best," said her stepson. "Their worst is something quite different."

"Well, let us say good-night to the victims of our indecisions."

66

"Dear, dear, is that still the word?" said Mr. Firebrace.

"So it is as bad as that, to be afforded ordinary advantages?" said Lesbia, turning to Clemence and using an almost friendly tone. "What do you think of the new prospect, Clemence?"

"We never know what to think of prospects, until they become something else."

"We can use our imaginations," said Lesbia, with quiet gravity, keeping her eyes from the parents.

"I don't think I can. Or not in any way that would show me how things are to be. I have never been inside a school."

"Well, then you have not much to build upon," said Lesbia, meeting simple truthfulness with cordiality. "We cannot do quite without a foundation. So you will wait and let the new world break upon you in all its unexpectedness."

"I shall not be able to prevent it."

Lesbia laughed readily and followed the others from the room.

"Good-night, my little ones," said Maria, folding her children in a close embrace.

Sir Roderick followed her example, and it was felt that a seal had been set upon the coming change.

"Well, it is good to be with my own flesh and blood," said Mr. Firebrace, as he sat down amongst his family. "It may be that they will leave us for a spell."

"We must not resent their presence in their own home," said Lesbia.

"If I had such a thing myself, I should not need to do so."

"Roderick has never filled Mary's place. And I mean no disrespect to Maria, when I say so."

"I call it gross disrespect," said Oliver.

"Maria has a place of her own."

"And Mary has the same by now," said Juliet. "When things are people's own, there is never much to be said for them. 'A poor thing but mine own,' was a natural saying to become established."

67

"Poor Maria!" said Lucius, looking surprised at himself, and incurring looks of surprise.

"Yes, poor Maria!" said Lesbia. "I have often thought it."

"It is terrible that we reveal our thoughts," said Oliver.

"So have I," said Juliet, "but I have never said it, because I knew it was insensitive to pity people."

"Pity may be a healthy and natural feeling," said her sister.

"It certainly flourishes," said Oliver. "I pity most people. I mean, I think how dreadful it would be to be them."

"Do you pity me?" said Juliet.

"Yes. You are a woman and older than I am. You have less of your life left."

"Do you pity your father?"

"Yes, he is sixty-eight, and he loves the treacherous land with a man's simplicity."

"And the children?"

"They are always pitiful."

"And me?" said Lesbia. "Am I subject to a woman's subtlety?"

"There is no such thing."

"But if you admit a man's simplicity, you must admit a woman's corresponding quality."

"I do admit it."

"And what is it?"

"Simplicity," said Oliver. "But I do not pity you or Grandpa. I am not quite sure of the reasons, but they are the same for both."

"And yourself, my boy?" said Mr. Firebrace.

"Well, self-pity is too deep a thing to be broached in words. I envy you for being able to do it. It shows how simple your causes for self-pity are. Mine are the knotted and tangled kind, that lie fallow in the day and rise up to torment people at night."

"Mine do their business by day, it is true. And they are

68

active at the moment," said Mr. Firebrace, as steps sounded on the stairs.

"Well, we have left the two little martyrs," said Maria.

"Come, that is too strong," said Lesbia. "Thousands of children are martyrs, if that is the truth."

"And is that impossible?" said her nephew.

"Yes, I think it is, Oliver. I think we may say so. The force of such a weight of suffering would react and end the cause."

"Oliver takes a pride in taking a gloomy view of everything," said Maria.

"Well, no one would be proud of looking at the bright side of things," said Juliet. "It leads to saying that poverty is a blessing in disguise—as if a disguised thing ever served its purpose—or that sacrifice is its own reward, or even that we should not grieve at people's death. It is simply a cover for what we are ashamed of."

"I wonder if we should send the children to school, if we put ourselves in their place," said Maria. "You will all forgive my harping on the same thing. It must fill my mind."

"I hardly think they will forgive it much longer," said her stepson. "Certainly not all of them."

"Well, no one would do anything then," said Sir Roderick. "A murderer would not kill, or a thief steal, if they did that. If we all formed the habit, the world could not go on. Of course we should not send them."

"A pessimistic presentation of human activities," said Lesbia, with a laugh.

The door opened and Sefton entered, holding his jacket together to cover an early stage of undress. He went to a bookcase and appeared to fumble for a book.

"What do you want, my dear?" said Maria.

"I wanted a book. I thought it was here. I was not quite sure if it was," said Sefton, with his hands on his knees and his back to the audience. "It is a book about the way things happen because people think they are happening. I forgot what the thing is called. And it could not be like that. If someone thought someone was ill, thought it in the night, when he was away from home, that person would not be ill and perhaps die because of it."

"Come here, my little son," said Maria.

Sefton went to her at once, brushing his hand across his eyes.

"Now say what is true, my dear. There was no book there that you wanted, was there?"

"No," said Sefton, sinking into tears.

"You wanted to know if imagining things at school could make those things happen to someone at home?"

"I did want to know. I felt I had to. It is in the night that the thoughts come, when you can't help it."

"Well, it could not, my dear. It would not make any difference. Except that trying to be contented and cheerful would please your mother and help her to be happy and well. Nothing that you cannot help, will do any harm. And another time you will ask a question straight out, and not pretend to be doing something else."

"Yes, I will."

"It does not matter if a question is odd or unexpected," went on Maria, in an easy almost offhand manner. "We all want to ask those questions sometimes. It shows we are thinking people. And we can say anything to our mothers, can't we?"

"Yes."

"So run away to bed with an easy mind. And do not think about changes until they come. You will find they bring their own help with them."

Sefton left the room, still holding his jacket together, and without glancing at the onlookers. Maria turned to them with a sort of triumph in her face.

"So that had to happen to prepare me for being a school-master," said Oliver.

"So harm is already being done," said Sir Roderick.

"It is possible that the swifter life of school may do something for him," said Lucius. "I think we may hope that it may."

"His life has been too stagnant, as you say," said Lesbia.

"Did Lucius say it?" said Juliet. "I hardly think he should have. And it is not like him to have positive thoughts."

"I wonder what Clemence is imagining," said Maria, still with the exultant touch.

"She is three years older than Sefton," said Lesbia. "Not that that would prevent imagination. But it might alter its channels. Yes, you must wonder, Maria. But, as Lucius says, a fuller life will do its work."

"Lucius is really getting garrulous," said Juliet. "And rather dogmatic as well. I hope he is not going to lose his touch. He almost recommended the school. If he begins to do that, there will be an end of everything. Fancy keeping a school that needs recommendation!"

"It may need it the less, that it can have it," said Lesbia. "Anyhow from its owner."

"Where are you going, Roderick?" said Maria.

"To see that it is well with my little man and woman upstairs. I should not sleep if I did not see them."

"I suppose I might have had a father like that, if I had been the child to invite it," said Oliver.

"You had the same father," said Maria.

"I did not, and you know it, and are glad about it."

"Your father never spoke a harsh word to you."

"No, but I do not think he spoke words to me."

"You must have had the ordinary intercourse of daily life."

"I do not call that speaking words. And I see you do not."

"Did you ever try to do anything for him?"

"No. What could I have done? He had power; I had none. He had everything; I had nothing. It could only have been a farce."

"He always did everything for you."

"Of course. What other arrangement could have been made?"

"You could have pleased him in many little ways."

"That is where I did not please him. And where I do not. He is not attracted by the little touches that make up my personality."

"And are you by those that make up his?"

"I do not think he has any. The whole of his personality is one touch. And everyone is attracted by it. He does not need to have any more. If he did, he would have them."

"You make him sound a simple person."

"I should hardly have thought I did."

"I can never follow your talk. I suppose you know what you mean yourself?"

"That is how I should put it."

"To be contemptuous is to be contemptible," said Maria.

"Well, it is probable that I am that. I do not say I know I am. I am really not quite sure."

"Perhaps you were for a moment, Oliver," said Lesbia.

Sir Roderick had mounted to the schoolroom and paused outside the door. He sustained this violation of his instincts to gain light on his children's minds. Adela's voice came to him, low and carrying a crooning sound, that suggested it was an accompaniment to rocking someone in her arms. Sefton's, coming from the same point, succeeded hers.

"I have always thought you might be ill, Adela, when I have woken in the dark. Sometimes I have thought you were dead."

"When I was young, I thought so too," said Clemence. "But I never do now. Or I should not, if I did not remember doing it."

There was a sound of movement, as though Adela contrived a place for her elder charge. The crooning was resumed, and Sir Roderick for the first time in his life tiptoed away from a door.

"Well, how were matters upstairs?" said Maria.

"I heard their voices through the door, and I thought I need not go in."

"I will go up myself. It is better to be on the safe side. I cannot have Sefton lying awake, fancying that his mother has been reft from him. And Clemence imagining the same thing on the other side of the wall."

"I should not, my pretty," said Sir Roderick, laying a hand on her arm. "They do not think so at the moment, and we need not put it into their minds. We will leave them to adapt themselves to the future in their own way. Adela is with them."

"Adela is the right person, Maria?" said Lesbia, in a tone that held nothing beyond the question.

"Yes, I think so. She is kind and trustworthy and attached to them. And they are fond of her, or fond enough. More we hardly want. A nurse should not take the mother's place."

"I suppose in a sense that is what she does," said Sir Roderick. "She gives what the mother would naturally give."

"In a savage state," said Oliver. "Why do we set up that as an example, when we spend thousands of years in getting away from it?"

"We see to whom Sefton turns in his real needs," said Maria.

"Yes, we do, my pretty," said Sir Roderick, perhaps feeling he had a right to say this.

"There may be the more need to keep schools, that children are rendered so vulnerable by life at home," said Lesbia, as if as the result of thought.

"Of course, if it is a duty, it has to be done," said her sister.

"I think—I hope it becomes so," said Lucius. "Much of what is done in the world is begun as a means to live."

"Most of it, if we think," said Lesbia, with an air of doing this. "I suppose Shakespeare earned by his plays and began to write to gain his bread."

"It is so pleasant always to be compared to Shake-speare," said Juliet. "It is a nice instinct always to take him as an example. There really seems to be nothing between him and savages."

"Well, everyone knows about him," said Sir Roderick. "We only half-know about the other people, though so much more is known."

"Father is one of those people who show how much better it is to be uneducated," said Oliver. "By that I mean, of course, to have had education and not profited by it, not really to have had none."

"Schools seem necessary on either ground," said Lesbia.

"Teaching at home would do," said Sir Roderick. "What are schools but places where people teach?"

"There are the lessons of communal life," said Lesbia, on her almost mysterious note. "And the safeguard against eccentricity and exaggerated individualism."

"But I thought those were the people whom we were so sorry to see passing away," said Juliet.

"I went to school," said Sir Roderick, simply.

"Oh, Roderick, why should people always be talking about you?" said Lesbia, shaking her head.

"There are surely reasons," said Oliver.

"I thought she meant me," said his father. "And I do not bear out her view. We do not all profit by the same thing."

"That is true. That is one of the first of our problems," said Lesbia, looking at the window. "I have even met cases in which I have actually advised that pupils should leave me. And people do not expect it, do not expect honest advice. I have found they do not. I do not know why they should not. To me there can be no reason."

"I do like people to pay tribute to themselves," said Oliver.

"Then you like your father to assume that our talk must refer to him?" said Lesbia, smiling.

"Yes, I do, but not so much. Anyone may think that

people's talk refers to him; everyone does think so. But not many people would refer to themselves as you did."

"I hope a good many would in their hearts."

"Yes, in their hearts. But I do not count that. Anyone might do anything there. And in their hearts they know better. They know they are imagining other people referring to them."

"People say we should see ourselves as others see us," said Juliet. "But it is better to tell them how to see us, and save the effort. Especially as they are looking forward to our making it."

"Is this talk supposed to be clever?" said Maria.

"Why, yes, Maria, it is," said her stepson. "Aunt Juliet is right. We must tell you how to see us."

"Was your speech supposed to be polite, my pretty?" said Sir Roderick.

"I am so wearied by this quibbling with words that mean nothing, when there is a real problem hanging over us."

"And what is that?"

"The children's going to school," said Maria, raising her eyes.

"Well, the term must begin sooner or later," said Mr. Firebrace, "and bring its solution."

"Then it will be their staying at home," said Lesbia, in an amused tone, "as it will be too late to make the adjustments. But let us allow the subject a rest and come to it fresh later. Sleep on it, as they say,"

"Then you are not in form at the moment?" said her father. "Sleep would mean another day."

"My children are going to school," said Sir Roderick. "It is settled and the subject is closed. It tires and tries my wife, and that is enough."

"So we must have another subject," said Oliver. "How nice subjects are! I do appreciate them. And I did like to hear Father speaking like a man. I find there is so much pleasure in life."

Sir Roderick rested his eyes on his son. He sometimes

thought he was easily pleased, and had need to be, and almost felt he owed him gratitude.

"I hope you like to hear me speaking like a woman," said Maria, "because I am going to do so. Could we manage without a subject and just talk of anything that comes into our heads?"

"Well, honestly, Maria, that is what we have been doing," said Lesbia, raising her brows.

"You cannot be governesses for a generation and bear no signs," said Mr. Firebrace. "We all carry our scars."

"To be natural is known to be the rarest of all things," said Oliver.

"We can be natural on different levels," said Lesbia. "There may be no point where we meet."

"I think our standard of naturalness is very high. And I agree that it is the greatest of all charms."

"I think I am a natural person," said Maria, in a tone that made no particular claim.

"So you are, my pretty. We should all bear witness to it," said Sir Roderick.

"So we should," said his son.

CHAPTER III

"Well, Maud—Esther—Verity—Gwendolen," said Lesbia, taking the hands of her pupils in turn. "I hope your holiday has been a success and that the term will be so in its own way. They should supplement and support each other. This is Clemence Shelley, a new companion—a connection of mine, but we are to forget that during the term. The relationship is only a shadow, but a shadow is not always easy to elude. Can I leave her in your charge?"

"Yes, Miss Firebrace," said the four girls, glancing at each other before they looked at the newcomer.

"Maud, you have the advantage in years and experience," said Lesbia, uniting the hands of Maud and Clemence. "And—I think I may say it—the advantage in some other ways as well. Can I appoint you guardian-in-chief without misgiving? I have other claims on my time."

Maud had a tall, thin figure, small, brown, honest eyes, average features that failed to result in average comeliness, and an air of following virtue, irrespective of current opinion.

"Yes, Miss Firebrace," she said, in a tone that ranged Lesbia and herself on one side against the rest on the other.

The latter stood by without signs of competitive feeling or need to suppress them.

"Well, I will leave you to what is apparently silence. Thank you, Gwendolen," said Lesbia, passing through the opened door and leaving her pupils to something that was different.

"Why did you come to a school kept by a relation?" said Esther, in a rapid monotone, tossing back a pale plait of hair from an oval face and speaking with a gleam in her opaque, blue eyes.

77

"There is no relationship, Esther. Did you not hear what Miss Firebrace said?" said Maud.

"I also heard her say there was one."

"There is a sort of connection," said Clemence. "No blood relationship."

"Blood relationship!" said the third girl on a mocking note.

"It is quite an accepted phrase, Verity," said Maud.

"Why talk about what does not exist?" said Esther.

"I am sure I do not know," said Clemence. "It was quite unnecessary."

"Why, is it anything to be ashamed of?" said Gwendolen, her round, happy face taking on a happier line.

"No, Miss Firebrace is simply the sister of my father's first wife."

"And are you any relation of his second?"

"Yes. I am her daughter."

"And what about the relations of his third?" said Verity.

"They do not exist and neither does she. My mother is still alive."

"There is no relationship at all. Miss Firebrace was right," said Maud. "It is, as she said, the shadow of one."

"She also said it was not easy to elude, and was also right," said Verity, who had a noticeable face and head, long, fine hands, clothes too good for her age, and an air of being or feeling apart from the rest.

"Are you very clever, Clemence?" said Gwendolen, as if struck by something in Clemence's replies.

"I daresay I am as clever as the rest of you."

"Well, why did you come to a school kept by a relation, or by somebody who thinks she is one, and knows she is not?" said Esther, in one rapid breath.

"Well, we knew about the school. We had not heard of any other."

"On that basis none of us could be educated," said Gwendolen. "We have no relations who keep them. I wonder how people do hear of schools. I have no idea how we knew of this."

"Naturally people would know more about a school kept by a connection," said Maud. "And would be more likely to go to it. And Miss Firebrace said the matter was to be forgotten during the term."

"Then why did she remember it? And why do you?" said Esther. "Why put it into our heads, just to give us the trouble of getting it out again?"

"You do not seem to be taking the trouble," said Clemence, affording some amusement to Verity and Gwendolen.

"A spurious connection seems to make more confusion than a real one."

"It makes no confusion, Esther," said Maud, who had the school habit of using people's names with courteous frequency and deliberation. "Indeed, I have never known a point emerge with greater clearness."

"Is it anything to be ashamed of?" said Gwendolen, again. "I don't see so much disgrace in keeping a school. Perhaps there isn't any."

"I should say there is no occupation that carries less disgrace, Gwendolen. Miss Firebrace merely meant that no difference was to be made."

"Does it make any other difference to come to a school kept by a relation, by a connection?" said Esther, in a tone at once blunt and innocent.

"I suppose not, if it is to be forgotten," said Clemence.

"I meant any difference of any kind."

"Does Miss Firebrace do you charity, or do you do her charity?" said Gwendolen, laughing at her own openness.

"Oh, I expect we do her charity," said Clemence, finding the situation taken in hand by something outside herself, and surprised at her ease in it. "That is how it would be."

"Have you been in the habit of doing her charity?"

"Oh, I don't know. My father may have a certain sense of responsibility towards her," said Clemence, uncertain where instinctive knowledge stopped and invention began.

"Clemence, be careful that you do not betray anyone's confidence," said Maud.

"Do your people do a lot of charity?" said Esther.

"Yes, a good deal, or I expect they do. That is how it would have to be. I know my father says it is a drain on the family resources," said Clemence, trying to strike a happy mean in her suggestions.

"Why do they do so much charity?" said Gwendolen. "I don't think my parents do. I believe we keep all we have, for ourselves."

"We could hardly do that, as we are placed. I mean, we have to do what the family has always done. I don't think we should have any choice."

"'That is how it would have to be,'" quoted Verity.

"Is your father the lord of the manor?" said Esther, with her eyes on something in her hand.

"Oh, I daresay he is. It is the sort of thing he would be amongst other things. But it would not make much difference. He is what would be called the squire, though it sounds an old-fashioned term."

"An old-fashioned term!" said Verity.

"Well, it is the word for something that no other term gives, Verity," said Maud.

"Who calls him that?" said Esther.

"The people in the village and about the place."

"Do you choose your own clothes?" said Esther, throwing her eyes over Clemence and as rapidly withdrawing them.

"No. My mother chooses them. I have not troubled about such things yet. Or sometimes Miss Petticott does."

"Who is Miss Petticott?"

"The governess. We call her the Petticoat."

"To her face?" said Gwendolen.

"No, behind her back, but I think she knows."

"Are you very rude people in your home?" said Gwendolen. "Ruder than we are here?"

"No, about the same," said Clemence.

There was a sound of mirth.

"I suppose Miss Petty-something will leave now?"

"No, she will stay to help my mother and to be with us in the holidays."

The girls exchanged glances, as though this shed a real light.

"What kind of things does your mother do?" said Esther.

"Esther, Clemence will think we are unable to put a remark except in the form of a question," said Maud.

"Oh, there are notes to write, and lists to make, and messages to be taken, and all kinds of things to manage in the village."

"Has your mother a high sense of duty?" said Gwendolen.

"Yes, I believe she has. She is always thinking of the welfare of everyone about her."

"I suppose in her position she has to," said Esther, with a glance at Verity.

"Yes, she would hardly have any alternative."

"Who mends your clothes?" said Esther.

"Adela, the maid I share with my brother."

"Your brother?" said more than one voice.

"Oh, he is only eleven. She is a sort of nurse."

"And do your father and mother share a maid?" said Gwendolen.

"Gwendolen, I wonder if you realise the impression you are giving," said Maud.

"No, I think my mother has one to herself," said Clemence, finding the fiction spring to her lips of its own force.

"Are you not sure?"

"Well, I think a maid who does other things waits on her as well."

"And does your father have another maid?" said Esther.

"Perhaps it is time," said Verity, under her breath, "as he has had so many wives, and a maid is a sort of nurse."

"No, Aldom looks after him in so far as he needs looking after. He does not want much done for him."

"Who is Aldom?"

"He is called the butler, or calls himself that. He is all kinds of things. He is the only man we have in the house."

"Isn't your father a man?"

"Oh, you must know the use of the term, man, for manservant."

"I do not wonder if Clemence is losing her patience," said Maud.

"Was it your mother who was getting into a cab at the door just now?" said Esther. "Or did the governess come with you?"

"I expect that was the governess," said Clemence, meeting the truth that one falsehood leads to another, as Maria's appearance and the possession of a maid were incompatible.

"She looked like your mother. She was rather like you in the face. Her eyes were like yours."

"Well, I don't know who it was. They both came with me."

"Then did not they both have to go?"

"Miss Petticott went early to the station to do some shopping on the way. But she may have come back to go with my mother. I said good-bye to them both in the drawing-room."

"Did you cry?" said Gwendolen.

"Well, perhaps I did a little," said Clemence, glad to be released from the effort of invention, though she had found it lighter than she could have hoped.

"Poor Clemence!" said four voices, though Esther's was a little distraught.

"How old are you?" said Gwendolen. "I should think you are about fourteen."

"I shall be fourteen in about two months, I think," said Clemence, unused to the school custom of exact estimation of age.

There was some mirth.

"Are you not sure, Clemence?" said Maud, with a note of admonition.

"Yes, I suppose I am; I had not thought much about it. I shall be fourteen on November the twelfth."

"What a dull sort of day for a birthday!" said Esther.

"Well, Clemence had not much choice in the matter," said Maud.

"I had none that I remember," said Clemence.

"You will be the youngest in the form," said Gwendolen. "You sound as if you would be that. We are all fifteen except Maud, who is sixteen and a half. I was the youngest before you came; I was fifteen yesterday. You have ousted me from my place."

"Have you a very good brain? I suppose you have," said Esther, in a resigned tone.

"I don't know why I should be different from the rest of you."

"The relation of a headmistress would hardly be quite the same," said Verity, her tone not disguising the ambiguity in her words.

"I fail to see why, Verity," said Maud.

"I wish my head was as large as yours, if it would mean I had a better brain," said Gwendolen. "But I should cover it with my hair."

"Why do you have your hair like that?" said Esther.

"Clemence might ask us all that question, Esther," said Maud.

"No, she might not. She is the only one who wears it in an odd way."

"Oh, I don't know; I had not thought about it," said Clemence. "I do not do it myself. Does it matter how I have it? I suppose I shall have to manage it now."

"The matron can do it for you, if you tell her how. I don't see how she could know."

"If Clemence understands the theory of the matter, she can soon put it into practice," said Maud.

"Well, is that better?" said Clemence, pulling at her hair with both hands, as though in the recklessness of indifference.

83

"You do look nice, Clemence," said three voices, as all the girls but Maud linked arms and regarded the new comer.

"Let us go upstairs and see Miss Tuke unpack for her, and look at her clothes," said Gwendolen, leading the line to the door.

"Come along, Clemence," said Verity, stretching out an arm from its end. "Don't stand and look like a person apart."

"This is our usual way of progressing, Clemence," said Maud, allowing herself to be attached to the line, as though having no wish to hold aloof from anything that was not wrong.

"Miss Tuke, Clemence Shelley refuses to walk upstairs with us," said Gwendolen, entering the dormitory with her usual vigorous tread. "Do you like us to be treated with contempt?"

The matron was a pale, preoccupied woman, who seemed to defy description by having so little to be described, whose age could have been placed between thirty and fifty-eight. She was standing, in complete personal neatness but with a dishevelled air, in a room containing five beds and the corresponding pieces of furniture, and a medley of rods and curtains that seemed designed to undo the effect at a moment's notice.

"Now what is this? No nonsense at this stage of the term," she said, coming forward and kissing Clemence with an affection that had the merit of being spontaneous. "And what are you all doing upstairs at this hour?"

"We want to see you unpack Clemence's clothes. We take a great interest in her, though she takes none in us. I am afraid she has a cold heart. But have you ever seen hair like hers, Miss Tuke?"

"Yes, it is very pretty; we must take care of it," said Miss Tuke, almost looking at Clemence's head.

"Is that her box?" said Verity, with a return to her faintly mocking tone.

"Now what do you think it would be? A very good old box it is. I wish things were made as well in these days. I expect it has many associations, hasn't it, Clemence?"

"I don't know. It just came from the boxroom. There are a lot of old things up there."

"It must be more than a hundred years old," said Maud.

"Then the associations are other people's rather than Clemence's," said Gwendolen. "Perhaps her family had boxes before our families existed."

"We have an old box at home that was made in the reign of Charles the Second," said Miss Tuke, not feeling it necessary to enlarge on this light on her lineage.

"What are those things?" said Esther, indicating some linen in Miss Tuke's hands. "Underclothes?"

"Now what do you think they would be," said Miss Tuke, shaking them out.

"I don't know," said Verity, in a low tone, as though good manners deterred her from going further.

"Little window-curtains," said Esther, in a tone of suggestion. "The kind that hang by those windows that open like doors."

"I fail to see any resemblance, Esther," said Maud.

"It must be a lot of trouble to press and iron them like that," said Esther, in a manner of making some atonement.

"I don't think anyone would do it for me."

"Who does it for you, Clemence?" said Verity, with the idle note that seldom veiled her mind.

"I do not know. I suppose someone must do it."

"Indeed someone must. That is quite true," said Miss Tuke.

"Don't you really know?" said Gwendolen.

"Now why should she?" said Miss Tuke.

"She must know, of course," said Esther.

"I don't think I do. Perhaps it is Adela. Or perhaps they are done in the village."

"Well, why should we want to know?" said Verity, giving a yawn, or causing herself to give one.

"I cannot tell you," said Clemence, "but you evidently do want to. I have never wanted to know so much about anyone as you want to know about me."

"That is right, Clemence. Show spirit," said Miss Tuke, putting some pins into her mouth with no further apparent purpose for them.

"Why do people eat pins?" said Gwendolen. "No wonder children swallow them, with the example always before their eyes. Do they taste nice, Miss Tuke?"

"I have not three hands," said the latter, continuing to use the two she had.

"I hope they are wholesome," said Gwendolen. "Dressmakers have a habit of eating them."

"Hasn't she any dresses?" said Esther to Miss Tuke.

"Now what do you suppose? You might as well ask if she has any shoes."

"Well, has she? I don't see any. Have you, Clemence?"

"I expect they were put in, those I am supposed to have here."

"Don't you have all your things here?"

"Oh, I don't know. No, I don't suppose quite all of them. This is only school, after all."

"So it is Clemence," said Miss Tuke, in a tone of absent but warm approval.

"I have things bought for me especially for school, that I should not have, if I were at home," said Esther, covering with rapid lightness what seemed to be an extreme admission.

"I have one or two things kept at home, that are supposed to be too good to wear here," said Gwendolen. "They are just stored up and go out of fashion, and they are the things that suit me best."

"Dear, dear, that is the way of the world," said Miss Tuke.

"I wear all my things both at home and at school, or I should not have enough," said Verity, lifting her shoulders.

"Fortunate people that you are, to have everything arranged for you!" said Miss Tuke.

"What do you do, Maud?" said Verity.

"I had not thought, Verity. I may not always do the same thing. Is it such an interesting subject?"

"Yes, of course it is," said Gwendolen. "It throws light into all sorts of shadowy corners. I am fascinated by it."

"We must learn to look things in the face," said Verity. "We are the future women of England."

"Now what nonsense next?" said Miss Tuke.

"Well, what is the subject?" said a rather deep, dry voice. "It seems to be one of great interest."

"It is of the greatest interest, Miss Chancellor," said Gwendolen, turning at once to the door. "Clemence Shelley does not bring her clothes to school because they are too good to wear amongst people like us. What do you think of it?"

"I do not think of it at all, Gwendolen. The clothes are not my province," said the new-comer, adjusting her glasses in a manner that suggested others, as she regarded the scene with steady, moderate interest. "So this is Clemence Shelley? How do you do, Clemence?"

"Quite well, thank you," murmured Verity, as though this would be Clemence's natural rejoinder.

Miss Chancellor appeared not to hear, and continued with her eyes on the latter.

"I think you are the only addition to my form this term."

"Are you not sure?" said Esther.

"No, I am not sure, Esther. I only know that there is one extra name on my list, and that it is probably that of Clemence," said Miss Chancellor, on her way to Miss Tuke as the centre-point of the group. "How are you, Miss Tuke? I hope you are rested after the holidays. You set us an example by being at work so soon."

"Other people's work cannot begin until some of mine is done," said Miss Tuke, taking the pins from her mouth in rapid succession.

"How do you do, Maud?" said Miss Chancellor, on an equal and cordial note. "Can you say that you are glad to be back at work again?"

"Yes, thank you, Miss Chancellor. On the whole I am very glad."

"Are you glad, Miss Chancellor?" said Verity.

"Well, my feelings are mixed, Verity. I cannot quite emulate Maud's wholeheartedness," said Miss Chancellor, turning her glasses on Verity in a somehow unsparing manner.

Miss Chancellor had bright, near-set, near-sighted eyes, a bony, irregular nose, with glasses riding uncertainly on it, and a suggestion about her of acting according to her conception of herself. She looked older than her thirty-six years, and seeing the circumstance as the result of weight of personality, was not without satisfaction in it.

"When do we have tea, Miss Chancellor?" said Gwendolen. "I am beginning to think of nothing else."

"I do not know, Gwendolen. I had not thought. But I suppose at the usual time. You all seem to assign to me a good many provinces that are not mine. And I am far from being a person of general activities like Miss Tuke. I am rather a specialised individual."

"You have a high opinion of yourself, haven't you, Miss Chancellor?" said Verity.

"Have I, Verity? I do not know what I said to imply it. And I hope I have no higher a one than is healthy and natural, and gives me a standard to live up to. We are none of us the worse for that. I hope you are not without it yourself, and I should not have said you were."

"I suppose you think I am a conceited creature."

"So that was the idea in your mind," said Miss Chancellor, with a laugh.

"Things are different on the first day," said Gwendolen. "I wish the bell would go. Don't you want some tea, Miss Chancellor?"

"Well, I shall be glad of a cup, Gwendolen, now that you

speak of it," said the latter, as though such a desire in herself were dependent on suggestion.

"I shall be glad of a good deal more. I had luncheon early, and I was crying too much to eat."

"I can hardly imagine it, Gwendolen," said Miss Chancellor with a smile.

"I am longing for the plain and wholesome school fare."

"I am not," said Esther. "I am dreading three months of it. The holidays are hardly long enough to recover."

Maud looked out of the window, as though a thing better not said were better not heard.

"Are you tired after your journey, Esther?" said Miss Chancellor, as though seeking an excuse for something that needed it.

"Yes, I am rather, Miss Chancellor."

"Poor Esther, she is easily tired," said Miss Tuke, her eyes on a garment she was holding up before them.

"Are you tired, Clemence?" said Miss Chancellor.

"No, thank you."

"Was your journey a long one?"

"No, quite short. Only about an hour."

"Did your mother bring you?"

"Yes. She has gone back now."

"Well, well, we can't keep everyone with us," said Miss Tuke.

"Especially if you have as many people as Clemence has," said Gwendolen. "Her mother and her governess brought her, Miss Chancellor. One person was enough to bring the rest of us, and Maud came alone. That shows that Clemence is twice as important as we are."

"And how many times as important as Maud? Really, Gwendolen, your method of estimating relative importance is an odd one. What do you think of it, Clemence?"

"Well, of course it has not anything in it."

"It is usual to use people's names, Clemence, when you are talking to people who are older than you, and who are going to teach you," said Miss Chancellor, in an even, pleasant tone, that hurried towards the next words. "Is this your first experience of school life?"

"Yes, Miss Chancellor."

"She will be the youngest in the form, Miss Chancellor," said Gwendolen, urged to compliment by the reproof. "She is still under fourteen. Don't you find yourself looking at her hair?"

"Well, if I may make a personal remark, it is very pretty. I hope she will take care of it. Do you manage it yourself, Clemence?"

"I have not done it yet. But I think I could learn. I am supposed to be careless with it."

"Dear, dear, we must have an end of that," said Miss Tuke. "What a confession!"

"I am sure you could learn a good many things, Clemence," said Miss Chancellor.

"Twelve weeks of term!" said Esther, sinking into a chair. "Shall we, any of us, survive?"

"Yes, I think I may say you all will, Esther. Anyhow your having done so several times is a reasonable ground for supposing it. And this happens to be a short term. Christmas is not so far away."

"Three months to plum pudding," said Gwendolen, "and I am ravenous already."

"Really, Gwendolen, the unvarying line of your thought!"

"She is growing, poor child," said Miss Tuke.

"I wish it was not necessary to be educated. Why is it, Miss Chancellor?"

"Now I do not think you expect that question to be answered, Gwendolen."

"If it were not, our parents could have the advantage of us. And mine find me a great pleasure. I think being educated is rather selfish."

"Well, it has that side, Gwendolen," said Miss Chancellor, in an unbiased tone. "It is true that it has. But the result should give you more for everyone in the end."

"If we were not being educated, Miss Chancellor would not have to be here—would not be here," said Esther, rapidly. "She would be as glad as we should."

"Well, it would have its bright side, Esther," said Miss Chancellor, in a dispassionate tone. "But there are compensations in every life, if we look for them. I have always found them in mine and been grateful for them."

"You want compensation for being with us, Miss Chancellor. That is a cruel thing to say to hungry and helpless children," said Gwendolen. "The tea-bell! The sound that cheers so much that it almost inebriates!"

"That is an individual turn to the expression, Gwendolen," said Miss Chancellor, turning her instinctive movement to the door into a smiling advance towards her pupil.

"Are you going out, Miss Chancellor?" said Maud, pausing in the doorway.

"Thank you, Maud. I suppose we must obey the summons," said Miss Chancellor, leading the way with another adjustment of her glasses.

"What would happen to Miss Chancellor's spectacles, if she did not keep on attending to them?" said Gwendolen.

"They would fall off, Gwendolen," said Miss Chancellor, turning with some liveliness. "That is what would happen. My nose is the wrong shape for glasses, and my eyes the wrong kind for doing without them. And they are glasses, not spectacles."

"Would spectacles interfere with your personality?" said Verity.

"Yes, in the sense that most people would see them as you evidently do, Verity."

"Miss Chancellor is really as eager for food as any of us," said Esther, in a whisper, or what she intended to be such, breaking off as she observed a modification of Miss Chancellor's bearing.

The latter paused, threw back her head, and emitted a little peal of mirth.

"Well, really, Esther, what a way of expressing yourself! I hope we all have good appetites, and shall satisfy them to the extent of keeping well and being equal to our work. I never heard that an appetite was a thing to be ashamed of. Indeed, I was taught that that kind of refinement belonged to another sphere."

"Yes, Miss Chancellor," muttered Esther, glancing at her companions.

"And I am quite content to do my duty in that station of life to which—to which I am called," said Miss Chancellor, adapting the quotation to the lightness of the moment, and taking her stand in readiness for grace, with her eyes held above the board, as though disregard of food were natural in certain conditions.

Lesbia came to the table and looked at its supplies before she bent her head. Meals were a welcome break in her routine and she did not disguise it, thinking it a healthy view of them.

Gwendolen murmured to her neighbour as she took her seat.

"There was an old woman and what do you think?
She lived upon nothing but victuals and drink."

"What did you say, Gwendolen?"

"I said that—we lived upon nothing but victuals and drink, Miss Firebrace."

"Well, have some of both, Gwendolen. I am sorry we can offer you nothing else."

A thin, dark, grey-haired woman at Lesbia's hand, who was a partner in the school, turned absent, grey eyes on the newcomer.

"Clemence Shelley? Your little cousin, Miss Firebrace?"

"Yes," said Lesbia, in an audible tone of saying what was of sufficient, but not excessive interest. "Or my little connection by marriage. She is to be in Miss Chancellor's form and so will be with you for some subjects."

Miss Laurence smiled at Clemence in automatic, kindly interest, and appeared to sink into abstraction, a state that so often claimed her that it had come almost to be required of her, and tended to be less complete than it seemed.

"I think she is adapting herself easily to her new surroundings," said another voice, as the third partner smiled at Clemence. "And that is a great art."

The number of partners in the school was in excess of its resources. It had been necessary to bring it into being, and was still so, to maintain it in this state. Lesbia drew a veil over it, and tended to pass over her partners' existence, when they were not there to establish it.

Miss Marathon's upright figure, pronounced nose and prominent, expressionless eyes gave her a somewhat forbidding aspect, that was hardly borne out by her pupils' demeanour towards her. She sat among them and supervised their needs in a. manner at once precise and kindly, critical and tolerant. Miss Laurence was recognised as too intellectual for tangible affairs, and remained aloof and did nothing, thereby both creating and fulfilling a part. Her pupils regarded her with affection and fear, or merely with the latter. Miss Marathon they regarded with neither, and with no other particular feeling.

Miss Chancellor sat by Miss Laurence, and seemed to identify herself with her aloof attitude, and indeed with any other that she displayed.

"Clemence, do have some victuals and drink," said Gwendolen. "I hope you do not feel as if every mouthful would choke you. Clemence feels that every mouthful will choke her, Miss Chancellor. And it is not reasonable when she is not taking any mouthfuls."

"It sounds as if you were right to urge her to modify her course, Gwendolen."

"All the attention will be for Clemence now, I expect," said Esther.

"What did you say, Esther?" said Lesbia, in a tone of according interest to everyone's utterance.

"Nothing, Miss Firebrace."

"Then it is of no good for us to pursue it. But how you

managed to observe something and say nothing, I do not know."

"An answer unworthy of your years, Esther," said Miss Chancellor.

"Did you enjoy your holiday, Maud?" said Miss Marathon, going on to safe ground with a safe companion.

"Yes, thank you, Miss Marathon. I have never enjoyed a holiday more. But I find I am glad to get back to work again."

A sighing sound, as of incredulous consternation, went round the girls, and Lesbia turned her eyes on them.

"Now which of you is acting in accordance with her real convictions? Or is 'acting' the right word in another sense? Do you really feel such an objection to being educated, Gwendolen?"

"Yes, Miss Firebrace."

"Do you, Esther?"

"Well, Miss Firebrace, it is not the pleasantest part of the year, and it is two-thirds of it."

"And you, Verity?"

"Well, I do not agree that our schooldays are the happiest time of our life, Miss Firebrace. Or anyhow I hope they are not."

"Neither do I agree, Verity. I hope that will not be the case. I hope there are fuller and more useful—yes, more useful, Verity—times ahead of you, more useful to other people. But the foundations of them have to be laid. I should have thought you were old enough to realise that. We may not always be enough in ourselves to come to our own fulfilment without help."

"I don't expect people ever realise that the times they are living are foundations of other times," said Clemence.

Miss Laurence and Miss Marathon smiled towards her, welcoming her entry into the talk, faintly deprecating any advance upon the freedom of it.

Lesbia remained grave.

"We must beware of presenting ourselves according to

some rule of our own, and not in our true colours," she said, as she rose from her seat. "That is at best a mere lip-service to convention."

There was silence, and Miss Laurence and Miss Marathon raised their eyes.

"And at its worst a simple acting for effect," said Lesbia, leaving the table.

Her partners looked at their pupils almost in sympathy for the consequences of their heedlessness.

"So we are under a cloud already," said Esther. "The storm has rolled up in the first few hours."

"That is very graphic, Esther," said Miss Marathon, in an uncertain tone.

"I feel I managed to bring it on you all," said Maud.

Miss Laurence and Miss Marathon rose and left the room, leaving what was irrepressible to find its outlet.

"No, Maud, you need not feel that," said Miss Chancellor. "You spoke the truth simply and sincerely, and no one can be asked to regret that."

"I ask Maud to regret it," said Gwendolen. "She startled us into betraying ourselves. We could have told Miss Firebrace we were glad to languish in exile."

"If you did not feel it, Gwendolen, it was better not to say it."

"It was probably better not to say that," said Clemence.

"It did not seem so much better," said Gwendolen.

"We suffered for the faith that was in us," said Verity.

"And what faith is that, Verity?" said Lesbia's voice.

There was the slightest pause.

"Faith in the value of freedom, Miss Firebrace."

"That was ready, Verity," said Lesbia, in a tone of giving ungrudging approbation where it was merited. "I do not know how far it was the expression of the truth, but I hold to what I say; it was ready."

Verity suppressed a smile.

"Miss Firebrace felt she had gone rather far," muttered Esther. "She is trying to retrieve her position."

Lesbia turned her eyes on Esther, kept them on her for some seconds, and withdrew them without speaking.

"Esther, you and I are the only ones who do not attain any credit," said Gwendolen.

"Is that so, Gwendolen? Then take some credit for bringing back to us a cheerful face," said Lesbia, smoothing Gwendolen's hair, and then turning to Esther with a different expression.

"Are you very tired after your journey, Esther?"

"Yes, Miss Firebrace; I cannot endure travelling."

"Poor child!" said Lesbia, putting out her hand with a similar purpose, but seeming to reconsider the matter and withdrawing it. "I shall be glad to feel you are in bed. I think you had better go up to Miss Tuke now. Yes, go straight upstairs, Esther. If you are so tired, that is the right course for you."

"Good-night, Miss Firebrace."

"Good-night, Esther."

The girls bade Lesbia a formal good-night, and received each a separate and full response. She stood and watched them as they left the room, and meeting a glance from Miss Chancellor, nodded as though in agreement. As the latter went to the door, there was a sound of Gwendolen's voice.

"My movements were stiff and self-conscious under Miss Firebrace's eyes."

Lesbia and Miss Chancellor yielded to amusement, and the latter followed her pupils to the dormitory.

"I suppose Miss Firebrace is really our second mother," said Gwendolen. "Anyhow I do not know who is, if she is not. And I think people generally have second mothers. It is second fathers they do not seem to have. I don't know why."

"It is not the term I should apply to her," said Esther.

"Now, be careful, Esther," said Miss Chancellor. "You are over-tired, and may say things you will regret."

"I will have Miss Tuke for my second mother. I think her feelings towards us come more from the heart. It is a mistake to come to bed so early. We shall have to cry for so long."

"Well, really, Gwendolen, what a very odd compulsion!"

"You ought not to brush other people's troubles lightly aside, Miss Chancellor. We have been torn from home and kindred."

"Well, so have I, Gwendolen, and I am not going to cry."

"Yes, but, Miss Chancellor, you can do as you like," said Verity. "You are not forced to spend three months away from your natural surroundings."

"No, I cannot do as I like, Verity; you are mistaken," said Miss Chancellor, looking straight at her pupil as she made her admission. "I am also the victim of compulsion, a different one from yours, but quite as binding."

"And then people say the age of slavery is past," said Gwendolen, sitting down on her bed.

"Slavery, but not service, Gwendolen. I hope we shall never get beyond that."

"Gwendolen, your quilt!" said Miss Tuke. "It is fresh today, and the bed has not been turned down."

"I knew we had come upstairs too soon."

"You are too old for such carelessness, Gwendolen," said Miss Chancellor.

"I am too old for the things I do, and not old enough for the things I want to do. Fifteen is an intolerable age."

"Indeed it is not, Gwendolen, if you would realise its opportunities. I wish I had realised them at that age and made the most of them."

"So do I, Miss Chancellor. I already wish it," said Maud.

"Well, I think that is rather premature, Maud. You can put off your regrets a little longer. You have still plenty of time to make up for any you have lost."

"Poor Maud! Carrying a load of regret for a wasted youth!" said Verity. "I could see she carried some kind of burden."

"What would you have been doing, Miss Chancellor, if you had used your opportunities?" said Esther. "Not what you are doing now?"

"The same sort of thing, Esther, but on a different plane and in a wider sphere," said Miss Chancellor, looking fully at the speaker and using her unsparing note.

"You wish you had not seen any of us, Miss Chancellor. I shall cry longer than I thought."

"Now that is not quite a fair way of putting it, Gwendolen. As you will see, if you think."

"Of course we are unbearable creatures, and no one can tolerate us," said Verity, approaching her bed to throw herself upon it, but dragging off the quilt before she did so.

"Thank you, Verity," said Miss Tuke.

"I don't know if it is very rude to ask you to speak for yourself, Verity," said Miss Chancellor, laughing.

"Are those Clemence's dresses, Miss Tuke?" said Esther.

"Yes. They are all together in her cupboard. Now no one is to interfere with them."

The girls gathered round the wardrobe and handled the garments as if they had received the opposite injunction. Verity lifted herself off the bed and came with a languid stride to join them.

"What is that dress?" said Esther. "I mean, what kind of a dress is it?"

"Well, surely you can see that, Esther," said Miss Chancellor. "A muslin dress meant for rather better occasions. There is no mystery about it."

"I think there is one," said Esther rapidly. "It is not good enough for a party and not much good for anything else. I find it a mystery."

"It did for little, garden tea-parties," said Clemence, just glancing at it.

"It would be most suitable for those," said Miss Chancellor.

"Why did you bring it here?" said Gwendolen. "Did you expect to have garden-parties at school?"

"Oh, I suppose it was put in."

"Don't you see your own packing done?" said Esther.

"No, I do not trouble about it. Of course I have never had it done before."

"Have you never been away from home?"

"Not alone, so that my things had to be packed separately."

"Do you see your packing done, Maud?" said Verity, in her idle tone.

"I do it myself, Verity. There is no one to do it for me."

"Cannot the servants do it?" said Esther, as though her bluntness were sufficiently established to justify itself.

"There are only two, Esther, and they have not time. My mother is not strong and needs a good deal of attention."

"Could not your mother help you?" said Gwendolen.

"I should not dream of asking her, Gwendolen. I would rather manage by myself."

"Has your mother a cold heart?"

"Well, really, Gwendolen! What will Maud think of you?" said Miss Chancellor.

"No, but she has not a strong one," said Maud, her gravity unshaken in the face of a sound of mirth. "I feel it is for me to take things off her rather than put them on."

"Gwendolen, you do not know the difficulties and demands of other households," said Miss Chancellor, gravely.

"No, but I am trying to learn them, and my sympathies are growing wider."

"I hope Maud's are wide enough to embrace your childishness."

"Did you bring more than one trunk, Clemence?" said Esther.

"I do not know. I am not quite sure."

"Now I do know, Clemence," said Miss Chancellor.

"You brought one large, interesting one. I saw you and your mother arrive from my window. I happened to be looking out."

"And the governess with them," said Esther. "Clemence travels with an escort."

"No, no governess, Esther. Clemence simply came with her mother, as you all did. You let your imagination run away with you."

"Mine is not the only imagination that does that," said Esther, in a light tone, separating the dresses with her hand.

"Where is your party dress, Clemence?"

"I expect at home. That kind of thing would be there. Do you have real parties at school?"

"There is the break-up party at the end of this term. It is regarded as the climax of the year."

"Well, twelve weeks will give Clemence plenty of time to send for a dress," said Miss Chancellor.

"I believe the muslin is her party dress."

"Why, what a tone to use, Esther! You sound as if you were accusing her of a crime."

"I should not mind if it was. What is the matter with it?" said Clemence, preparing the way for any eventual climax. "It is only a little, schoolgirl party, I suppose."

"Well, that is what it would be, Clemence, in our present situation," said Maud.

"What kind of parties did you have at home?" said Gwendolen.

"I hardly did have them. There were no little, ordinary ones. And I am not old enough for the others."

"Don't you have a Christmas tree and things like that?"

"Yes, but they are mostly for the villagers. It would not do to dress for those," said Clemence, giving a little laugh.

"Clemence's life has had duties as well as pleasures," said Miss Chancellor.

"What is your real party dress like? Describe it to us," said Esther.

"I thought you said the muslin was my party dress."

"Well, I think you deserved that, Esther. You brought it on yourself," said Miss Chancellor.

"Do tell us what it is like, Clemence," said Gwendolen.

"Oh, I don't know. I have hardly seen it. It has been so little good. And I daresay I have grown out of it."

"And you do not care if you have, Clemence," said Miss Chancellor, smiling.

"Will you have it at the end of the term?" said Verity.

"I suppose it will be sent, if I ask for it, or one something like it. I don't much like party dresses. They are too different from the ordinary kind."

"That is a reasonable criticism of some of them, Clemence," said Maud.

"Maud has never worn one against which the criticism could be brought," said Verity, in a murmur that seemed designed to escape the general ear, and apparently did escape Maud's, as she gave every sign of not hearing it.

"Things that are grown out of, and cannot be seen, might just as well not exist," said Esther "I daresay they often do not."

"Esther, we know you are over-tired," said Maud. "Otherwise we should not be proud of you."

"I hope the same excuse can be made for you, Verity," said Miss Chancellor, "but you do not look over-tired."

Verity moved to her bed and sank down on it, giving colour to another view.

"Well, I don't mind if it doesn't," said Clemence, with a laugh. "It would be a fussy-looking thing. And I like things that are old and comfortable." She settled her shoulders in the dress she wore.

"You said it did exist," said Esther. "Or you implied it."

"Well, it may have found its way to the rag-bag by now."

"We could all have plenty of dresses on that understanding."

"Or it may be unearthed and lengthened and altered and given to me instead of a new one. Then you will have the pleasure of seeing it. Though I should not think it would be much pleasure."

"It is easy to see you have not been to school before, Clemence," said Miss Chancellor. "But I understand you have done a fair amount of work at home."

"Yes, with a governess, and with my brother's tutor."

"You have learned Latin and Greek?"

"Yes, up to a point. Of course, not very much of them."

"Greek?" said Gwendolen. "Then are you going to do something, when you grow up?"

"Do something? How do you mean?"

"Well, I hope she will not do nothing, Gwendolen," said Miss Chancellor.

"Do some sort of work for a salary," said Esther.

"No, I do not suppose so. Why, are the rest of you going to?"

"No, but we do not learn Greek."

"I envy you Clemence," said Maud.

"So do I, Maud," said Miss Chancellor. "I wish I had had such opportunities when I was young. We shall see if Clemence has made the most of them. Or rather Miss Laurence will tell us in her own good time, or will tell herself. What she tells us is her own affair."

"I hope she will not tell me," said Clemence.

"You need not be afraid, Clemence. There is nothing to fear in Miss Laurence's teaching, for those who can respond to her influence. That there may be for those who do not, I do not deny. It would be idle to do so."

"I do not know what her real influence is," said Gwendolen. "She rules me by fear."

"You are very fond of Miss Laurence, are you not, Miss Chancellor?" said Verity.

"Yes, very fond, Verity. She taught me when I was your age, and it was an experience not to be forgotten. I certainly shall never forget it."

"Being taught by someone does not always make people fond of the person," said Esther.

"No, it does not, Esther. I do not flatter myself, for example, that any of you are very fond of me. But I can do my work and find it interesting, in spite of that. Indeed I do not find that that sort of feeling plays much part in my life."

"People are supposed to be proud of odd things," said Verity. "And I suppose a failure to inspire human affection is one of them."

"But Miss Laurence is another matter," went on Miss Chancellor. "She has the gift of inspiring her pupils, or some of them, with a strong feeling."

"I do not call it a gift," said Gwendolen. "It is a vice."

"Well, but, Miss Chancellor, you are not very fond of us, are you?" said Verity.

"No, I am not, Verity," said Miss Chancellor, with the unsparing note. "As I have said, affection is not necessary, and perhaps not natural, to me in such a relation. I neither inspire it nor feel it. But Miss Laurence often does both. Clemence is fortunate to meet with teaching on that level."

"And are not the rest of us fortunate?" said Esther.

"You can answer that question for yourself, Esther. I cannot do it for you."

"I wish you would stop boasting of things you ought to be ashamed of, Miss Chancellor," said Gwendolen. "You are fond of us, aren't you, dear Miss Tuke?"

"Dear, dear! What should I do without you all?" said the latter, continuing her occupations under existing conditions.

"You are unfeeling, Miss Chancellor," said Verity. "You make no attempt to come near to us."

"No, I do not, Verity. It is the last thing I should think due from me to you," said Miss Chancellor, going to the door. "Now, I hope you will all sleep well and appear punctual and bright in my classroom in the morning."

"I hope you will sleep, Miss Chancellor," said Gwendolen, "but I do not see how you can, with such a burden of remorse upon you."

"Miss Chancellor has taken a fancy to Clemence," said Esther.

"And promised her that Miss Laurence shall do the same," said Verity.

"Now how much more time are you going to waste?" said Miss Tuke. "The other girls will wonder what has happened to me."

"I wish you would ignore their claims and sit with us until we are asleep," said Gwendolen. "This harsh bringing-up will make hard women of us. We shall want other people to suffer as we have."

"I wonder what you would say, if you had one," said Miss Tuke, going round the beds and imprinting a kiss on each cheek. "Now no more chatter until the morning. I put you on your honour not to say another word."

"Why did you say that your governess came with you to school, when really only your mother did?" said Esther to Clemence, as the door closed.

"Did I say so? I got so muddled by all your questions. And she did come. She did some shopping while my mother was here, and they were to travel back together."

"Then she did not come to the house?"

"Yes, she came and went away again. They were to meet at the station."

"Then she could not have been getting into the cab at the last. You knew it was your mother."

"I did not know who it was. She might have come back at any time. She is always here and there and everywhere."

"But if she had come back, you would have seen her."

"I might not have. I did not stay in the drawing-room all the time. It seemed that my mother and Miss Firebrace wanted to talk without me."

"As was to be expected, Clemence," said Maud.

"But wouldn't you have gone back to say goodbye to the governess?" said Esther. "Or is yours an old-fashioned family where she is not treated like other people?"

"We said goodbye in the morning, before I started."

"But you could not have, if you were to travel together."

"Oh, indeed we could. You don't know the Petticoat's goodbyes. They stretch right over the past and future. Nothing that we could have said here, would have added to them."

"We all know that sort of goodbye," said Maud, "and it was a very natural occasion on which to have one. Now do leave poor Clemence alone, Esther. Anyone might find the first day confusing, and you are not doing anything to make it less so. And naturally she knows her own affairs."

"Well, if she does not, she can easily produce some others," said Esther, in a rapid undertone. "And I do not think she is confused. And I quite agree with everyone that she is clever."

"Can you call Miss Petticott by the old nursery name without getting a lump in your throat?" said Gwendolen.

"I do not think about it; we have done it for so long," said Clemence, her voice uncertain, as this condition threatened her.

"Poor Clemence! She has had a long day, and we have all been teasing her," said Maud.

Esther turned her pillow and closed her eyes, dissociating herself from a situation to which she had perhaps sufficiently contributed.

"I am going to get you a glass of water, Clemence," said Gwendolen. "I think a cup of cold water is what it would be called."

"Gwendolen, are you thinking of what you are saying?" said Maud.

Clemence rose in the morning with a sense that a cloud threatened her world, and that she must walk warily until it was dispelled.

Things passed as she would have expected, until they assembled in the classroom. Miss Chancellor checked the names and set matters on foot, and waited for Miss Laurence, who was to succeed her. She had a tendency to welcome encounter with the latter, and was not expected to withdraw until it had taken place. Miss Laurence entered a little behind her time, a little absent and distraught, and more than a little dishevelled, which last circumstance was accepted as an occasional adjunct to a picture that as a whole invited no criticism. Miss Chancellor rose, collided with her, made a full apology, and was repaid by a more perfunctory one. Gwendolen opened the door for Miss Chancellor and received a courteous acknowledgment, which she did not take as directed to herself. Miss Laurence confronted her class and proceeded to fulfil her character.

"Now have I left my books behind? Shall I have to teach you out of my head? I hope I have not forgotten all I know, as I have no doubt you have. Perhaps we had better all begin at the beginning."

"There are your books, Miss Laurence," said Verity, indicating a pile that Miss Laurence had just put down.

"So they are, my good, observant child. Now we can make our impression on Clemence. She is used to masculine tuition, and is ready to look down on us. Will you read the Latin in turn and then translate the passages? I know you are not prepared, and that it will be painful to hear you, but we have to get through the hour. Maud, Verity, Esther, Gwendolen, Clemence. That is your order on the books. I wonder what it will be at the end of the term."

"I expect Clemence will be the first, and before that date," said Esther.

It looked as if this might be the case. Clemence was in advance of the rest, and when she had a private lesson in Greek, also acquitted herself well. She was treated with ordinary, unexaggerated approval, but she felt her success, saw a word exchanged by Miss Laurence and Miss Chancellor, and had bright eyes and cheeks by the middle of the morning.

"Nothing succeeds like success," said Esther. "Would anyone think that Clemence was the same person as she was yesterday?"

"Well, you are rather different yourself, Esther," said Maud. "And it is not too much to say that we hope you will remain so. You and Clemence were both over-tired, though she gave less evidence of it."

"Her memory was odd," said Esther. "That is a sign of fatigue."

"Perhaps it is as well not to talk about the different signs of it, Esther."

"Miss Chancellor, I have conquered myself," said Gwendolen. "I have got over my jealousy of Clemence. It belongs to a self I have left behind."

"I am glad its life was such a short one, Gwendolen," said Miss Chancellor, finding her amusement echoed by Lesbia, who stood, as she frequently did, in silent attention.

"Her success shall be sweeter to me than my own."

"Your success would be sweet to me, Gwendolen," said Lesbia, advancing and speaking gravely. "Yes it would. And I mean what I say. I hope you will try to attain it this term."

"I am not a clever person, Miss Firebrace."

"No, you are not. That is not your word. But you have your own capacities, if you would use them. And I am asking you to do so."

"Yes, Miss Firebrace."

"I hope you will all act up to the best that is in you," said Lesbia, looking from face to face. "This is a small form, and each of you has a chance to make her mark, and leave it. That is not always the case and may not always be so. You should make the most of it."

"The forms seem to get smaller and smaller. I suppose the school is going down," said Esther, after allowing time for Lesbia to withdraw.

"And why do you think that, Esther?" said the latter, who had not availed herself of it.

"Well, if the numbers get less, I suppose that is how it must be."

"Our numbers are larger," said Lesbia, in a cool,

incidental tone. "We have arranged small forms, and more of them, for your benefit. We hope to be able to maintain the arrangement, but questions are involved that are beyond your scope. That is why I have advised you to make the most of it."

"I suppose our parents do not pay enough," said Esther, after waiting again for Lesbia's withdrawal, and this time ascertaining that it had taken place.

"Well, there must be a certain correspondence in things, Esther," said Maud.

"My father says the bills increase. And I cannot see any advantage in such small forms myself."

"Well, I can, Esther," said Miss Marathon, entering with her books under her arm, and in no doubt of their whereabouts, "if I may answer a speech that was not addressed to me. It prevents pupils from getting to the back of the class and taking advantage of it in their own way. I think we remember some incidents of that kind."

The girls just glanced at Esther, who had figured in one of these, and silence ensued while Miss Marathon chalked a problem on the board. As the girls took it down, Esther's voice was again audible, though intentionally only to her neighbour.

"This place is a nest of professional eavesdroppers."

Miss Marathon raised her eyes in complex feeling, and a voice came as though in response to the mute appeal.

"It is true that I have a profession, Esther, but it is not that of eavesdropper. I have a right to walk where I will in my own house, and I shall continue to use it. And it is a pity you so often say things that you do not wish to be heard, that is, that you are a little ashamed of. If you broke yourself of the habit, you would not need to be concerned about what you choose to call eavesdropping."

There was silence over this choice of Esther's, and Lesbia continued in an even, distinct tone.

"I do not take a harsh or narrow view of the intercourse amongst you. No, I do not, Esther. You are allowed more latitude than is often the case. You would not meet it every-where. I know that young people must talk, and that it is idle to look for much weight or worth in what they say—or to listen for it, if you will." Miss Marathon just raised her eyes at this open appraisement. "But things must be kept within certain bounds, and within those bounds they will be kept. Do you understand me, Esther?"

"Yes, Miss Firebrace."

"Do you not all agree with me?" said Lesbia, looking round.

There was no reply, and Lesbia repeated her question in a manner that necessitated one.

"Yes, Miss Firebrace."

"Well, I will leave you to your mathematics. Indeed, I am due elsewhere," said Lesbia, taking out her watch and turning on her way. "You will forgive the interruption, Miss Marathon; it was not of my seeking."

"Now here is Clemence working away by herself, while the rest of us have been wasting our time," said Miss Marathon, more concerned with restoring normal conditions than with doing justice to her partner. "Now let us see how she has managed. What is her answer to the question?"

Clemence gave it, and Miss Marathon smiled in approval.

"That is very good. We have all been set an example. And now we will have an easier problem, as we have been a little disturbed. Clemence has done it in her head! So I will ask her not to answer the next one. We must all be given a chance, and mere quickness is not everything. Not that I know why I use the word, 'mere'; it may be based on something deeper. That is right, Verity; I am glad some-one else has managed it. And now here is one that calls for something more than quickness. Write the answer in your books, and I will come round and see. No, do not give up without making an effort, Gwendolen. Trying in itself has its educational value. Verity and Clemence have both managed it. We must accept them as our leaders. Maud, it is time that you made some contribution to our success."

"I am not good at mathematics, Miss Marathon."

"I know it is not your strong point. But Clemence is good at other things as well. Indeed, she refutes the theory that classical and mathematical ability do not meet."

"Miss Laurence has both," said Esther, as though the combination were not so rare.

"Yes, there is nothing mutually exclusive about them. And now our time is at an end. Of course it got a little wasted—a little—at the beginning. Yes, Miss Chancellor, you will have your hour. I am not encroaching upon it."

"Clemence goes from strength to strength, Miss Chancellor," said Gwendolen. "My heart swells with pride in her."

"That is more than my heart does in any of you, when I look at last term's history papers. Apart from Maud, you might all have gone back to your childhood."

"I thought I was still in my childhood."

"I am afraid you are, Gwendolen. You are remaining in it a little too long. You must try to get beyond it. Now I am going to read some history aloud, and then you can write a summary of it. That will show me how Clemence competes with the rest."

"Clemence, Clemence, Clemence!" muttered Esther. "I thought her being Miss Firebrace's cousin was to make no difference."

"And you were right, Esther. It is to make none. And she is not Miss Firebrace's cousin. And 'compete' was the wrong word. I am sure she has none of the feelings that it suggests. Now will you all give me your attention?"

"I wish I were having luncheon instead of writing this history," said Gwendolen, as the hour advanced. "Don't you wish you were, Miss Chancellor?"

"No, Gwendolen, the wish had not occurred to me. And have I given you permission to interrupt the class?"

"No, Miss Chancellor. But I thought you would be sorry I was tired and hungry and make allowance."

"Well, if that is really the case, Gwendolen, you may break off and have a rest before luncheon. Now I think of it, you do look a little tired. Has anyone else come to the end of her tether?"

"Yes, Miss Chancellor," said Esther and Verity together.

"No, thank you, Miss Chancellor," said Maud, continuing to write.

"Are you tired and hungry, Clemence?"

"No, thank you, Miss Chancellor. But I have finished the account."

"Well, that is a good reason for leaving it. So we will leave Maud working in solitary state and go into the passage for a breathing-space. Perhaps we do deserve it. The morning is rather long. Not that I do not often wish we could get more into it. So it is ungrateful of me to complain of its length."

"Miss Chancellor was betrayed into uttering an ordinary human sentiment," said Verity.

"Yes, I do rather feel that happened to me, Verity," said Miss Chancellor, laughing and leading the way into the corridor, unconscious of the extent of her self-betrayal. "Why, there is your luncheon bell, Gwendolen, three minutes before its time! Are we to congratulate you?" She laughed at the idea as she directed her steps to the dining-room.

"I am glad the bell is not only Gwendolen's," said Clemence.

"Why, so am I, Clemence," said Miss Chancellor, in a tone of realising something about herself. "I find I am quite glad, now that the moment comes."

Clemence followed in a mood of exaltation and doubt. She had attained success, but was unsure of its foundations. She had put out her effort, shown her resource, and felt they were seen as the basis of further things. Would she be able to go from strength to strength? Could she keep this distance that might be less than was thought? Was her father so anxious for her success? Was her mother as anxious as she said?

She settled to the work and talk that seemed to constitute her life; paid little heed to the games that did not touch her pride; and took the second place on the weekly lists with a plausible appearance of content, as the first was dedicated to Maud and toil, and held less glamour. No one but the latter, who sometimes had a sense of pursuit, suspected that she strove for the first place. Her mother's letters moved her to further effort, one from her father to tears. The last rendered her distraught for a day, and showed how easily her ascendance might be lost. Her companions were not without parts, and worked with less pains; what they did not do easily, they left undone; and they could add to their stature when she had to struggle to maintain hers. She began to seek further methods of advance, and one day put an open book, with some lists she was supposed to know, just inside her desk, more to give herself a sense of security than with any definite purpose. Miss Laurence noticed the raised lid, opened it and thrust the book within, giving a rapid glance at Clemence and as rapidly withdrawing it. The latter attended to the lesson without sign of discomposure, though she noticed that Esther and Verity observed the incident and exchanged a glance. At the end of the hour Esther approached.

"Why did you have that book of rules open inside your desk?"

"Oh, it is best to glance over things at the last moment. Don't you find it is? I find it makes all the difference. It brings things to the front of your mind, that have got to the back. Everything can't always be in the foreground."

Verity stood with her eyes on Clemence, and said nothing.

"Miss Laurence shut it up and put it away quickly enough," said Esther.

"Perhaps she thought Clemence might open her desk and take a peep," said Gwendolen with a laugh.

"You should not say things like that, Gwendolen, even as a joke," said Maud.

"Many a true word is spoken in jest," said Esther.

"But many more untrue ones," said Clemence.

"Yes, I think that is so, Clemence," said Lesbia at the door, where she had heard the last speeches without their context.

"True words are more often spoken in a more trying spirit," said Clemence, causing Lesbia to laugh, and feeling she had strengthened her position.

Miss Laurence's manner hardly altered to Clemence; she gave her the benefit of an obvious doubt; and the latter came to believe she had not been doubted. The placing of an open book inside her desk became a practice, and several times obtained her an increase of credit. Esther suspected her methods, but nothing was said, though there were whispers within her hearing. She hardly realised their menace, took the reluctance to speak as a sign of uncertainty rather than discomfiture. One day the whispers took a more open form. Lesbia commented on the standard of the class, and mentioned Clemence, who was now at its head. When she had gone, Esther spoke in a casual manner.

"Do you like to be first in the form, Clemence?"

"Well, it is as good as any other place."

"It must be better than that to you, or you would not take so much trouble to get to it."

"Clemence only does what we all do, Esther," said Maud, who had missed the whispers and was at pains to show no chagrin. "We all like the first place better than any other."

"I should not like it, if I were Clemence."

"Nonsense, Esther, of course you would."

"I should be too little at home in it to be comfortable," said Gwendolen. "And if my parents saw it on my report, the shock might outweigh the pleasure."

"Try it, Gwendolen, and see if that is the case."

"I don't see why you should not say what you mean, Esther," said Verity, drawing with a pencil on her desk.

"Oh, I can't go any further. I don't know what words to use. It is not fair to have to find them."

"What is it all about?" said Gwendolen, opening her eyes.

"Nothing at all, Gwendolen, I should say," said Maud.

"Things are not often about nothing," said Esther. "There is no smoke without flame."

"No, Esther, but there may be a good deal of smoke with very little flame," said Lesbia, at the door. "We should be prepared for that, as life goes by. It may lead to broader judgment."

"Words may give rise to thoughts, as well as thoughts to words," said Clemence.

Lesbia rested her eyes on her and passed on her way.

Esther said no more at the time, felt she might get into personal disrepute, and things went on until the examinations.

Then Clemence resorted to her method when answering a paper, arrested the eyes of Esther, Verity and Maud, and the resulting tension brought the mistress from her desk, and the matter into the open. The book was confiscated and the examination proceeded, Esther working with an easier heart and Clemence with a heavier one, Maud with an air of keeping aloof, and Verity and Gwendolen with covert communication, as the latter sought explanation and was accorded it. At the end of the hour the mistress collected the papers with a single glance at Clemence, and the girls hardly waited for the door to close before they formed a group.

"Clemence, you cannot go on like this," said Verity. "No one will speak to you or know you. And there is no meaning in that kind of success."

"It is worse than none," said Esther. "It can't give you any satisfaction."

"Why do you need to do it?" said Gwendolen. "Don't you do well enough without it?"

"That is what I should have thought," said Esther. "If I were as clever as she is, I am sure I should be content."

"Why stand there like a molten image for us all to worship, Maud?" said Verity. "There is nothing to be proud of in not saying what is in your mind."

"I have nothing to say, Verity. I could not help what I saw."

"And could the rest of us help it? You talk as if being mute about it would make any difference."

"I made no such implication, Verity. But I sometimes think that talk about a thing does have its own effect. And so I would choose to be silent."

"Well, it is nothing to do with us," said Verity. "It will be carried to the ears of authority, and there it can rest."

"It will hardly do that," said Esther. "Or Clemence will be fortunate if it does. But she is a fortunate person, and I daresay it will."

"If it does, you should let it do so," said Maud.

"Why should I interfere with it any more than you? You talk as if I were the guilty person. All I did, was to see first what all of you came to see afterwards. Somebody had to be first; somebody always has to. We can't all be equally blunt."

Clemence was not a fortunate person and the matter did not rest. It developed with a simple directness that seemed inconsistent with the complexity of life. She was summoned to the presence of the three headmistresses, and found them in open conclave concerning herself. The directness of their outlook and the experience behind it came home to her and pointed to a simple ruthlessness of fate. Miss Marathon was looking harassed and distressed and was lost in the situation. Miss Laurence stood with her elbow on a bookcase and an air of being present only in the flesh. Lesbia spoke with a compassion in her sternness, that defined and enhanced the occasion.

"Now, Clemence, I ask you to give me your own account of this matter. You know what it is; and I shall not tell you or expect you to ask. Give me your account in your own words and in your own way. Take your time and do justice to yourself."

"Oh, do you mean that book inside my desk?"

"Yes, Clemence, I do mean that. And you know I do," said Lesbia, keeping her eyes on Clemence's face.

"I often put an open book just inside my desk, to look at at the last. I find it is a great help. Things get pushed to the back of my mind and it brings them to the foreground. Then I find I know them quite well. Of course, if you did not know them, it would be no good. And I opened the desk to settle the things inside. It was too full and I could not write on it. And I saw the book, of course; I could not help it. But it did not make any difference; it was not open at any place that helped."

"It was open at a place that bore on the question that Clemence was answering at the time," said Miss Marathon, with obvious reluctance to say what must be said.

"Yes, Clemence, we know you put open books inside your desk," said Lesbia, revealing that Miss Laurence did not live apart from the world. "But do you think it is a good thing to do? To help yourself in a way the others would not? Do you think it is free from an attempt to give a false impression?"

"No, I suppose it is not; of course it is not. But people often do look at things at the last. It is the kind of wrong impression that everyone gives."

"And it is looking at a book during an examination, that is the case in point. We see how one thing leads to another. What do you think of that, Clemence? What have you to say about it?"

"I saw the book by accident when I opened the desk. I did not think what I was doing."

"No, I believe you did not think; I am prepared to believe you did not. Had you done so, you would hardly have ventured on a thing that involved so much risk. But think now, Clemence; you are old enough to think. Does it seem to you that putting open books inside your desk, and looking at them during an examination, is conduct worthy of yourself, of your parents, of anyone to do with you?"

"No, Miss Firebrace, but I did not plan to do that. I just saw the book when I lifted the lid of the desk. It was not anything more than that. It did not mean anything."

"It seems there have been other incidents of the same kind," said Miss Marathon, still with the obvious effort. "I do not see that we can leave them out of account, in justice to the other girls. It seems they have borne a good deal. If Clemence had not been popular, I do not know what would have been the result."

Miss Laurence raised her eyes and threw them over Clemence's face.

"They tried not to make more of it than they were obliged," said Miss Marathon, in a tone of indulgent affection. "I do not say there has not been jealousy of Clemence; I have noticed it in Esther more than once. But they spoke of her cleverness and said that she seemed the last person to have to do such things." Miss Marathon smiled at Clemence and smiled in recollection of her other pupils, and seemed to recall herself from feelings of general appreciation. "Indeed, it was only Esther and Verity who said anything. Maud is quite aloof and Gwendolen hardly seemed to realise that anything had happened." Here Miss Laurence turned her eyes about with a smile, as though seeking Gwendolen, to bestow it upon her. "But we must recognise that in a sense a charge is brought against Clemence, and that we cannot see it as without foundation. And there will be a reference in Clemence's report to the matter. We cannot avoid that."

Clemence lifted her eyes in incredulous consternation. Surely human beings could not have such power over each other and wield it thus without thought or mercy. She shrank from betraying her fear of her home, her fear of her parents, her fear of the trust and hope that had cradled her, but could only grasp at the chance of averting an ordeal that was too great.

"Need we trouble people at home with what happens at school?" she said, in a voice that carried sufficient, but not excessive urgency. "The point of school is that it takes such things off them. They mean to entrust them to other people."

"There are things that they would wish to know. They will not see it as a trouble," said Miss Marathon, taking the words at their surface meaning. "We cannot leave them ignorant of anything that comes so near to them. They would see it as failing in the trust."

There was a pause, and Clemence broke out, as if on an impulse.

"Miss Marathon, they are both so worried by the troubles of the house and place, and all the general anxieties. It seems hard that they should not have freedom from these other things. It was to be their reward for giving us up."

"Yes, it does. But there are exceptions to every rule," said Miss Marathon, in a sympathetic, almost social tone. "This is, perhaps, the exception that proves this one."

Lesbia's eyes were also on Clemence, seeing more than Miss Marathon's, divining a shade of Clemence's feeling; and what Clemence saw as relentless and shallow penetration, struck her pride and gave her a calm front. She made no further protest, and left her judges to conduct their case, experiencing a faint sense of triumph, as their resource failed.

"Well, the holidays are upon us," said Miss Marathon, in a more cheerful tone, as though seeing some solution in a fact that for her pupil certainly carried none. "And we shall start afresh next term and forget this has ever happened. I am sure nothing will occur to remind us of it. And the girls have agreed not to speak of the matter, Clemence. Miss Chancellor does not know and we hope never will. We can spare you that and spare her the disappointment the rest of us have felt." She smiled and almost bowed towards Clemence in reference to the compliment in her words.

Clemence felt the irony of sparing Miss Chancellor and sacrificing her parents, of saving the easy disappointment and causing the hard one; but supposed it escaped her judges in their simplicity and ignorance. She wondered they had gone so far in life, saw herself as inevitably going further, pictured her mother's joy in her advance, and fell with a shock to the certain truth.

"And we must make clear, Clemence," said Lesbia, maintaining the note that had been relinquished by her partner, "that if anything of the kind should happen again, the excuse of not thinking, or of acting on the spur of the moment, will not hold. We accept it this once, believing it to be the true one, but things would take on a different complexion a second time."

Clemence made no acknowledgment of an acceptance that went so short a way, and Miss Laurence seemed to divine her thought, and turned as if to speak, sent a ray of hope through her heart, and was silent.

"Oh, there will be no second time, I am sure," said Miss Marathon.

"I hope we shall be able to be sure, as time goes by," said Lesbia; "and I will say, Clemence, that I believe we shall."

Clemence returned to her companions, careless of the ordeal in view of the greater ones ahead. They gathered about her, too curious to hold aloof, not unfriendly in the face of the reckoning that had come.

"What did they say?" said Esther.

"Oh, just the ordinary things that would be said by any-one."

"How many of them were there?" said Verity.

"All three, but Miss Laurence did not say anything."

"Didn't she speak at all?" said Gwendolen.

"Not a word; she might have been struck dumb."

"She is angry with us all," said Esther. "More than she is with Clemence."

"Miss Chancellor is not to know about it," said Verity. "Did they say that?"

"Something was said. I am sure I do not care if she knows or not."

"I hardly think that can be the case, Clemence," said Maud. "It is clearly better both for you and for her that she should not know."

"Oh, what difference does it make?" said Clemence, feeling that to the main and desperate truth it made none.

"Will your people at home know?" said Esther.

"Yes, I suppose so. There was some talk of something on the report, or I think there was. But home is not like school."

"I should have thought it was a good deal worse in some ways."

"Well, homes differ, Esther," said Maud. "Clemence knows her own."

"Won't your parents really mind?" said Gwendolen. "Mine would care very much about a thing like that."

"Well, I don't think they trouble much about things at school. They don't seem to think they are very important, somehow. And I am sure they are not."

"I should have thought certain things were equally important everywhere," said Maud.

"Why did they send you to school, if they felt like that?" said Gwendolen.

"Oh, well, I suppose we all have to be educated somehow. And I daresay they would not have done it, if Miss Firebrace had not suggested it, and carried it through."

"Perhaps she wanted another pupil," said Gwendolen.

"And got one of a kind she may not much have wanted," said Esther.

"Perhaps it is as much your parents' fault as yours, that things have happened as they have," said Gwendolen.

"I should advise your reconsidering your attitude to school before next term, Clemence," said Maud.

"You might have been expelled," said Esther.

"Well, I should not have minded that. I have no great wish to be here."

"I hardly think that is the case, Esther," said Maud. "Things would have had to go further."

"And would soon have done so, if they had not been checked. They were moving apace."

"I don't think there was any talk about it," said Clemence, in an indifferent tone.

"Miss Firebrace would hardly want to lose Clemence after taking all that trouble to get her," said Gwendolen.

"People would hardly keep schools, if they wanted to lose their pupils," said Maud.

"What an odd conversation this is!" said Verity. "Are we in sympathy with Clemence, or are we not?"

"I hope we are, Verity," said Maud. "The more we regret what has happened, the more we should be, in a way."

"Oh, that kind of sympathy! I wonder if Clemence is grateful for it."

"I don't think Clemence is easily grateful," said Esther.

"You would hardly have an opportunity of judging that. About me or anyone," said Clemence. "You are not a person to inspire gratitude."

"You frighten me, Clemence," said Gwendolen. "Maud, forbid her to tell me her opinion of me. I am nervous of people who do that."

"I think a great deal more of you than I do of Esther," said Clemence.

"Clemence's tongue is unloosed," said Verity. "She will make us all nervous. It is a good thing that Miss Chancellor is coming."

"Well, what is the subject of discussion? You seem very earnestly engaged in it."

There was the slightest pause.

"Clemence's parents do not mind how well she does at school, Miss Chancellor. They think it does not matter."

"Well, that is a pity, Gwendolen, as she seems likely to do well. I hope she is mistaken, and I think it probable that she is. People do not always say all they think, before their children. There are many reasons why they might not."

"We might get to feel that our own affairs were too important. Especially as we are allowed no concern in any others. I am sure I hope my affairs at school are not important. It would be a sad thing if they were."

"Well, perhaps that sort of success is hardly in your line, Gwendolen. I should say it is more in Clemence's, and she shapes well towards it."

"Clemence, Clemence, Clemence! Suppose we all copied her!" muttered Esther.

"Well, you might do worse, Esther. Do you not think you might, yourself?"

"I wish I were as clever as she is," said Esther, in her rapid monotone.

"Well, the break-up party is in four days," said Gwendolen.

"And is that a continuation of the subject, Gwendolen?" said another voice.

"No, Miss Firebrace. But I wanted a change of subject."

"Then there was no reason why you should not have it. Break-up parties merit our interest as much as other things. They depend on people's thought and effort. We do not ask you to be indifferent to them."

"Will you have a new dress for the party, Clemence?" said Esther.

"No, I should not think so. There is not enough time, is there? Only four days."

"What about the one you said you had at home—the one you left at home?" said Esther.

"Yes, Esther, your phrasing needed correction," said Lesbia.

"Oh, I should think I must have grown out of that. It has been about for so long. And it is such a fussy thing. I would rather wear the old muslin that is upstairs. That is at any rate ordinary and simple."

"There is time to get a ready-made one," said Verity, as Lesbia withdrew into the background, keeping her eyes on Clemence, as though to receive light on her character. "And they are much better than they were."

"Write now and catch the post," said Gwendolen. "Miss Chancellor will give you permission. Say you forgot it in the stress of the examinations. There is sure to be something at home, to give the measurements."

"May I write, Miss Chancellor?" said Clemence, yielding to the mood of recklessness induced by her position.

"Yes, certainly, Clemence. I see nothing against it."

Clemence wrote to her mother and stated the case, unable to think of another pretext under scrutiny and on the spur of the moment. Gwendolen ran to the hall and returned with an air of relief.

"I was just in time. The box was being cleared."

"I am glad, Gwendolen," said Miss Chancellor, "and as much for you as for Clemence. I think you take the matter more seriously than she does."

A pair of eyes at the door rested gently on Gwendolen.

"I wish I could command a new dress at a moment's notice," said Verity. "Mine has been brought up to date, with the result that it is a medley of dates. It is better not to give people time to think. Their thoughts run to contrivance, which is an indulgence for them and not for us."

"Clemence may not have her request granted, Verity," said Miss Chancellor. "I shall think she is fortunate, if she does. Such short notice involves both trouble and expense."

The term moved to its end. The examination lists were read. Clemence was given the place second to Maud, that her marks warranted, without question or sign of doubt. The course was involved in the policy of silence, and she supposed that any unfairness or false impression was balanced by the exposure on the report, and did not see the scale as weighted on her own side. She sat through the applause in awareness of the thoughts about her, feeling her uneasiness a shadow of the real thing. She imagined prisoners awaiting their doom, with a sort of envy. Here was dignity of fate, simple, strong trouble instead of subtle and humbling.

An unfamiliar gleam of light pierced the darkness. A dress arrived from Maria, chosen indeed with haste, but with a care prompted by regard for its cost and its future usefulness. A letter hinted surprise and a sense of lavishness, and enjoined care of the garment. Clemence felt the irony of the pleasure cankered at the root, but gave herself to the moment. The form hailed the parcel, and proceeded to Miss Tuke to be present at the unpacking. Miss Chancellor followed, as though she hardly knew where her steps led her.

"Do you take an interest in clothes, Miss Chancellor?"

"I am quite interested in seeing Clemence's dress, Verity. It is a signal instance of what can be done at a moment's notice."

"It is a charming dress, Clemence," said Maud. "And I think it should be becoming."

"I am jealous of it," said Verity. "I wish we had not reminded Clemence to send for it."

"Well, really, Verity, what a very odd line for a joke to take!"

"It is not a joke, Miss Chancellor. Our dresses will suffer by comparison."

"I do not think you need trouble about a comparison that no one will make, Verity."

"People ought to make it. They ought to put themselves in other people's place," said Gwendolen.

"It was really clever of Clemence's mother to manage it in so short a time," said Miss Chancellor, with a reference in her tone to her momentary glimpse of Maria.

"Have you a new dress for the party, Maud?" said Verity.

"Yes, I have one this year, Verity."

"Then why did you not show it to us?"

"It did not strike me as a very interesting object. And I think I will hold to my own view of it."

"One that is apparently unique in your present company, Maud," said Miss Chancellor.

"Dear, dear, how proud I shall be of you all!" said Miss Tuke.

"What are you going to wear, Miss Tuke?" said Gwendolen.

"Oh, I shall have too much to do in supervising other people's clothes, to worry about my own."

Miss Chancellor looked towards the window with an easy expression.

"What are you—have you thought about your dress, Miss Chancellor?"

"Yes, I have thought, Verity. I gave quite proper attention to it at one moment, though I admit it has escaped my mind since. I shall be wearing a velvet dress with lace touches, that I think will meet the occasion."

"The one you wore—the dress I think you wore at the spring concert?" said Esther.

"The very same, Esther. Not a stitch or a button altered. To my joy it was not held to be necessary. No thought, no trouble, no expense! It was a great relief."

Clemence went through the evening with a sense of suffering a dead form of the pleasure that might have been hers. She marvelled that the girls assumed her enjoyment to be of the same order as their own. The lack of imagination staggered her and wrought in her a lasting change. Her growing sense of superiority would have startled the arbiters of her fate. The farewells and the actual departure followed with the same unreality. Miss Tuke kissed numbers of girls without sign of discrimination, and Miss Chancellor shook hands with her form, as though the prospect of travelling with them gave no cause for dispensing with the observance. The principals bade each pupil a cordial farewell, and Miss Laurence held Clemence's hand for a moment longer than was usual, and looked into her face. Lesbia said an extra word to Clemence at the last, as though they might now resume their relationship.

"You and I are to be re-united in a week, Clemence. I shall meet you next in the capacity of a guest. It is quite a turn in our affairs."

Clemence smiled in acceptance of the words, disguised the sinking of her heart, wondered if Lesbia would see the visit as imposing silence, or as affording scope for violation of it. She felt the impulse to put the question, to plead the code of host and guest, but found her courage fail. She did not care if Lesbia read her thought, almost hoped she did, that she might recall and act upon it. She followed her companions to the cab and the train with no sign of her inner tumult. They were to travel with Miss Chancellor to London, there to be met and conducted onwards. Clemence was the only one whose destination was earlier, and it seemed a part of the ruthless hastening of fate.

"You are fortunate to get home so quickly," said Verity. "This is a dreary stage of the term."

"Why not call it the first stage of the holidays, Verity?" said Miss Chancellor.

"I find it the best of all moments. Nothing over, and everything to come," said Gwendolen, striking at the pain in Clemence's heart.

"School seems a long way off already. I have almost forgotten it."

"Well, really, Clemence, that is evidence of a very shallow heart," said Miss Chancellor. "And when school so soon afforded you a niche of your own!"

"It must be odd to have Miss Firebrace to stay," said Esther. "What is she like in the house?"

"Why should it be odd?" said Miss Chancellor. "I suppose Miss Firebrace may pay a visit like anyone else. And no doubt she is like herself, Esther, and so an entertaining guest. I expect Clemence will enjoy having her."

"I hope she will not broach awkward school affairs," said

126

Esther, breaking off as she realised where her words might lead.

"I failed to see what school affairs have been awkward for Clemence, Esther. And I do not know why Miss Firebrace should take another view."

"I shall not see much of her," said Clemence. "My brother and I will be together. We are not a great deal with guests. We are still looked upon as children."

"Won't your being at school make a difference to that?" said Esther.

"No, I don't think so. School is not much regarded. And we like our old ways best."

"But you see your father and mother?"

"Yes, we can go to them when we like. But Miss Petticott is with us in the schoolroom."

"I suppose it is a very large house."

"Well, it seems to be divided into parts. I suppose houses in the country are like that."

"We live humbly in London," said Gwendolen.

"I do not see anything humble in living in the greatest city in the world, Gwendolen."

"There are slums in great cities, Miss Chancellor."

"But you do not live in one, so I fail to see how that is on the point."

"We live in a watering-place," said Verity, lifting her shoulders.

"We live in a suburb," said Esther, speaking as though she did not spare her bluntness in her own case.

"Maud lives in the same place as I do, and we never meet," said Verity, as if in mockery of the circumstances.

"We move in a different milieu, Verity. My mother and I live in another part of the town. Those things count in a place of that kind, even if they do not count in themselves."

"As they do," muttered Esther.

"Where do you live, Miss Chancellor?"

"Also in a suburb, Gwendolen. And very pleasant I find it, and very anxious I am to get there."

"Have you parents, Miss Chancellor?" said Verity, in a tone that recalled the one she sometimes used to Maud.

"Yes, indeed I have, Verity. And they are eagerly awaiting me. I am going back to be a child at home again, as Clemence is."

"But you are not kept upstairs in a schoolroom?"

"No, not quite that. I have enough of schoolrooms in the term. But I believe my father would think it was rather my proper place."

"Have you not had enough of them, Clemence?" said Verity.

"No, not of my own schoolroom. I have had nothing of it for three months."

"But everything of it for years before," said Esther.

"It is a natural feeling, Clemence," said Miss Chancellor. "You are fortunate to have a sanctum of your own. It is one of the things for which I envy you."

"Here is Clemence's station!" said Esther. "The porter is looking out for her. I saw him recognise her as we passed. He is talking to a lady, and pointing her out. Is that someone who has come to meet you, Clemence? I think I once caught a glimpse of her at school."

"Yes, it is my mother. I am at home at last," said Clemence, preparing to leave the train.

"Well, really, Clemence, your journey has not been such a long one," said Miss Chancellor, laughing, and helping with Clemence's possessions. "I will just get out and see you into your mother's hands."

"Miss Chancellor likes to make new acquaintances," said Esther. "And may not have much opportunity in the house where she is a child again."

"I do not know why we should deduce so much from her seeing Clemence out of the train," said Maud.

"This is Miss Chancellor, Mother. I am in her form," said Clemence, when she and Maria had embraced.

Maria turned at once and grasped and retained Miss Chancellor's hand.

"Why, I find this a closer tie than many older ones. And Clemence's father would feel with me. Perhaps Miss Firebrace would let Clemence bring you here at some time, or let you bring her, in whichever way it is seen. I suppose we are all under discipline."

"I think we should have to bring each other, Lady Shelley. And in the spring it would be a delightful plan. The winter days are rather short. We were sorry not to see you at our party on Tuesday. We hoped you would be able to come."

"You will have to see us in our home, to know us. I should think we can see you anywhere. You are not a person who has to be in one spot, to be yourself."

"No, Lady Shelley. One advantage of my work is that it has taken me into different parts of the world we live in. It is one of the things I asked of life, and it has not been denied me."

Maria talked until the train moved on, and beyond this stage, calling out invitations and suggestions, as it gathered speed. The girls leaned from their seats and called their farewells.

"Lady Shelley is very charming," said Miss Chancellor, as she returned to her place.

"I should hardly have thought that was her word," said Esther.

"And it is not, Esther. You are right. Cordial, genuine, with a quality of her own. That is a much better way of putting it."

"It was clever of Esther to suggest so much in a word," said Gwendolen.

"Or without one," said Verity.

"Lady Shelley suggested it, Verity. Esther simply saw something of what was there. And it comes out much more in actual contact with her, both what is there and what is not. And the one definitely outweighs the other. I quite feel we shall meet as friends another time, and that is good work for a passing encounter."

"The girls seem fond of you," said Maria to her daughter with a mingled pleasure and dubiousness, that drew Clemence back in a moment to her home world. "I am glad you are making friends. Is there anyone whom you especially like?"

"No, not yet. There has hardly been time. But I have got to know all my form. There are only five of us, and we see a good deal of each other."

"They are all nice to you, are they?"

"Yes, very nice," said Clemence, realising for the first time how far this had been the case.

"You are pale and thin, my little girl," said Maria, putting her arm about her. "It is time you were back in your mother's hands. Are you glad to be in them again?"

Clemence felt an impulse to yield her mind as well as her body to this keeping. The flatness of this homecoming seemed to offer protection to the truth. But the very ordinariness broke her courage, and her load was the heavier as the impulse passed.

Sir Roderick came on to the steps with joy in his face, to fold his daughter in his arms, and resume their relation without thought or question of the intervening time, or any idea that she had any thought of it. She yielded with a relief that was sapped at its roots by the impending doom. She served her parents' pleasure and pride with the knowledge that her efforts would emerge as placing her in a false light. Maria saw something new in her, and spoke of it to Miss Petticott.

"The change seems to have brought out the best in her. Or is it the pleasure of being at home again? We should like to think it is that."

"And I am going to think so, Lady Shelley. Especially as a still, small voice within me tells me that it is the truth."

"I met rather a nice governess—mistress I suppose she is called—at the station," said Maria, as though Miss Petticott's presence prompted the recollection. "I think she takes Clemence's form. I hope she will come to see us at some time."

"Oh, I shall hear all about her, Lady Shelley. I shall not need to see her, to have a clear glimpse of her personality. Clemence is good at conjuring up characters for my benefit, and very entertaining I find it, especially when her little spice of mischief creeps in and leavens the whole."

"You will always be the first and the foundation of them, Miss Petticoat," said Sir Roderick, giving the word that was needed.

"I believe you think I am jealous, Sir Roderick. And, as you say, as you imply, it would hardly be possible without any cause."

"School is the wrong thing for Clemence. She looks the worse for it. It has her no more good than I expected. I shall take her away. I shall talk to Lesbia about it."

"You will not do one thing, if you do the other," said Maria.

"No, it would not be the best preliminary step," said Miss Petticott, not disputing that some step might be taken.

"Then I shall think of another, or you shall do so for me. Between us we will outwit them," said Sir Roderick, again not affecting to misunderstand.

"It is surely not my business to outwit anyone. Sir Roderick."

"I might write a letter and say I will do what is best for my own child," said Sir Roderick, his tone faltering over this extreme suggestion.

"Clemence, would you like to go back to school or to settle down at home again?" said Maria, later. "If the question arose, that is to say."

Clemence looked at her mother with a flood of feeling surging into her face. Could connection with the school be broken before the report came? Might Lesbia be estranged and cancel her visit? Could the people who knew her secret pass in a moment from her life?

"It is a change that would have to happen at once, or not at all."

"It could hardly come about in a moment. It would have to be considered and discussed. I wonder what Miss Firebrace would say, and who would have the courage to ask her. Of course she will be here in a week."

Clemence's heart sank once more, and rose again almost in exaltation at her solitary confronting of the extreme thing.

"Oh, what did you think of the dress?" said Maria. "Was it what you wanted? You did not allow us much time."

"Yes, it was just the thing. We have to dress for that party, silly though it seems, when only a few people come. It is a kind of unwritten law that is never broken. I only found it out at the last."

"I thought you did not really want it. I should have had more pleasure in getting it, if I had thought you did. As it is, it was rather an expense, and will be very little good. Miss Petticott was afraid the muslin might fall short of their requirements."

"Oh, I have my own knowledge of the ways of school-mistresses, Lady Shelley. They are not alive to the realities of life as we normal mortals are. They live in their imaginary world, and draw their pupils into it."

"I am going to draw one pupil out of it," said Sir Roderick. "And I am sure I wish the world was imaginary."

Clemence received her parents' fondness at night as a thing undeserved and destined to emerge as such. She slept from exhaustion, and the waking in ease and joy was succeeded by the fall of hope. Oliver and Sefton were to return that day, and their presence would end her respite. Sefton's innocence would reproach and isolate her, when her hour came.

CHAPTER IV

"I hope I am not disturbing you at your luncheon, Mrs. Cassidy."

"Thank you, Miss James. It is so kind to cling to the hope."

"Please do not get up. I will sit down, if I am to keep you standing."

"I did not suggest it, because I thought you always stood."

"You see me at prayers, Mrs. Cassidy, and everyone stands then."

"Yes, of course; so reverent. I hope I look as other people do."

"You look yourself, Mrs. Cassidy."

"Yes, I was afraid of that."

"I thought you might like to approve the hymns for the first week of the term."

"I should like to, of course. I do like approving of things. It is disapproving of them that is disturbing. But is there anything about them to arouse approval? They make me feel uncomfortable and complacent and almost exalted, and that cannot be wholesome, and wholesomeness is important for boys."

"We have chosen our usual one for the first night. I do not know if you remember it."

"It will soon remind me of itself, and of many other things as well. Hymns do that more than anything, though it is supposed to be scents. And how independent of you to dare to be bound by custom! I knew we could rely on you."

Miss James certainly looked as if people could do this, as she stood with her notebook in her hand. She was the matron of the school, and the only woman in it, and the second capacity seemed to transcend the first. Her dark hair was arranged so plainly that it seemed to need a more negative word; her features seemed to be impregnated with her expression; her clothes were so suitable that no one saw them, and her figure so thin that the same thing might be said.

"It celebrates our coming together from our different homes to face the spell of work before us."

"But ought the boys to be reminded of those things? Ought we not to help them to shut their eyes to them?"

"The thoughts must be in their minds."

"Of course, and so it is healthier to give voice to them. And hymns would lead to that."

"I sometimes have a tiny suspicion, Mrs. Cassidy, that you are not quite serious."

"And that is shocking about hymns. But I am quite."

"Perhaps you would like to suggest a hymn yourself."

"I believe that speech was made in a spirit of revenge; I mean I have a tiny suspicion of it. And I was to approve of the hymns, not suggest them, though if you approve of something, you may as well suggest it. Well, that hymn about the encircling gloom, and the night being dark and everyone far from home—that seems to cover the ground; and there is something about not asking to see the distant scene, that might be in place."

"Is it not a little too pointed?"

"Of course it is, and your hymn has a merciful vagueness. You have the truer sympathy. And I was thinking it was myself. I am so ashamed."

"You are not fair to yourself, Mrs. Cassidy."

"I try to be. I think everyone does. And I hope I am sound at bottom. Being sound at the top would be more useful, but that seems too rare for us to hear of it."

"I believe we are to have two members of your family with us this term."

"I find it hard to believe. It seems so odd that our connections should trust us so far, after the glimpses they have had of us."

"And a good deal more than glimpses, I suppose."

"It was the glimpses I meant. And it seems that the plan must be to our advantage, and that has a flavour of discomfort."

"The advantage will be on both sides," said Miss James.

"Will it? That is dreadful. I hoped it was tacitly assumed that we were to get nothing out of it."

"Things were arranged on the usual basis," said Lucius.

"No wonder it was all so tacit. Truth does drag one down. I do not think it can be best."

"We shall have to make a demand of your nephew as soon as he arrives in the house," said Miss James. "We have no one to play the harmonium now that Mr. Eaton has left us."

"And he left for his own ends without any thought of the instrument? And he was very happy playing it. You could tell by the way he swayed. I used to think how nice it would be to abandon oneself."

"Did we let him go without thanking him for his kindness?" said Lucius.

"We tried to induce him to stay," said Juliet. "And when he refused, it did not occur to us to thank him. It did not seem to be due to him. We forgot it was due to ourselves."

"You are confusing the issue."

"So I am. We did confuse it."

"A vote of thanks was passed by the boys," said Miss James. "I suggested that one of the masters should propose it, and I seconded it myself. I thought it was in place."

"We are indebted to you," said Lucius.

"And so is Mr. Eaton," said Juliet, "and so will Oliver be when he goes. Because I am sure Miss James will second it for him too."

"If I am here then, Mrs. Cassidy."

"What a cruel thrust! Surely Mr. Eaton has not had an unsettling influence. I should have thought all the influence would come from you."

"It was merely the natural rejoinder, Mrs. Cassidy; it

meant nothing. I have never been happier than I am here."

"I wish I could say a generous word. But my tongue is tied. It is that foolish sort of shyness."

"We all understand you, Mrs. Cassidy. And as for Mr. Cassidy, I never knew anyone speak with more economy and point."

"Lucius, thank Miss James, and tell her that Oliver will be glad to play the harmonium. I know he plays something at home that is not the piano, and those people always play everything. And we always render services when they are not simply expected of us."

"Will he bring his brother with him?" said Miss James.

"Yes," said Juliet. "He is thirty-eight."

"How is that on the point?" said Lucius.

"He is past the age when he would be ashamed of the charge of a child."

"Surely always an odd thing to be ashamed of," said Miss James.

"But people are ashamed of the oddest things," said Juliet, "though they are supposed only to be proud of them."

"It is a good thing I am not ashamed of that, Mrs. Cassidy. I have been in charge of as many as twenty children. But, of course, I am past thirty-eight," said Miss James, flushing as she ended, as an odd thing she was ashamed of, was her age of forty-seven. "So no parents are coming. That is a good thing. I do not mean they are not always welcome, of course."

"Of course not," said Juliet.

"But we shall have enough of them for this occasion. Do you mean to hold to your rule that the new boys are to sleep by themselves?"

"Well, it does make me proud to have made a rule, when it is a thing so useful in a school. Though modern people do say the boys should make them for themselves."

"They cannot know much about it," said Miss James.

"They would make the same ones," said Lucius, "and be too hard in enforcing them."

"I never quite see the reason for a separate dormitory," said Miss James.

"It is to prevent brutality," said Juliet.

"The new boys do not meet that here."

"Might they not be asked the number of their sisters and their fathers' Christian names? The rumours cannot be quite without foundation."

"That would not hurt them."

"I never know why it hurts them so much. But it seems to be recognised."

"They will never be anywhere at the right time. There will be no one to tell them anything."

"Cannot they read the notices on the walls? Or do they only write things on them? I suppose they mean those to be read, though one might hardly think so. I am sure you do not. It must all be part of the elusive charm of childhood."

"I think this school has a healthy tone, Mrs. Cassidy, though there are always a few things we cannot prevent. There is none of that furtive atmosphere that prevails in some schools, as if everyone had something to hide."

"That is not hidden from you. It is shocking that we do not protect our womanhood. It is so untrue that to the pure all things are pure. They are particularly impure, of course."

"Would you like to approve the other hymns, Mrs. Cassidy?"

"I do approve of them. I see it is what must be."

"Well, I think I understand the needs of boys, and the way to meet them."

"And you are the matron in a boys' school! So you are not a square peg in a round hole. And I should have thought you would be. I mean, you are not of the stuff that martyrs are made of."

"There is no need for that here, Mrs. Cassidy. And I feel I have found my sphere. I am always so sorry for people in a wrong place."

"So am I. I am in one myself. The school touches no responsive chords within me."

"But you have the wisdom to keep aloof. So no harm is done."

"I did not know I was quite such a failure. I believe I thought I shed my own influence in my own way. That is a kinder way of saying that I shed none, but it is much kinder."

"Oh, but you do, Mrs. Cassidy. You quite misunderstand me. The difference when you are away would hardly be believed. Something that permeates the school from top to bottom, is gone."

"I did misunderstand you. Thank you so much. Is my husband's influence felt at all? We should not ask for compliments, but people who do not ask for them do not have any."

"Mrs. Cassidy, a word or a look from him does more than torrents of words from anyone else. We sometimes feel it is quite unfair that natural gifts should go so far, and make all our efforts seem superfluous. Though that is unworthy of us, of course."

"I should have thought everything was unworthy of you. It is so good of you to come down to our level."

"I never mind coming down to any extent. I think we never know where real importance lies, or what may constitute a real need. I do not call it coming down."

"I will never call it that again."

"I do not mean to give the impression that I am a lofty-minded person. I should almost feel I was praising myself, if such a thing were possible."

"I have heard that all things are possible, but I have never thought it was true. Is that a ring at the bell? Why do we put it like that, when we know it is?"

"It is the first of the masters," said Miss James, going to the window. "It is Mr. Dalziel. How tall and thin he looks!"

"I daresay he does," said Juliet. "He did, I know. How nice of him not to put off coming until the last moment! It is almost as if he were not ashamed of being willing to return."

"You are always the first of all, Miss James," said Lucius.

"My term begins earlier and ends later than anyone else's, Mr. Cassidy," said Miss James, going to the door with a glow on her face.

"Miss James said that a word from you did more than a torrent of words from anyone else," said Juliet. "And I saw it doing it."

"How do you do, Miss James?" said a deep, soft voice. "It is too bad of me to begin the term by almost knocking you down."

"It is dreadful what thoughts go through one's mind," said Juliet. "I almost thought how kind it was of the masters to be so nice to Miss James. I did not quite think it, of course."

"It was my fault, Mr. Dalziel. I saw the cab arrive, and ought to have guessed you would come straight to the study. It is what we all do, of course."

"Yes, she ought to have guessed it," said Juliet.

"How do you do, sir? How do you do, Mrs. Cassidy? You see I have arrived betimes."

"We were saying it was kind of you to be willing to rejoin us," said Lucius, anticipating his wife, but not disguising his debt to her.

"I never travel late in the day in the autumn. I mistrust the evening air at the fall of the year."

"I mistrust all air," said Juliet. "It is what winds and draughts are made of. And it is always morning or evening or some kind of air. I do not know what air in itself would be like, but no doubt very bad. Lucius, shut the window; Mr. Dalziel will feel the air."

"Thank you, sir. I am serious about such matters. I find it is the only thing to be," said Mr. Dalziel, unaware that he had no further choice of feeling.

"My wife is serious too in her heart. As you know, she does not wear it on her sleeve."

"I have gone into the matter of the textbooks, sir, if she

will forgive our broaching such matters before her."

"I thought textbooks were expurgated, when they were for boys," said Juliet.

Mr. Dalziel turned his pale, broad, full-browed face towards her.

"And Lucius never intrudes into the sphere of the school, except in so far as his presence is a liberal education."

"I endorse the last indeed. And surely 'intrude' is not the word in his case."

"Watch him next time you see him doing it, and tell him what is the word."

"Did you meet Miss James?" said Lucius.

"I am afraid I charged into her, sir. She was already about her duties. She is a saint on earth."

"I used to want to meet one, before I knew her," said Juliet. "Now, of course, the desire is fulfilled."

"I mean it seriously, Mrs. Cassidy."

"Then it was all the nicer of you to say it."

"I am a great admirer of simple goodness."

"I admire all goodness. I believe everyone does. And of course we like to say that kind hearts are more than coronets, as if we met both. But why is it better for being simple? I should admire complex goodness as much, though no one speaks about it. I suppose people know they are wicked, and they will not consent to be simple, and so they think the two cannot go together."

"Everything is commoner in its simpler forms," said Lucius.

Mr. Dalziel looked at him in some relief.

"I will go and unpack, if Miss James has not forestalled me. I sent my luggage in advance."

"I saw her engaged on what appeared to be that very task."

Mr. Dalziel lifted his shoulders in helpless resignation, and left the room.

"Would you like to see Mr. Bigwell, Mr. Cassidy?"

said Miss James at the door. "He would prefer to know, before he disturbs you."

"Yes, yes, we should like it," said Lucius, glancing at his wife.

"Well, I wanted to be sure of my welcome, before I broke in upon the conjugal privacy," said a deep, unmodulated voice, as a short, dark, simply rough-featured man entered the room and looked about with a critical, unimpressed air. "It must be such a dreary business starting the concern, that I did not want to force it on you before the time. Well, the respite is over, and we must make the best of the world where we find ourselves."

"Did you not enter it of your own will?" said Lucius, as he shook hands.

"Well, those progressive universities put you into something useful, whether you will or not," said Mr. Bigwell, who dealt with the fact that he had not been to Oxford or Cambridge, as well as he could, indeed was always dealing with it. "And the life may not be more circumscribed than any soft-handed life must be. In a way, the further you go up the scale, the further you go down."

"Are you a pessimist, Mr. Bigwell?" said Juliet. "Perhaps we ought to stipulate for optimism, when we hold our interviews."

"Well, there is scope for the quality in the routine of a private schoolmaster. I don't take any other view. But I never see so much in life to throw up one's bonnet about. Your term may be the one for me. And those of us who live below a certain point, as we all do here, have to adapt ourselves to a certain degree. There are points below, of course."

"Yes, that is true," said Lucius, resting his eyes on the speaker, as though the latter might have a right to speak of these. "I hope you had a holiday that pleased you?"

"Yes, thank you. That is how I should describe it. My idea of a good time is to follow my own bent, and not to do things because they are done, or because it is time one did them. I hope you can say the same."

"We spent our time with relations," said Juliet. "In the house of my former brother-in-law, where my father still has his home."

"I hope you gave satisfaction," said Mr. Bigwell, in the manner of a man with his own knowledge of life.

"I hope so too. At least I am not without hope."

"Hope is not dead in your breast."

"By the way, Bigwell," said Lucius, "a nephew of ours is to take Eaton's place this term. A man of your age, the elder son of the house where we were staying. I hope you will make him welcome."

"We will not prejudice him against the life. But, situated as he is, I am at a loss to know why he has chosen it."

"It is only for a while. And he is easily spared from home. His father is a vigorous man."

"Yes, there would only be occupation for one," said Mr. Bigwell, as he ran his eye over the situation.

"And his young half-brother is coming to the school as a boy."

"You are using your family to bring in new blood," said Mr. Bigwell, rising and drawing a pipe out of his pocket in preparation for leaving Juliet's presence. "Well, I hope your nephew and I will bring out the best in each other."

"What is the best in Mr. Bigwell?" said Juliet, as the door closed.

"He is a worthy fellow and has made a good fight."

"I wish he had been more victorious. And it is quite a kind wish."

"People who remain in the one place do not measure the advance of those who rise to another. If 'rise' is the word."

"Of course it is the word. What word would Mr. Bigwell use?"

"He has gone further than I have."

"But you have not gone anywhere. I would not have married a man who had conquered in the battle of life. I could not live with the scars of victory. May I ask an impossible question? Why would it have mattered, if Mr. Bigwell had stayed where he was?"

"It would have mattered to him. He did not like the place."

"I wonder how he knew he did not. That was rather clever of him. But his effort has only been for himself. Why do we have to admire him so much?"

"I see no sign that you do so."

"But I am ashamed of not admiring him. You are not, and you almost betrayed it. Is that a cab at the door?"

"Two cabs," said Lucius, rising. "Oliver and Sefton in the first with their baggage. And Spode by himself in the second. Why did Spode not walk? His things came yesterday. What care he takes of himself!"

"It is odd how much that sounds to a person's discredit. I think he is taking even more care of his umbrella. Does that matter as much? He and Oliver are not unlike. They look as if they might be fond of each other. Sefton looks as if no one had ever been fond of him. Why do new boys look like that, when more affection than ever before has been lavished on them? How do you know so much about people's luggage, Lucius? No wonder your influence permeates the school, when you go and put it everywhere."

"So a mile is too far for you to walk, Spode?" said Lucius.

"Walk, sir? From the station?"

"Yes. Was a mile too far? It is a fine day."

Mr. Spode looked out of the window, as though he had not considered this.

"Does one walk from stations?" said Oliver. "Cabs are always there. And what is the good of them, if people walk?"

"Many people have luggage," said Lucius, "Spode had the expense of sending his luggage in advance and of taking a cab."

"If you call it expense," said Mr. Spode.

"What would you call it?"

143

"Expense," said Mr. Spode, a smile creeping over his face.

"I was thriftier than you at your stage."

"I should hope so," said Juliet, "or your talk would have no meaning."

"I took care of the pence. I hope Spode's pounds take care of themselves."

"I take care of them," said Mr. Spode, at once.

"Pounds are made of pence," said Lucius.

"No," said Oliver. "Nothing is made of two hundred and forty parts."

"Well, I see what you mean," said Lucius.

"Do you?" said Juliet. "How n ce to be able to talk like educated men!"

"How is Miss James?" said Mr. Spode.

"I think she is well," said Lucius, with a faint note of surprise.

"She looked exhausted at the end of last term. Not that she ever talks of herself."

"That is one excuse for my husband's not knowing about her," said Juliet.

"I must hear more about Miss James," said Oliver.

"Well, pay attention," said his aunt.

"We are dependent on her," said Mr. Spode.

"For your creature comforts," said Lucius. "Does your your work come anywhere in your lives?"

"Mine hardly does," said Mr. Spode. "I am too far above it."

"Why did you choose it?"

"Because it was a blind alley. I was afraid of anything that led to further things. I shall only need it during my mother's life."

"How old is—how is—is your mother well?"

"Of course she is," said Juliet. "Or Mr. Spode could not speak as if she would not always be."

"She is seventy. She was forty when I was born. I am her only child and the child of her old age."

"Well, I hope she will remain herself for a long time," said Lucius.

"She hunts," said Mr. Spode, on a deeper note, "and her horse has an Irish strain."

"Perhaps she will give up hunting soon," said Juliet. "No, do not interrupt me, Lucius. I must say something to comfort Mr. Spode. After all, I am a woman."

"Do not tell me she is wonderful," said Mr. Spode. "It is not that to misuse power."

"I see that her failings have endeared her to you," said Oliver.

The two tall, heavy young men stood side by side, looking as if they would be alike, if Mr. Spode's hair had not been light, his complexion fair, and his eyes grey instead of dark. Sefton's eyes rested on them, as though he saw them as a pair.

"Will you take your brother to Miss James, Oliver?" said Lucius. "Spode will act as guide."

Mr. Spode put his hand on Sefton's collar to direct his steps, and as they reached the passage turned to Oliver.

"I ask you——" he said, taking up his umbrella and breaking off to look at it with interest.

"Is anything amiss with your umbrella?"

"The boys," said Mr. Spode, putting the umbrella under his arm with a look of relief. "They are what is amiss with many things. I ask you if it is proper for my mother to keep her income, and give me only an allowance, when we are equal human beings of mature age."

"How does the money come to be hers?"

"Her father left it to her, because she was his daughter, and I was only his grandson. Such a shallow reason."

"But hardly an unnatural one."

"He should not have allowed it to influence him. Suppose we all did what was not unnatural! And he did not like my not hunting. He said I was afraid of the risk."

"And were you not afraid?"

"I shrink from all danger. I have high imaginative power.

My mother does not see the pictures that rise before me. That is why I look so old for my age. My face carries its experience."

"An accident might be instantaneous," said Oliver.

"Sometimes horse and rider are entangled," said Mr. Spode, losing hold of Sefton and opening the door of the common room. "Dalziel, Bigwell, Shelley! Know each other."

"We have followed hard on each other's heels," said Mr. Daiziel, rising to shake hands.

"Each name has two l's," said Mr. Bigwell, as he shook hands without rising.

"And does that constitute a bond?" said Oliver.

"We can do with one, as the term goes on," said Mr. Bigwell, on an almost retaliatory note.

"Surely we are not on each other's nerves already?"

"Nephew of the Head?" said Mr. Bigwell, turning his thumb in the direction of the study.

"Of his wife. She is my mother's sister, my Aunt Juliet."

"You are giving up a leisured life at home, I understand?"

"Yes, I need a rest from it."

Mr. Bigwell nodded several times, as though he could follow this.

"I did not know that masters were put through a catechism. I thought it was only the boys."

"A certain foundation is necessary to an acquaintanceship. And sharing a common life involves as much as that."

"I like to tell you all about myself. I only meant I did not know it was customary."

"So you two knew each other?" said Mr. Bigwell, indicating Oliver and Mr. Spode.

"No," said the latter.

"But you were walking arm-in-arm."

"An affectionate impulse," said Oliver. "It helped me a good deal. I only left my home this morning."

"Parents?" said Mr. Bigwell.

"Two living. One dead," said Oliver.

"Beyond the average," said Mr. Bigwell, not permitting himself further enquiry.

Mr. Dalziel raised his eyes.

"Father, mother, and now stepmother," said Oliver, looking at the latter.

"Stepmother any good?" said Mr. Bigwell.

"Yes, too much good. Now please tell me all about yourself."

"Both parents living in the North. Member of a large family."

Oliver nodded in Mr. Bigwell's manner, and Mr. Dalziel gave a gentle, almost guilty laugh.

"Religion?" said Mr. Spode to Oliver.

"None. Village church at home. Sometimes play the organ. Play the harmonium here."

"None. Chapel at home. I am not ashamed of it," said Mr. Bigwell.

"Surely you must be," said Mr. Spode.

"I should not confess it, if I were."

"People are always ashamed of things they confess. Otherwise they would be easy in keeping them to themselves. I confess I have not a penny in the world, apart from what my mother allows me. But I am ashamed."

"Then why are you not quiet about it?"

"People might expect me to help them on their way," said Mr. Spode.

"I have nothing but what I earn," said Mr. Bigwell.

"Then you must be ashamed and glad to have got the confession over."

"I think independence is a good thing, though it may be an arrogant attitude."

"If it were arrogant, it would be very nice," said Oliver. "But it is brave and sad, and makes other people ashamed for us. I am ceasing to be proud of depending on myself."

"Have you a religion, Spode?" said Mr. Bigwell.

"I have tried many things in my search for support. But I have had no encouragement. My mother is a sceptic."

"I am a Catholic," said Mr. Dalziel.

"Believing?" said Oliver.

Mr. Dalziel turned his eyes towards him.

"Believing, as we see," said Mr. Bigwell.

"I do not try to convert people."

"Do you not think you ought?" said Oliver.

"I see what you mean. I fear I am but a feeble witness."

"Confession," said Mr. Spode, as if to himself. "Confession. Such an outlet."

"Well, since you say so," said Mr. Bigwell, with a laugh.

"Do people confess the truth?" said Oliver.

"People always ask that," said Mr. Dalziel.

"It is my turn to be ashamed."

"Why should you not be as other men?" said Mr. Bigwell.

"It is because there are no reasons, that I am ashamed."

"What are your ideas for the future?" said Mr. Bigwell. "Inherit, I suppose?"

"If things can be kept together."

Mr. Bigwell nodded once more.

"How did you gain universal understanding?" said Oliver.

"Well, I keep my eyes open, as I go through life. I may as well learn what I can, whether or no it is any good to me."

"What are your ideas for your own future?"

"Stick to my work and get where I may. Nothing else for me. I suppose you expect me to be ashamed."

"You must be. And all through no fault of your own. What are your ideas, Dalziel? This keeping nothing from each other is such a success."

"I shall have enough to live on in the end. And I can't help being glad of it. My own efforts would not take me far."

"You need not pretend to be ashamed," said Mr. Spode.

"Well, I am glad I have no reason to wish my parents dead," said Mr. Bigwell.

"Everyone wants the reasons," said Oliver. "Of course we need not be influenced by them."

"My mother's death will tear up the roots of my life," said Mr. Spode.

"But it will give you other support for it," said Oliver.

"There, that is what I meant," said Mr. Bigwell. "Always that idea in your heads! I repeat that I am glad I have no reason to desire the death of those who gave me life."

"Yes, yes, you do repeat it," said Oliver, in a soothing manner.

"You do not really seem to like it much," said Mr. Spode.

"I am glad I shall have enough to offer a woman one day," said Mr. Dalziel.

"I would rather earn it," said Mr. Bigwell. "But women—that takes us into another sphere."

"Not those we can offer enough to," said Oliver.

"Well, well," said Mr. Bigwell, half-laughing, "a man's life is his own."

"Surely not here," said Oliver. "I do not want to go back to my old sense of isolation."

"Well, a man is a man," said Mr. Bigwell.

"That is rather sweeping," said Oliver. "I am not."

"Neither am I," said Mr. Spode. "And I should not think Cassidy is."

"Of course not," said Oliver, "when he keeps a boys' school. And my meaning is simple, not sinister."

"Well, Dalziel and I will keep our own counsel," said Mr. Bigwell.

"I should be surprised if Bigwell were a man," said Mr. Spode, in an absent tone.

"You can speak to me, and not of me, when I am here."

"I found I could only speak of you."

"So it is true," said Oliver.

"What?" said Mr. Dalziel.

"The relation of masters in a school together."

"I am not sure that I agree with Spode's conception of himself," said Mr. Bigwell.

"I like you to speak of me, and not to me. I follow my mother's conception of me. I am an adult human being."

"She is an unusual parent, if she conceives of you as that. My mother does not think of me as far on the road."

"And she is right," said Mr. Spode.

"Now what do you mean by that?"

"I mean what I say. That your mother is right."

"Well, you would not have him say she is wrong, Bigwell," said Oliver. "A man does not speak against another man's mother. If he does, I believe he is not a man, and we hardly want any more of that."

"I know what he meant," said Mr. Bigwell. "And it is true that I started behind the rest of you, and have to go further."

"I really did not know," said Oliver. "And he was talking about what your mother meant. Do you think that was it? What are you holding in your hand, Spode? Some precious thing?"

"It is a jewel," said Mr. Spode, in a deep tone. "My mother wants me to sell it for her."

"She wishes to part with it, does she?" said Mr. Bigwell, on a faintly corrective note.

"She wishes me to do it for her. It embarrasses her to part with things. She fancies that people look at her as if she were in debt."

"Well, as long as she is not."

"But she is. That is her reason for the step. I do not think people often have any other."

"What is the good of a single earring?"

"It could be made into something else. Ever since I can remember, that has been the case. But it is the kind of thing that is never done."

"True," said Mr. Bigwell.

"Is it true?" said Oliver. "I should not have known that either. I believe I have seen an earring like it."

"You cannot have," said Mr. Spode. "It is unique."

"Unless you have seen its fellow," said Mr. Bigwell. "It must be somewhere. Well, good luck to the barter. Is that someone at the door?"

"Is this Miss James's room?" said a boy's voice.

"No, but come in," said Mr. Spode. "We will try to take her place."

Four boys obeyed the word and looked about them.

"Is Miss James here?" said the same voice, as an open-eyed boy, with a large, round face and head, detached himself from the group.

"What would you think?" said Mr. Bigwell. "If you cannot believe your ears, you must use your eyes."

"She is not here. There are only men."

"True," said Mr. Spode; "and you have just been torn from your mother and sisters. But do not despise the rougher sex. It is your own."

"Where is she?"

"You must call me 'sir'. You must do as the Romans do."

"'Do you know where she is, sir'?" prompted Mr. Dalziel, in even tones.

The boy repeated the words with a glance of humour at his companions.

"You are laughing at us," said Mr. Spode. "But I shall not tell you that you will soon laugh on the other side of your face, because I could not say a vulgar thing. And I daresay it is not true."

"She is in her own room along the passage," said Mr. Dalziel. "She will solve your problems."

"You detect in us no feminine grace?" said Mr. Bigwell.

"Hasn't he got it?" said the boy, indicating Mr. Dalziel.

There was some mirth.

"What is your name, my man?" said Mr. Bigwell, in a tone of giving the correct turn to the proceedings. "And how many summers have you seen?"

"Francis Bacon, sir. I am eleven."

"Your namesake was the greatest, the wisest and the meanest of mankind," said Mr. Spode. "Which of those do we expect you to be?"

"The first, sir. The first two."

There was further mirth.

"The last, sir," said Bacon, with less confidence.

"The next boy," said Mr. Bigwell. "Your name, my son?"

"Sefton Shelley, sir."

"Yes, he is my half-brother," said Oliver. "My step-mother has sent me here to keep an eye on him."

"You will not often see him."

"Then I cannot do as she said."

"Are you the boy I dropped in the passage?" said Mr. Spode, in faint surprise, as if he had hardly expected Sefton to emerge.

"Yes, sir. But I met the others."

"That was a resourceful boy."

"Next young man?" said Mr. Bigwell.

"Hubert Holland, sir. Nearly eleven."

"Colin Sturgeon, sir. Ten and a half."

"A tall, pale, aquiline boy, and a short, snub, rosy boy." said Mr. Spode in a dreamy tone. "The old story that is always new."

Bacon glanced at Holland and then at the men.

"You could describe us as well as we can describe you?" said Mr. Spode.

"Yes, sir."

"Well, remember that a pleasant description is more difficult than an unpleasant one," said Mr. Bigwell. "You want to do the difficult thing, don't you?"

"Yes, sir."

"Why?" said Mr. Spode.

"Because fewer people could do it, sir."

"May you never have a worse reason for doing things than that," said Mr. Bigwell. "Now you may go to Miss James. And remember that she is always there, and we are always here."

"Yes, sir."

"Miss James will make them feel at home," said Mr. Dalziel.

"She will make them feel at school," said Mr. Spode. "She will show them the truest kindness. That is cruelty in a condensed form."

"I had no idea that schoolmasters were so alive to boyish troubles," said Oliver. "I thought they became callous to suffering they constantly witnessed."

"They may become sharpened to it," said Mr. Bigwell. "I wish that could be said of the little ruffians themselves."

"Well, they would hardly be tender with a man's tenderness," said Oliver.

The four boys outside the room paused and looked at each other. Their pursuit of Miss James seemed to have fallen from their minds.

"What relation did he say you were to him?" said Bacon to Sefton. "The darker one of the two large men."

"Half-brother. That means that one parent is the same, and the other is not. We have the same father and different mothers."

"Then has your father more than one wife?"

"No, of course not. The first wife has to die before a man can have a second. Oliver's mother was the first."

"Then your father does not keep a harem?"

"Of course not. He has only had one wife at a time. Oliver's mother died and he married again later."

"But she was still his wife. So is your mother his concubine?"

"No, of course not. A second wife is as much a wife as the first. Just like a second husband."

"When he happens to be a wife," said Holland.

"We want to get at the truth," said Bacon, with a frown. "Perhaps his father is a Mohammedan."

"Of course he is not," said Sefton. "He is just like any-one else."

"Then he is a commonplace man," said Holland.

"That is what you will be," said Bacon. "But Shelley can't make things true by just saying 'of course'. His mother is probably a concubine. He might not be told about it. I don't suppose he would be."

"It may be like Agamemnon bringing back Cassandra when he already had a wife," said Sturgeon.

"It is not," said Sefton. "The first wife died before he married my mother, before he even saw her, years and years before."

"Is your brother treated differently from you?" said Bacon. "I mean apart from his being older. Does he have more of everything?"

"He will have the place in the end. But that is because he is the oldest."

"You see," said Bacon, nodding at the others. "That is how it would be. The brother is the child of the real wife, and is more important. Won't you have any share of things at all, Shelley?"

"Has he any right to be called that?" said Holland. "Perhaps his mother called him Sefton, to give him a sur-name."

"My name is Sefton Shelley, just as my brother's is Oliver Shelley. Sefton is my mother's surname."

"Well, there it is," said Bacon. "His mother's surname is the one he has a right to."

"I shall have a profession, and he will have the place, because it is the law."

"Of course it would be. The child of the real wife is the only one the law recognises. You are what is called a natural son. That is why you are to have work of your own. Natural sons are often made quite important in that way. There is a lot of it in history."

"He ought not really to be at the same school as we are," said Sturgeon. "He ought to be at one for the sons of concubines. There are schools for the sons of almost all kinds of people."

"I expect his mother managed it for him," said Holland. "Concubines are often more spoilt than ordinary women."

"Is his father a gentleman?" said Sturgeon.

"Yes," said Bacon. "It is gentlemen who do these things. They are the only ones who can afford to do them. They cost a great deal, though they are generally not mentioned."

"Do all men who can afford to, keep concubines?"

"No, only in China. In England only a few keep them. And they are generally kept outside the house. Sometimes the real wife does not know about them."

"I am the son of a real wife," said Sefton, with tears in his voice. "My father's first wife died before he ever saw my mother."

"Well, there is no need to cry about it," said Bacon. "Your father may love your mother the best. That does happen with concubines. I daresay Agamemnon loved Cassandra better than Clytaemnestra. Indeed it seems as if he did."

"How do you know so much about concubines? Do all your fathers keep several?"

"What is all this noise?" said Miss James, opening her door. "No talking is allowed in the passage. Oh, it is the four new boys! Well, even you can read the rules. Were you looking for my room?"

"Yes," said Bacon, as he recalled this purpose.

"'Yes, Miss James,'" said the latter, putting things at once on a proper footing. "Why are you crying, Shelley? You are Shelley, are you not? I saw you arriving with your brother. What is wrong?"

"My mother is not a concubine."

"Well, of course she is not. Who said she was?"

"All of them. All of them, Miss James."

"Well, he said our fathers kept several," said Holland. "Several, Miss James."

"I never heard of such talk. I was never so shocked in my life," said Miss James, rapidly. "And new boys, and one of you related to the Head! I should complain to him, if I liked to talk about such things, if I wished to be degraded by them. And telling tales of each other on your first day! I can hardly believe it. Are you not ashamed of it yourselves?"

"Yes, Miss James."

"Well, it is best to say no more about it. Indeed, it is not fit to speak about. Here is the key of your playbox, Bacon. And of yours, Sturgeon." Miss James here waited for the keys to be accepted, to attach names to their owners, a capacity taken by them as part of a general unfathomable power. "You have yours, Shelley. Then Holland will lead us upstairs. You are to have a dormitory to yourselves. There is a playbox by each bed, and you must claim your own."

Miss James kept her eyes on Holland, to register her impression of him, and the boys gave their first signs of interest in their new world.

"Now I am going to put you all on your honour," said Miss James, her eyes now resting easily on the claimants of the boxes. "I am sure you know what that means. You are on your honour as gentlemen not to mention the word, 'concubine', again."

"The word comes in the Bible," said Bacon.

"And so do a great many words that are not fit for you to use, that are not suitable for people who do not understand how to use them," said Miss James, with the rapidity that was frequently her resource. "And you want a great knowledge of the Bible to understand its language."

"Suppose we have to read the word aloud?"

"Then you will do so without giggling or exchanging glances," said Miss James, to the discomfort of her hearers, who recognised in her some power of divining their nature. "And in ordinary conversation you will not mention it. You are on your honour not to do so. Do you understand?"

"Yes, Miss James."

"And now here are the rules of the school," said Miss James, with the faint sigh of one approaching the last and most arduous stage. "Here is the printed list on the wall. Now can you all read?"

"Yes, Miss James."

"You need not say it too easily. I have often met boys who apparently could not. This is an important thing," said Miss James, who had disposed of such matters as could be settled through the medium of honour. "Will you read the first rule, Bacon?"

"'Rise on hearing the first bell.' How do we know it is the first?"

"Well, you can count as far as one, can you not?"

"Yes. But we might be asleep when it went. Miss James."

"The bell would wake you. That is its purpose. Read the second rule, Shelley."

"'Leave the dormitory on second bell, and descend in silence to classroom.'"

"And the third, Sturgeon."

"'Observe silence in passages and on stairs.' Suppose we observe a noise, Miss James?"

"You do not know that use of the word?" said Miss James, in a tone that mingled kindliness, suspicion and resignation, in case any of these qualities was called for. "It just means 'keep'. You can remember that."

"'Observe silence in dormitory after lights are out,'" read Holland. "'and when visiting dormitory during day. Observe punctuality at meals.' Suppose we do forget what the word, 'observe', means?"

Miss James took a pencil and altered the word to 'keep', and on second thoughts produced a pen and traced it where it occurred.

"*Keep* punctuality at meals?" said Holland, as if to himself.

"It is an old use of the word. You would not know it," said Miss James, going to the door. "Now, if you want me, you know where I am. Remember all I have said."

"If we do not want her, we forget where she is," said Holland.

"As is true in many cases," said Bacon.

"Not a bad old dame," said Sturgeon.

"She might be better-favoured," said Bacon.

"If she was, she would not be here," said Holland. "There would be a risk of the masters' falling in love with her."

"She would not be chosen for——for what must not be said," said Sturgeon.

"You are breaking your promise," said Bacon.

"He is not. He did not say the word," said Holland. "And we did not really give the promise."

"We did in effect. There is a point beyond which we do not go. Now I am going to open my playbox."

"The size of mine is in keeping with myself," said Sturgeon, getting over what had to come.

"You are of a wizened stature," said Bacon. "Perhaps you will grow up a dwarf."

"Then you could earn your living in a show," said Holland. "Indeed, you might have to. I don't think a dwarf would be employed in ordinary ways."

"Should I be paid enough for that?"

"You would not want much," said Bacon. "You would not have family expenses. No one would marry a dwarf."

"Dwarfs sometimes marry each other," said Sturgeon. "Sometimes their children are dwarfs, and sometimes not. It happens in the big circuses, and I might succeed in my profession."

"And what profession is that?" said Miss James, returning with the air of one who had expected to do so.

"When you cannot remember a simple thing for a few minutes!"

"A dwarf in a fair, Miss James."

"Well, what extraordinary characters you think of! First a—and then a dwarf, first one thing and then another. And did I, or did I not, tell you to read the rules, and hear you reading them?"

"Yes, you did, Miss James."

"And did you read the one about keeping silence in the dormitories during the day? Or did you miss that one out?"

"No, Miss James. But that was *visiting* the dormitory," said Bacon. "We are unpacking in this one and settling down."

Miss James again produced her pen, made an alteration on the list, and turned on her way. A bell rang as she reached the door, and she looked at the four boys engaged with their boxes.

"What sound was that?"

"A bell, Miss James."

"And what bell would it be at this hour?"

"A bell for tea?" said Sturgeon, in a dubious tone.

"And did you miss this rule out?" said Miss James, tapping her pen against the list. "Will you please read it again, all together?"

"'Observe punctuality at meals.'"

"Well, what are you going to do about it?"

Four pairs of eyes met hers and sought each other.

"Ought we to go down?" said Holland, in a tone of hazarding a just possible suggestion.

"Perhaps our tea will be brought up to us on our first night," said Sturgeon.

"Go down, all of you, and let me have no more nonsense," said Miss James, tapping her pen on his head and almost smiling. "You will miss grace now. You can say your grace to yourselves. You all know a grace, don't you?"

"Yes, Miss James."

"Then mind you do not forget to say it. And talk among yourselves and not to the other boys. That leads to trouble."

The boys went down and followed a hum of voices to the dining-room. An elder boy leaned from his seat and pointed them to their place. They took their seats and turned their eyes on the table.

"If we were made truly thankful, we might get on better," said Sturgeon, with no thought of attending further than this to Miss James's injunction.

"They should have warned us that the school was for coarse feeders," said Bacon. "Perhaps that is true of all schools. Only coarse feeders can be educated."

"What is this, boys?" said Miss James, coming late to her place, with her habitual, hurried disregard of her own comfort. "What is this I hear about coarse feeders? It does not sound a polite way to talk. I hope you can all behave properly at table. Is no one going to pass anything to me?"

The boys, who had assumed that Miss James arranged matters for herself in arranging all things, handed plates with signs of discomposure.

"Miss James also feeds coarsely," muttered Sturgeon.

"I beg your pardon, Sturgeon?" said Miss James, in a new tone.

"I said—I only said," said Sturgeon, realising the interpretation put upon his words; "we were talking about the food, not about the people who ate it."

"Oh, I see. That explains it. But I hope you were not finding fault with the food put before you. We eat what is provided for us, without discussion or criticism. Did you all remember your grace?" Her tone suggested that such an observance might have ensured subsequent propriety.

"No, Miss James," said Bacon.

"Did you actually forget it?"

"No, Miss James," said Holland, feeling that Sturgeon's allusion saved them from this.

"Then what was your reason for not saying it?"

"I don't know, Miss James."

"Now I think I can tell you," said Miss James, leaning back and surveying the faces turned towards her. "I think it was that you felt a little ashamed of saying it in front of everyone, of standing to your colours in public. And as that is not a feeling to be proud of, you will not yield to it another time. Are you going to leave that butter on your plate, Sturgeon? Is it not wholesome food?"

"Yes. No, Miss James. It is the fat on the top of the potted meat."

"It is butter. The meat is potted in the house. Put it on a piece of bread and eat it."

"No, Miss James. It is against my nature, and I must stand to my colours in public," said Sturgeon, realising too late the various baseness involved in his speech.

Miss James rose, a flush mounting her cheek, and walked down the table towards the presiding master.

"I am about to suffer for my colours," said Sturgeon, grinning at his companions.

"You have time to hide the butter and say you have eaten it," said Bacon, not pretending to accept this lightness.

Sturgeon looked about him, but saw that the moment had passed. Miss James was returning with a gowned figure in her wake.

"Do you ask me to countenance direct disobedience, Mr. Spode?"

"No disobedience of any kind. It would be an improper requirement. In what way has obedience been withheld?"

"Sturgeon refuses to eat the wholesome butter on his plate."

"Why did he take it, the boy called Sturgeon? He was called that a little while ago. So he is a wasteful and un-biddable boy. In my employers' house are many monsters."

"I did not take it. It was on the potted meat. Sir," said Sturgeon.

"And you took it upon yourself to separate them? Do not take matters upon yourself in future. You are not a person to judge. You are a person to be enjoined and directed. You are the least of all persons. Do you grasp this truth about yourself?"

"Yes, sir."

"Then render to Miss James the thing that is Miss James's, the submission of people such as you. Take bread place the butter upon it, and carry it with you after the meal. Do not keep a lady waiting while you eat it. Grace is about to be said." Mr. Spode took a step apart, stood for a space with bowed head, and withdrew without a glance behind.

Sturgeon spread the butter, with remorse welling up within him, and Miss James surveyed him with similar experience. There is a rule that no human being is perfect, and a tendency to hastiness saved Miss James from upsetting it.

"You see, Sturgeon, the view a master takes of your behaviour. Now all go up to the dormitory, and I will follow. There are still some things to be arranged."

"I will eat the bread-and-butter for you," said Holland on the stairs. "I don't mind it as much as you do. I thought the other things were worse."

Sturgeon relinquished it with a shudder and wiped his hands. Miss James was aloof and preoccupied, her geniality destroyed by the recent passage and her compunction for it. She began to sort some clothes and to ask curt questions concerning them.

"I feel sick," said Sturgeon, in an uncertain way. "I feel sick, Miss James."

"Oh no, you do not," said the latter, rapidly threading one thing through another. "Sick boys are not rude and obstinate. Use your handkerchief and stop choking like that."

Sturgeon obeyed the first injunction, but the smell of butter on the handkerchief disposed of the second. The other boys surveyed him, rigid and silent, and it occurred to him to wonder if they would do anything to succour him, if his life were at stake, as possibly it was. Miss James dealt with him with an efficiency and absence of fuss, that aroused his gratitude, and finally stood back and regarded him in her usual manner.

"Well, I am glad of this sickness, Sturgeon, if it does sound an odd thing to say. It proves you were not yourself when you behaved as you did. I should be sorry to think it was your real self that you showed me."

"I am not glad of it," said Holland.

"Sturgeon's real self has not everything to recommend it," said Bacon.

"Now do not be foolish, boys. It might happen to you at any time. And you should never say anything to add to anyone's discomfort. Your first thought should be to lessen it."

"We were not showing you our real selves, Miss James."

"You should have said you were not well, Sturgeon; then I should not have told you to eat the butter."

"Holland ate it for me. It was the smell of it on the handkerchief," said Sturgeon, now beyond any stage but simple truth.

"Well, I am glad it was not wasted."

"As it would have been, if Sturgeon had eaten it," said Bacon.

"Now will you all get to bed? I want you off my mind before I go to the other boys. You are only four out of sixty. I cannot give you all my time."

The boys, with an incredulous acceptance of the ordinary nature of their experience, prepared for the night, now finding every step an obstacle in the way of darkness and their different means of relief. These varied from tears to prayer, and rapidly ended in sleep.

The next morning the bell tolled—as they had agreed to describe the sound—and they rose with an unexpected feeling of being able to face the day. Bacon, forgetting the congestion of the new world, led the way downstairs with mimicry of Miss James.

"Whom are you imitating, Bacon?" said a voice in the rear.

"The—the housemaid at home, Miss James."

"And do you think that is a kind thing to do?"

"Well, she cannot see me, Miss James."

"And does that alter the essential quality of the action?"

"No. Yes. No, Miss James."

"Do you think it is a manly thing to bring ridicule upon someone of a weaker sex than your own?" said Miss James, who was at frequent pains to impress the frailty of her nature upon those who owed her subservience.

"No, Miss James."

"Someone too, who spends her life in working for your comfort," said Miss James, with a quiver of feeling, or fellow-feeling, in her tone.

"No, Miss James," said Bacon, with some feeling in his

"Well, if I try to forget it this once, will you give me your word that you will not sink to that level again?"

"Yes, Miss James," said Bacon, less affected by Miss James's self-betrayal than by fear that she might realise it, and hurrying into the breakfast-room.

"We are getting hemmed in by promises," said Holland. "It is a good thing we have not promised not to eat and drink."

"It might be a solution," said Bacon, looking at the dishes.

"I am the hungriest. I have a right to be," said Sturgeon, assuming that thoughts were on his late mishap, and surprised by the looks of question.

Letters were put on the table, and there was one at Sefton's place.

"You are a lucky boy. A letter already!" said Miss James, something in her tone suggesting disapproval of unsettling methods.

"It is from my mother," said Sefton.

"From your mater?" said Holland, in a tone that was just a question.

"Yes," said Sefton, tearing the envelope and surveying the round hand written by Maria for his aid.

"My little son—A word from your mother to help you through your first day. A happy day it may not be, but a brave and busy one it can, and I am sure will be, and the first step towards the success that means so much to Father and me. So you will forget yourself, and put your heart into your new life for our sakes.—Your loving Mother."

Sefton sat with his eyes on the words. Forget himself he could not; put his heart into his life he could; succeed he must. He crumpled the letter and put it in his pocket, conscious of reluctance for it to be seen, conscious in a way new to him, that indifference to his progress in his parents would be more to his credit than anxiety for it. To go to expense for a son's education, and then be unconcerned for his benefit, was the ideal thing. He felt strange knowledge welling up within him, knowledge that did not come from outside; knowledge of the world of school, of the world itself; knowledge that the parallel between them was a shallow thing. He was surprised by his perception; felt it could not be common to his kind, and set him apart; saw his parents' ambitions fulfilled, and himself rendered fitting dues. The mood of exaltation was fostered by prayers, a ceremony new to him and coming with consequent force. A passage of scripture, chosen it seemed, at random, was read by Lucius; and a hymn chosen in another manner, by by Miss James, was rendered by all with simple feeling, and supported by Oliver with his eyes on the keyboard. Sefton's emotions were fed, and he entered the classroom in a mood of high resolve.

Arithmetic was the subject of the first hour, and the master of the art was Mr. Spode, who suffered from resentful surprise that new boys could not proceed from the point where the last ones left off.

"Have you been taught?" he said.

"Yes; yes, sir."

"And have you learnt?" said Mr. Spode, as if it were not worth while to finish his sentences.

"Yes, sir."

"Then work that sum. And if it is wrong, do not mind about it. Others will not."

Sefton found the problem within his powers, looked up the answer and found it correct, and awaited and obtained approval.

"Try the next kind, and I shall begin to see what you are. I did not know what you might be. Do not look at the answers. They are to help me, not you. We both need them and I am to have them. In future you will use a book without them."

Sefton followed directions and again attained success, was put on to a further chapter and pursued his way. In the fourth he was less sure of himself, consulted the answer and worked at the question until the result tallied with it. Mr Spode saw the erasures.

"You were less sure of your ground?"

"Yes, sir. I saw the mistake myself. I thought the sum was wrong, and looked for it."

"Well, who else was there to see it? Now I am here to teach you, and I do not ask that the cup shall pass from me. Do another of the same kind, and take your time."

Sefton did so, protected by glances at Mr. Spode, and by means of his last method again achieved success. Then he went further, and finding a problem beyond his powers, appended the answer at a distance from it, filled in the intervening space with attempts at working, and achieved a plausible effect and another triumph. One more problem dealt with in this way, and the lesson ended, and he put his work into his desk in relief and exultation. He was too young to see his danger and joined his companions without misgiving.

"Who taught you arithmetic at home?" said Holland.

"Miss Petticott, my governess, my sister's governess."

"She must have kept your nose to the grindstone," said Bacon.

"Women do that," said Holland. "They are known to be harder than men."

"I don't think they are," said Sturgeon.

"Oh, your sickness is not the whole of life," said Bacon.

"No, but it is a part of it," said Sturgeon, betraying some feeling.

"There is not so much in early success," said Bacon. "It may be a bad sign. But you need not look disturbed, Shelley. I daresay you will not have much of it."

Sefton was silent, knowing he must have it, if he could.

"We have Latin after the break. We have it with Mr. Bigwell," said Holland. "Bigwell wastes his time and ours with it."

"He takes Greek too, for the boys who learn it," said Bacon. "I shall have enough of Bigwell, and he of me."

"I am not to learn Greek," said Holland. "I am not supposed to be clever. Are you, Sturgeon?"

"Yes. So I am to learn Greek, to let people know about it."

"Now what is this, boys?" said Miss James, appearing from no particular direction. "You do not want so much to eat in the middle of the morning. You have fetched enough from your boxes to last you all day. Anyone would think you had never had a meal before."

The boys, who had seen their appetites as casting an aspersion on the school fare, were silent as the slur was transferred to their home provision.

"No wonder you do not enjoy your meals, if you over-eat between them."

The boys grinned at each other, Sefton feeling shame for the first time that day, and repaired before they needed, to Mr. Bigwell's class.

"Well, I hope you are ready to face the term," said the latter, hitching his gown on to his shoulders as a hardly natural appendage. "I confess I am still inclined to indulge in the backward glance."

"It is easier for you. You have not anything to learn," said Holland.

"Have I not? Make no mistake," said Mr. Bigwell, who made none himself, and attended to his needs.

"I mean, you know all you have to teach. You don't have to keep on learning, as we do."

"Well, once I was in your pristine state," said Mr. Bigwell, giving further adjustment to the outward sign of his present one.

He set the boys to construe from a book of selections, to gauge their knowledge. The book was in common use, and Sefton had read it with his tutor, and obtained easy credit.

"Have you read that passage before, Shelley? Do you know this book?"

"No, sir. But I have read Latin something like it."

"Try this passage on the opposite page."

Sefton did so, with similar result.

"And now this harder one some pages further."

Sefton just managed it, or gave the impression that he did, making one or two false moves, and rectifying them in a manner of sudden perception.

"That is above the average. You may have a gift for languages. If so, you must see it as a responsibility. It is not a matter of credit for yourself."

"No, sir," said Sefton, who had no personal concern with it.

"We shall have our textbooks next week, and shall see how you manage then. That will be more of a test, but I do not think you will fail."

"I think you know more Latin than Bigwell," said Holland, when the latter had withdrawn. "He is supposed to buy cribs for every book, and keep them in his desk. The boys have seen them when he opens it. But he did not give himself away when I set a trap for him."

"It would hardly do to borrow them," said Bacon. "It would leave him without the means of taking his classes. He would have to take to his bed."

"And then we could not show off before him. So it would be no good," said Sturgeon. "And it would be beyond human courage."

"Yes," said Sefton, feeling that this might be the case, but that the matter could remain in the balance.

The rest of the morning was given to Mr. Dalziel, who taught Scripture, history and English, regarded as kindred subjects and appropriate to his gentler nature. Sefton did well without great effort, and saw these things would present no problem, a matter for relief, as problems gathered.

The dinner bell rang, and the four took their seats about Miss James in an uncertain spirit, feeling that a poor appetite would recall their gluttony, and a good one establish it. Miss James had forgotten the incident, or rather had got out of the way of remembering incidents, to avoid the strain on her memory.

Sefton's life thickened about him. Success was his, but success with a crumbling basis. He followed it along a way that wound hard and steep. Strategy and courage were demanded of him; danger claimed him for its own. Envy of his comrades, with their open and ordinary lives, filled his heart and looked from his eyes. By night he crept down to Mr. Bigwell's desk, to read translations, with his ear alert for sound; broached the desk of Mr. Spode for the answers to the problems to be faced by day. A visit from Maria, urgent and exultant, confirmed him in this course. More than once catastrophe dogged him, barely passed him by. He was heard, followed, all but seen. A reputation for sleep-walking arose and saved him for the time. He was discussed, questioned, physicked by Miss James. His lapses from his standard, when his strategy failed, were ascribed to improper sleep, and he bore the symptoms of it.

He settled down to the routine, almost coming to find it such, received his mother's letters with their pride and praise, wept over his father's simple words, and pressed forward on his path, resolved to sustain its rigours for his parents' sake. He longed for the end of the term; never forgot, as others did, to mark off the days; felt he could hold out so far and no further, shrank from imagining an extra day. He fancied the masters grew guarded in their praise, that their eyes rested on him in doubt and question, but was too young to know how far he was self-betrayed. If he could reach the end of the term, his troubles would end. The next term lay beyond his sight. Here his childhood protected him; it was part of the formless future.

The end of the term approached, and with it the examinations. He heard them discussed without any real conception of them, hardly knew the threat they carried. When they came, it emerged that his house was founded upon the sand. Elemental forces beat upon that house, and it fell. He was confronted by problems without an answer, by passages he had not seen. His place in the subjects passed without question, either from masters or boys. This was ill-omened, but the threat was not defined. The end was at hand; the hard road lay behind; enough success was assured to him to carry him home. He no longer envied boys who slept in their beds, slept himself in a delusive peace.

When the summons to Lucius came, he went with a sinking heart that he did not explain. The glances of the boys gave him a feeling he would not recognise. He could hardly believe it when he found his shadowy suspicions fulfilled. What was known as simple truth was simple indeed.

Lucius sat at his desk, with Mr. Spode and Mr. Bigwell at his hand. Their faces defined Sefton's foreboding. As Lucius spoke, his heart was still.

"Sefton, I ask you to speak the truth, to show me you are a person who can speak it. You have had answers to the questions set by Mr. Spode?"

"Yes—yes, sir," said Sefton realising that honesty was the best policy, at the usual moment of finding that other policies had failed.

"You have had books with the answers appended to them?"

"Yes; yes, sir," said Sefton, preferring this picture to

that of himself creeping forth by night to pursue the books to their place.

"Did you bring them from home?"

"They were with the books that were packed for me. I did not know what they were."

"Did you think that copying the answers and faking the work above them was the proper use of them?"

"I did not know how to use them, sir. I think Miss Petticott looked first at the answers."

Lucius looked him in the eyes, uncertain how far to accept this innocence. Mr. Spode and Mr. Bigwell kept their eyes averted, not being subject to the uncertainty.

"And had you translations of the books you read with Mr. Bigwell?"

"Well, I had read the book of extracts at home."

"You did not say you had read it?"

"No, sir," said Sefton, seeing that Mr. Bigwell recalled his saying he had not.

"And the other books you used? Had you translations of those?"

"I found some old ones in the classroom. I did not know at first we were not supposed to use them."

"But you did not show them to the other boys?"

"No, sir," said Sefton, weeping. "I wanted to do better than they did."

"Even when you realised you were gaining credit that was not yours, you did not show them?" said Lucius, his tone suggesting that honour among wrong-doers rendered the latter more acceptable to him.

"No, sir. I thought that would make it more likely that it would be found out," said Sefton, on an honest note.

"Well, go and fetch those books and bring them to me."

"I can't, sir. I have destroyed them. I put them on the fire. I wanted to stop using them before the examinations. I thought if I did not use them for those, it would not much matter my doing it before. And I did not use them for those. I did not open a single book all through them. I had not got the books any longer." Sefton raised his eyes with a childish openness that was echoed in his tone.

"There was no sign that you did use them," said Mr. Spode.

"You could not have done so," said Mr. Bigwell. "The invigilation would have made it impossible."

Sefton lifted his eyes again in innocent acceptance.

"So this was the reason of the sleep-walking and pallid looks," said Lucius. "It was what you had on your mind."

"Yes, sir," said Sefton, causing his shoulders to rise, as though he felt the burden rolling off them.

"What made you so anxious to do better than the other boys?"

"My mother wanted it, sir, because of my father," said Sefton, arousing in Lucius a familiar doubt whether to encourage parents in interest in their sons.

"We have never had to deal with such a protracted course of deceit."

Sefton broke into natural tears, as the long stretch of weariness and effort surged over him.

"Your parents will feel more sorrow in your wrongdoing than they had pleasure in your success. I need hardly say that to your father's son."

"No, sir," said Sefton, his eyes dilating as he grasped the possible result of his sacrifice.

"The masters cannot write a report of your work without mention of a thing so much involved in it," said Lucius, in an empty tone, as though getting through what must be said. "And we could not take it upon ourselves to keep such a thing from your parents. We must not fail them because you have done so."

"I suppose you do have to depend on them in any real thing to do with the boys."

Sefton spoke under some strange urge, surprised by the directing force within himself. He saw the shaft go home, saw a gleam of hope and saw it fade, knew without seeing it the comprehension in the masters' eyes.

"I am glad there has been no suggestion of trouble in your work for Mr. Dalziel."

"No, sir. There was nothing in the books I had, to do with that," said Sefton, as though the trouble in the other things were hardly to be referred to himself.

"You may go now. There is no more to say on the matter. I wish that words could mend it."

"It is a sorry thing to see a child at bay," said Mr. Bigwell. "We could only be ashamed of our own position."

"He saw us as secure and pitiless," said Mr. Spode, "and what is greater cause for shame? And a child is not what we think. We should not know, if we did not see it, that it was a child. That is a knowledge that has come to me."

"The childishness of the whole affair is its saving grace," said Lucius. "Thank you for giving me your time."

"So he does not want to give us his," said Mr. Spode in the passage. "He does not like to hear us doing justice to ourselves. Most of this trouble is saving grace. It is so gentle and aspiring a crime. That may be true of many crimes. It is righteousness that tends to lack quality."

"Oh, it has more on the whole," said Mr. Bigwell.

"The boy was surprised that it had not. I observed the boy."

"I wonder what he is doing now. I hope not crying in the dormitory."

"Your hope is realised. I can hear him with the other boys. He is vaunting himself and being puffed up."

"I do not see he has cause for doing that."

"I think I see why he does. The way of transgressors may be hard in a subtle sense."

Sefton had intended to go upstairs and face alone the death of hope. He was not yet versed in the ways of his present world. In the passage, at a considered distance from the study, stood the three partners of his life, if not of his experience.

"What had the Head to say?" said Holland. "You have not lost a relation, have you? I mean, nobody is dead at home? It is just that you did your papers less well than your ordinary work?"

"Yes, of course it is that. Don't you really know the game I have played?"

"We knew there was something. We began to guess. Had you cribs and keys and things?"

"Yes, of course I had. I have torn them all up now. I have watched their death in the flames. I wanted to see how far I could go without being suspected. And it was a pretty long way. What fools these masters are!"

"It is not a sign of intelligence to be easily suspicious," said Bacon.

"I got rid of the keys before the examinations. I could not use them for those. It would not have been fair on the rest of you. And there is such a thing as going too far."

"You did not stop far short of it. You went a pretty long way."

"And I expect the Head thought so," said Holland, "and said what he thought."

"And you were not so fair to the rest of us as all that," said Bacon. "We had to suffer through the term by comparison with you."

"With your keys and cribs, which was worse," said Sturgeon.

"Isn't there going to be any trouble about it?" said Holland, in a baffled tone.

"Allusions on report, and all that," said Sefton, in an airy manner, feeling this would satisfy any normal desire for justice.

"An instance of the all-in-one, indeed," said Bacon, showing it had done so in his case.

"Couldn't you run away instead of going home?" said Holland, in whose case it had gone further.

"No, thank you. I prefer the comforts of home to hanging about without a roof over my head."

"*Comforts* of home!" said Sturgeon.

"You might stay away just long enough to make them

anxious," said Holland. "Then they might be too relieved to see you, to say much."

"I have not enough money. And I can't very well ask for it for that purpose," said Sefton, implying that for any other it would be forthcoming.

"Ask for it for something else."

"There is not time. We go home in two days."

"Well, the sooner it comes, the sooner it will be over," said Sturgeon.

"True," said Sefton lightly, unable to imagine the latter stage.

"We could lend you enough between us," said Bacon. "That is, if you really think it is a wise course."

"No, thank you. I won't take it. You will need it on the journey. And, after all, I am accustomed to imposing my own ideas at home."

"You may find the idea of cheating through a term an exception," said Bacon.

" Oh, parents don't use those words about little, trivial, school affairs."

"I wonder what words the report will use."

"Two different people will write them, Spode and Bigwell," said Sefton, on a note of interest. "It will be amusing to see what they make of it."

"If amusement is your feeling."

"I suppose you began by wanting to be a success?" said Holland, puzzled by ambition in one under so little pressure to realise it.

"Something of the kind. I really can't quite explain. The whole thing was a novelty to me. And then the ball gathered force as it rolled. You know how it is."

"Yes," said Holland and Sturgeon.

"No, we do not know," said Bacon. "We are not versed in such courses."

"What does your brother say about it?" said Holland.

"Oliver? Oh, I don't know. I daresay he has not heard anything. What is it to do with him?"

"Will you go home with him?" said Sturgeon.

"We shall travel together in the normal way."

"Couldn't you intercept the report and destroy it?" said Holland. "It comes in the first few days. You could watch the posts and get hold of it. Your parents might not think of its coming."

"Hardly worth while," said Sefton, in a considering manner. "It would waste the first days of the holidays. I should have to think of nothing else."

"You know you will do that anyhow," said Bacon. "But it is not worth while to get any deeper in the mire. Your parents might be looking for the report too. It would not do for your all to intercept it together."

"They would hardly think so much about it. But my brother would know it would come, wouldn't he? Why he will have to write reports himself. That might put it into his head."

"It is a good thing that parents do not see the people at the school," said Holland.

"Or only on festive occasions, when it cannot be called seeing them," said Sturgeon.

"Or seeing the parents either," said Bacon.

"The Cassidys will come to us for part of the holidays," said Sefton. "They are related, you know, connections of some kind, really relations of Oliver's. But they don't talk about the school when they are with us. Before I came here I hardly knew they kept one."

"They must have talked about it, when it was arranged for you to come to it," said Sturgeon.

"This time you will know that they keep one, and that you are at it," said Bacon.

"Will you come back next term?" said Holland. "Or will you be expelled?"

"There has not been any talk of it. If I were, my life would be a perpetual holiday. There would be nothing to mind in that."

"Make no mistake," said Sturgeon.

"Shelley does not make as many as you think," said Bacon.

"Wouldn't you have your tutor again?" said Holland.

"Oh, yes, I suppose I should. Yes, that was a mistake."

"I wonder if the masters are discussing you at this moment," said Sturgeon. "I believe people are always talking about what we should expect."

"They are engaged with their own business," said Sefton. "I don't suppose they take so much interest in mine."

"Your affairs are interesting enough at the moment," said Bacon. "And I expect they think so. They would not be so different from other people."

It was Bacon who took the correct view, or took it openly. Sefton was the subject of the talk in the common room, where the group had been joined by Lucius and Juliet.

"Do I understand that the child has cheated through the term?" said Oliver. "For one thing, I should not have thought he had it in him."

"I agree that he must have a good deal in him," said Juliet. "Only a resourceful person could have done it. I do not know why he came to school, when he had progressed so far."

"I wonder if we ought to keep him there," said Lucius. "Why should pupils be expelled for wrongdoing? If schools cannot train them, what is their purpose?"

"We must think of his influence over the other boys."

"Well, that seems to be good. He kept all knowledge of evil from them. It is not his fault, if their ears have been sullied by it."

"Did you not suspect anything, Spode?" said Oliver.

"Not at first. I pampered him and spoke him honeyed words. Then I saw the cloud as big as a man's hand. And when he came down so much in his papers, I went to his desk and examined his work. And what I have told you, was made plain."

"How dreadful to be a child!" said Juliet. "Suppose someone went to our desks and examined our private papers! Because it must be said that these were private."

"It was leaving him so much to himself, that led to the trouble," said Lucius. "He should have been treated as a child from the beginning."

"So he should, if he was going to be in the end."

"And he hoodwinked you too, Bigwell?" said Oliver.

"Well, I did not think of his having translations," said Mr. Bigwell, as though this were not a likely line of thought. "He had no opportunity to buy them. He must have had them in his possession."

"Well, they are not rare things."

"No, I suppose not," said Mr. Bigwell, accepting light on the subject.

"I must not say that I wish it had been any other boy," said Lucius. "But its being the child of relations complicates the issue."

"Can't you wish it had been no boy at all?" said his wife. "And why must there be an issue? When we resent parents' interference in so many things, ought we to demand it in others?"

"Perhaps it is inconsistent."

"You are clutching at a straw. And when people do that, it does sometimes save them."

"But how can we write a report with any meaning, without allusion to the matter? And the boy should be checked in his course for his own sake."

"Are you really thinking what is involved for him? He will not see it as arranged for his benefit."

"And yet it is, Mrs. Cassidy," said Mr. Bigwell.

"The report must be written, including my own, as if for any other boy," said Lucius. "I cannot see my way to anything else. I should only be saving myself."

"And that, of course, you must not do," said his wife. "Sefton must be sacrificed to prevent it."

"The boy looks better for having the strain off his mind,"

said Mr. Bigwell, who did not know of the nightly demand on Sefton's body.

"Did you notice nothing amiss with him, Oliver?" said Lucius.

"My dear sir, I hardly ever see him. And relations are known to miss what is clear to other people."

"Oliver, remember you are not at home," said Juliet. "What an honest phrase that is!"

"I am glad he steered a straight course with me," said Mr. Dalziel. "I never leave my boys to work without supervision."

"You mean you steered his course for him," said Mr. Spode. "And naturally you steered it straight."

"I do not believe in treating boys as natural deceivers," said Mr. Bigwell. "If you trust people, they become worthy of trust."

"So they do. Sefton destroyed his keys," said Juliet.

"I know it is the Catholic view that boys should be watched from morning till night. But there is something repellent to a Protestant in such mistrustfulness."

"If I may say so, you know nothing about the Catholic view," said Mr. Dalziel.

"May he say so, Mr. Bigwell?" said Juliet.

"Well, suspicion is the keynote of the system."

"You know nothing about the system, as you call it."

"Well, what would you call it?"

"Giving something a name does not put it in its place."

"It is because it is in its place, that it has the name."

"I can't help being glad that Sefton only cheated two of you," said Juliet. "Or would it have been better if he had done the same to you all? It was nice of him not to cheat you, Oliver. People are generally worst to their own families."

"He does not learn music. My stepmother likes him to be different from me."

"Is your family musical, Mr. Spode?" said Juliet, with no suggestion of a change of subject.

"My mother is one of those people who do not know one note from another. That means that they do not concern themselves with notes. I do not know about my father. He died when I was born."

"What?" said more than one voice.

"It appears to have been the case. There is a primitive people, whose men take to their beds when their wives have children. It seems that my father followed that course, and never rose again."

"So your mother is a widow?" said Mr. Bigwell.

"That is one of the consequences."

"We must remember that Mrs. Cassidy is present."

"I did remember it. I was trying to cause her some amusement."

"Thank you so much," said Juliet. "You have quite taken my thoughts off our disgrace."

"Oh, the little boy's lapse hardly comes up to that, Mrs. Cassidy," said Mr. Bigwell.

"If lapse is the word," said Lucius. "It lasted for a term."

"It was a sustained one," said Oliver.

"It has been kind of you to let us come and discuss it," said Juliet. "And it was clever to find it out, when it had gone on for so long. It seems it might have gone on for ever. And it was nice not to have discovered it before. It shows so much undestroyed faith in boys. And Sefton must have had a lot of undeserved praise, and that is known to be the hardest thing to bear. And that must have been so salutary."

"It is always part of the gentlest method to find the hardest thing," said Mr. Spode.

"The praise was not that in this case," said Mr. Bigwell. "I am afraid we have found it, but what are we to do?"

"Convention is too strong for you," said Juliet. "It always is. If it were not, it would be no good. It is unfair to blame us for being the slaves of it. What else can we be?"

"The boy had given up cheating of his own accord," said Lucius. "That can be said for him."

"And for ourselves as well," said his wife. "It does show the influence of the school."

"I should not talk to the boy of the matter, Oliver. Leave it to his parents. They cannot be spared."

"I never talk to children of their failings. It implies that I have none myself, and they know the truth. Children and animals are never wrong."

"Neither are the working classes," said Juliet; "they always know. And women cannot be wrong, with their penetration. And doctor's and clergymen's testimony is always accepted. I wonder who *is* wrong. Perhaps it is only schoolmasters."

"Well," said Lucius, holding out his hand without any indication who was to grasp it, in his usual avoidance of preferential dealing, "we shall reassemble at the beginning of next term."

"And now we shall find ourselves outside the door," said Juliet. "And that will be so useful. It is such an awkward thing to have to happen so often."

"Will you and my nephew come with me for a moment, Spode?" said Lucius, in a tone so incidental as to sound like a rejoinder.

"Two handshakes wasted!" said his wife. "And worse. You will have to shake hands twice as much with some people as with others."

"The friendship between you—perhaps it is rather too evident," said Lucius, with his eyes on the ground.

There was a moment's silence.

"Is this a thing to talk about in the passage?" said Juliet. "Or couldn't it be talked about anywhere else?"

"It is not what I looked for," said Oliver. "I thought I might meet the sort of thing at school, even hoped to do so; but I never thought I should have to bring it with me."

"We should know better than to betray it," said Mr. Spode. "We are congenial to each other. We have much in common. It is a good thing in our lives, and we are lovely and pleasant in them."

"I was not suggesting anything else," said Lucius, faltering as he found himself committed so far.

"And we have the same Christian name," said Oliver.

"Have you?" said Juliet. "Oliver?"

"Yes. It had to be that, to be the same."

"Well, that is a coincidence of a kind," said Lucius.

"You should not speak contemptuously of anything," said Juliet. "And I am sure it is quite a good coincidence. Do they call each other by the name?"

"No doubt they can tell you?"

"Perhaps they modify it in one case. But there are no names like Oliver, but Olivia. And that would not do. You need not look at me, Lucius. I said it would not do."

"Am I to have no interest in life but what I produce myself?" said Oliver.

"That note is not in place," said Lucius. "I am merely suggesting that you should veil your intimacy. You do not misunderstand me."

"I wonder if they do," said Juliet. "I am not sure if I do or not."

"Well, that is all," said Lucius, still looking at the ground. "We have said goodbye."

"That may be fortunate," said Juliet, as they moved away. "It was better to shake hands before they refused to do so."

"It escaped me that you were here."

"It escaped me, too. But Mr. Bigwell was not here to remind us."

"Well, I have met the problems of school," said Oliver. "Cheating and this. And it has all been provided by my own family. It was not necessary to leave home at all."

"If Cassidy meant no more than he said, he would hardly have said it," said Mr. Spode. "It is a poor return for three terms' faithful service. We will revenge ourselves by having a lifelong friendship. He will not like us to have what he does not have himself."

"I believe he says just what he means. That is probably why he does not have the friendships."

The other masters were waiting in suspense, as the boys had done at another moment.

"Yes, we may turn our eyes to the holidays," said Mr. Bigwell, as though continuing the talk. "For me, four weeks of home, with a family who see me as a worldly success. And a few days of visiting, of course."

"Four weeks of visiting. I have no home," said Mr. Dalziel.

"Sad," said Mr. Spode.

"Four weeks at home with a family who see me as no success at all," said Oliver. "And when my uncle comes to stay, some of the school as well."

"Four weeks with my mother," said Mr. Spode. "One with affection and familiar chat; one with less; one with none; one with other things. Sad."

"I wonder that the Head wanted you, Shelley, when he was to have the further chance of unburdening himself," said Mr. Bigwell. "But, of course, he wanted you both."

"Yes, of course," said Mr. Spode. "And Mrs. Cassidy was present."

The four boys came along the passage, and Oliver addressed his brother through the open door.

"Ten o'clock on Thursday, and no doubt about it! I am not to be kept waiting."

"No, and neither am I. That is a bargain," said Sefton, in a distinct tone, glancing at his companions.

They paid him no attention. Their eyes were on Bacon, who was about to deliver his mind.

"Ought we to thank Miss James for all she has done for us this term?"

"Do people generally do it?" said Holland.

"It would be an awkward thing to do, if it is not done," said Sturgeon.

"Perhaps we ought not to think of that," said Bacon. "I don't think it can all have been included in her duties. And it would not do to take extra things as a matter of course."

"It might hurt her feelings," said Holland. "She is the sort of person who would notice it."

"And then we should suffer remorse," said Sturgeon, just blinking his eyes.

"Who would dare to begin?" said Holland.

"We must draw lots," said Bacon.

"No," said Sturgeon. "Shelley is under a cloud, and Miss James may know about it. I am too awkward and undersized. Holland is too ordinary. Bacon is the one. Miss James will think more of anything that comes from him. And people must fulfil the duties of their place."

Bacon turned his steps towards Miss James's door, his lips firm and his face pale, as he set himself to pay the price of that which was in him.

"Thank you very much for all you have done for us this term."

"Thank you very much," said Sturgeon and Sefton in one breath.

"Thank you very much, Miss James," said Holland.

"Well, this is nice of you boys," said Miss James, rising and coming to meet them. "I appreciate it very much. I shall not forget it. I shall think of it afterwards. And you will remember to knock at the door another time. And Holland remembered to say my name. Will you stay behind for a moment, Shelley?"

The last words just anticipated the closing of the door, and Sefton turned and faced her.

"Now, Shelley, I keep to my own sphere in the school. But a rumour has reached me, and I want to say one word to you, just as you wanted to say one to me. I am so sure that such a thing can never happen again, that you will rise above it, because you are above it in yourself, that I feel it must be as I say. Just because I feel so sure. Do you not agree with me?"

"Yes, Miss James," said Sefton, not questioning Miss James's part in the matter.

"Then thank you once more for what you said. And goodbye and happy holidays."

Sefton reached the passage, marvelling that a person on Miss James's scale should not see the irony of the last wish. He braced himself to meet the questions of the boys, with a sense that crowding trials almost lost their force. They did not cease their talk, and he had only to stand and hear it.

"I think it was a good thing to do," said Bacon. "It may be a small thing, but small things have their importance. They may have more meaning than bigger ones. Trifles make perfection, and perfection is no trifle. And it is a good thing to end up the term in the right way."

"It makes the average better," said Sturgeon.

"Yes, now we can feel that our level for the term is quite good," said Holland, while Sefton stood in silence, a person in a different place.

CHAPTER V

"My little son!" said Maria, standing on her steps. "So you are glad to see your mother."

"We got out of the train first. The other boys had quite a long way to go. It is better to live near the school. The holidays begin sooner. Being in the train is not really holidays, is it?"

"He is just the same," said Maria to her husband, confronted by no advance on the surface, and unable to see beneath. "We need not have thought he would change."

"People don't change, do they?" said her son. "Everyone is always the person he is."

"Out of the mouth of babes!" said Maria.

"How are you, my boy?" said Sir Roderick, shaking hands with his elder son, after his embrace of the younger.

"I am well, but I have changed."

"Have you retired from your profession?" said Mr. Firebrace, with no sign of his joy in the reunion. "Has it done for you what you hoped?"

"No, but it has done other things."

"You have gained your knowledge of life?"

"No, but I have gained knowledge of lives."

"And that is not the same thing?"

"No, it is a deeper, more demanding thing. It is a change from the shallow to the deep. It seems to add less to the person who has it, and really adds more. It has made me a student of human nature instead of a man of the world. I don't think I shall ever be a man of the world again."

"Were you ever one?" said Maria.

"I dare to answer the question. I still have my own kind of courage. Strange though it was in my useless, narrow life, that is what I was. It is a sheltered life that makes such people. If you think, they always belong to the privileged class. And if you think again, Father is one."

"Will you be a happier person for the experiment?"

"Not happier, but better. I shall see people's problems beneath the surface. And that is the last thing a man of the world does. He thinks that people do not have problems in their position."

"Well, they do not," said Sir Roderick, with a smile.

"Well, are not the brother and sister going to greet each other?" said Maria, passing to a point of interest.

Clemence and Sefton, who had done this at once in their own way, now did it in their mother's.

Miss Petticott came into the hall, and Sefton gave her an excited welcome, suffered the unavoidable salute and even returned it. Clemence looked on with feelings that she hardly defined. To her eyes there was a change in her brother. She seemed to see in him something that she knew in herself. He might almost be doing what she had done, might be laying the foundations for things that would need them.

"Well, the group is complete," said Maria, allowing the three to withdraw in their established way. "I wonder what we did in separating them? I suppose we shall never know."

"I have always known," said her husband. "We did a heartless and harmful and needless thing. We can never undo it, but I hope to end it when I can."

"Both the children are pale and thin. Did you see much of Sefton at school, Oliver?"

"No, I only caught a glimpse of his white face and wistful air from a distance."

"Do you think he was homesick?"

"I expect he was only schoolsick. I think that is what homesickness generally is."

"You are confusing your meaning. Anyone might be homesick, in your sense, when he was at home."

"So he might," said Oliver.

"Is that what you were yourself?" said Sir Roderick.

"What a sharp and pointed question, Father! I hope you are not becoming acute. I honestly do not know."

"Did you get the impression that he was happy?" said Maria.

"No, I don't think so. But I did not get much impression."

"Why did you not write and tell me?"

"He could have done so himself. It was not for me to come between mother and son, or to inform against an institution where I was a member of the staff. I was loyal to the school, and it seems that Sefton was too."

"It is easy to see you are not a mother."

"Well, yes, I daresay it is."

"Did you ever talk to your brother?"

"I think hardly ever."

"Do not the masters ever speak to the boys?"

"I had not thought of it, but I hardly think they do. What could they say to them?"

"They could ask if they were well and happy."

"Could they? Then no wonder they do not talk to them. They might find the words escaping their lips."

"What was the good of being at the school with Sefton?"

"It was none. But it was no harm either. He was not despised for the relationship. I carried off the position, even when I played the hymns."

"How do you know you did," said Sir Roderick, "when you held no communication with the boys?"

"It came through to me, and my instinct is never wrong."

"Why should you be so exceptional?" said Maria.

"Exceptional? No one's instinct is ever wrong. Everyone will tell you about it."

"Played the hymns?" said Mr. Firebrace. "Were there no waiting women?"

"Only to sing them. There were some for that. And they always sang the one I played."

"What other should they sing?"

"They might have sung many in the course of the day."

"You mean that they sang all day the one you played in the morning?"

"That is what I mean. And the one I played in the evening, they sang at night. I heard them, as they went up to bed."

"Why did you not stop them?" said Maria.

"Because I felt faintly flattered by it."

"Did Sefton sing?"

"No, but he moved his lips in time."

"Poor little boy!"

"That would not have hurt him. He does it in church at home. And if it were hurtful, fewer people would do it."

"I always do it," said Sir Roderick.

"I shall not let the children go to church in the holidays," said Maria. "They have enough of the sort of thing at school."

"I like a woman's inconsequence," said Oliver. "But only because it is really something else."

"You give me the impression that you could be more explicit, if you would."

"I dislike a woman's penetration. What credit is it to anyone to see what she is not meant to see, and not to scruple to reveal it? I cannot think why it is supposed to be any."

"I expect your uncle can tell me more."

"I daresay he can, and will do so. I dislike a man's simplicity."

"Are you free from it yourself?"

"Yes, quite free. I do not shrink from self-praise. It is so untrue that it is no recommendation."

"Well, come along my boy," said Mr. Firebrace, offering his arm to his grandson in his old way.

"Another group complete," said Sir Roderick.

"Not a very natural one," said Maria.

"As natural as any can be at a school. And depending on

human affection. Not simply on the impulse of some people to live, and of others to shirk the duties of their lives."

Sefton and Clemence ran to the schoolroom, uplifted by their reunion, living in the moment, trying to see an indefinite respite in the days ahead. Sefton ran into Adela's arms; Miss Petticott left a scene in which she had no part; Aldom appeared at the moment of her doing so, his instinct for succeeding her unimpaired by disuse.

"Well, what did they want to change this for?" said Adela. "What is wrong with it, I should like to know."

"It is well enough as far as it goes," said Aldom. "It does not go far enough. That is what was thought."

"No, it does not," said Clemence, whirling round on one foot. "It goes such a little way, if only you knew."

"Well, what have you learned, that you don't say?" said Adela.

"A good many things," said Clemence, pausing as the truth of her words came home.

"That sort of talk hasn't much meaning. If there is anything to be told, people tell it."

"Well, it may not mean a great deal," said Clemence, standing with her eyes on space.

Aldom minced across the room, recalling his earlier mimicry.

"Oh, it is not like that," said Clemence, again revolving. "You can't know things without knowing them."

"People don't think there is anything funny in teaching in a school," said Sefton. "And when you are there, there doesn't seem to be."

"Well, you miss one thing to gain another," said Adela. "And why have things so much on the common line? What is there in being what you are, if you just have ordinary knowledge?"

"I don't think the boys were different from me. I mean I don't think they were poorer. We seem to be rather poor."

"We don't spend as much as other people," said

Clemence. "The girls have better clothes than I have."

"Well, they may need them to compensate for having less background," said Adela.

"They have not so much less. We are not different from other people."

"Well, I am glad you sent for the right kind of dress. You were not called upon to go without it. And it was properly packed; I will say that."

"Miss Tuke does that sort of thing. The matron."

"Oh, and so I suppose you want no one but her now."

"I do not want her at all. She was thrust upon me, or I was upon her."

"There you see. That is her real mind," said Adela, turning to Aldom.

"I don't want the matron; I don't want the mistresses; I don't want the girls," said Clemence, with a sense of unworthiness in disclaiming the world that had welcomed her and lamented her downfall.

"And I don't want the masters or the boys," said Sefton. "And I don't think they want me. I should like not to remember any of it."

"Oh, and after all the trouble and expense," said Maria at the door, in a tone of reproach and joy. "Why, here are a girl and boy who like their home better than school, their mother and father better than masters and mistresses, and their own nurse better than the matrons. Well, their mother likes them in the same way, and would not change them. So Aldom has come to join in the welcome. I daresay you like him better than his counterpart too. But he will not have to impersonate teachers any longer. You know them at first-hand."

"Five more days to Christmas!" said Sefton, with a note of excitement, that he would have given much to have real.

"And we shall be a large party this year," said Maria. "Miss Firebrace and the Cassidys are coming to-morrow. I thought I should like to discuss you with them. And now

I find I would rather not talk about them and their schools at all. I want to enjoy our home, and not think of your leaving it. I hope it will not spoil our Christmas."

"It will not add to it," said Clemence, with a faint hope of averting the danger. "It will bring in things that have nothing to do with home."

"My poor child! How stupid I have been! You have had enough of them. And we ought to feel they have had enough of you. But you shall stay up there with Miss Petticott, and hardly see them. Miss Petticott, come and hear what your duty will be this Christmas. To protect these two little home-lovers from the school invaders. I promise to make it easy for you. That will be my expiation of the sin of asking them. But I do want to discuss the children's abilities and prospects. I promise not to do it in their presence, but I am looking forward to it, and I daresay you are too."

"Well, Lady Shelley, I have had my opinion about the children for too long, to need that of people who have only just known them. It can hardly be of much value to me. There is not much that I need to be told."

"You may find your own opinion confirmed, and that has its own satisfaction."

"It is much too unshakable to be strengthened by argument, or weakened by the lack of it. Indeed, opinion is the wrong word. It is a case of simple knowledge. And I am afraid poor Sir Roderick will be the chief sufferer from the invasion, if I am to use your word. He will not be able to take refuge in the schoolroom."

"Their success means a great deal to him. Only he and I know how much. Well, Aldom and I will return to our sphere, and leave you to settle down in yours."

The children could only pretend to do this, and used an apparent excitement to veil their restlessness. Miss Petticott found them docile and affectionate, as they established themselves in a favour that would withstand the shock to come. They seemed to be playing into each other's hands, but had no chance of a private word. It was evening when they found themselves alone.

"What is a report, Clemence?" said Sefton, as he turned a page.

"A report? A paper that comes from a school and tells about a pupil in it. I think one is sent at the end of each term."

"And will one come for us?"

"Yes, I suppose so. Of course it will. But it will make no difference, as the people themselves are coming."

"It is a pity we went to schools kept by relations, or we might have watched for the reports and intercepted them. That is what boys call it. It is a thing they do sometimes."

Clemence stared at her brother at this evidence of change in him.

"Is there anything bad on your report?"

"Yes. Yes, there is," said Sefton, with a burst of tears. "Clemence, I have cheated all through the term, and it has been found out. And it will be on the report, and Mother will mind so much, and there will be such misery. And Father will mind about cheating as much as she will."

"So have I cheated," said Clemence, in a tone that seemed to her strange for the words she said. "I wonder why we have both done it. It seems to be such an unusual thing, or they say it is. It is such a strange coincidence. I wonder if we are different from other people?"

"Have you cheated, Clemence? Then it will not be so bad. It will be the same for us both. The coincidence is a happy one. Coincidences are often that. It will all seem so much more ordinary. And I don't think it can be as bad as they say, if we both have done it."

"What exactly did you do?" said his sister.

Sefton gave his account, and she gave her own, and they heard each other without question or judgment.

"It will make great trouble," said Clemence. "We have dreadful things ahead, worse than we have ever had. We shall need great courage. We have thought such small things were bad. And the people from the schools will make it worse. No one but us would have to face that."

"Yes, we shall need great courage," said Sefton, almost with complacence. "But its being the same for us both will make a difference. Even the school people can't prevent that."

"It may not make it so much better. Why should Mother and Father like disgrace for both of us better than only for one? In a way it will be twice as bad. I wish we could run away or die. But we should starve if we ran away, and we don't know any way to die. We are not like savages, who can die when they want to."

"If we were, would you die?"

"Well, savages would never be in our place. It is only possible for civilised people. Miss Firebrace could not be a savage. Her way of making things worse, without seeming to want to, could not exist in one. I wonder if she knows what she is like, and what I really think of her. She seems only to think of what she thinks of me. But thoughts are possible in anyone."

Lesbia was unconscious of this verdict on herself, as she entered the Shelleys' house, followed in the usual way by her sister and her husband.

"Christmas, the season of childhood!" she said. "We have no excuse for coming, and so will make none. So Clemence and Sefton are not here to greet us. They are properly exercising their peculiar rights."

"Christmas is the season of everyone," said Sir Roderick, who almost adopted at this time the beliefs he did not hold at others. "We are all here to greet and serve each other. The children will be coming to do their part."

"I have a sense of guilt at Christmas," said Juliet. "We have nothing but pleasure that we have done nothing to deserve."

"A good definition of it," said her sister, speaking just audibly. "A sense of guilt is not out of place. And our having done nothing to deserve our benefits is also true."

"I never have such a feeling," said Oliver. "I am a helpless vessel tossed on the waves of life."

"I always have it," said his grandfather. "I am not entitled to my home or my bread."

"We all give thanks for our daily bread," said Sir Roderick.

"No wonder people dread Christmas," said Oliver. "Ought we to make it so much worse for each other? This is the sort of thing that gives it its name."

Maria took no part in the talk. She moved about her duties in a dreamlike way, and her manner had a zest and hint of suspense that were new to Lesbia and told their tale. The latter rendered the dues to convention, and then looked about her with a difference.

"Maria, I have an ordeal before me. I hesitate to ask you to make it easy for me, as I cannot do the same for you. Something of an ordeal it will be to me. Christmas, we have said, is the season of childhood, and the cloud over this Christmas must be the sadder for that. Your children have been a source of joy, and must be one of sorrow too."

"What is the trouble?" said Sir Roderick.

"Must it come so soon?" said Oliver. "Must it come at all? Why talk of Christmas as the season of childhood, and then forget it?"

"Oliver, if only it need not come! If only the choice were ours!"

"We all have our ordinary, human choice," said Juliet.

"What is it all about?" said Maria. "I have heard nothing."

"No?" said Lesbia, in gentle question, pausing as if this shed a certain light. "No? I could wish that you had, Maria, and not only because it would save myself."

"Give us the plain tale, Lesbia," said Sir Roderick. "Tell it simply and openly, as anyone else would tell it. Tell us the truth, and the whole truth, but also tell us nothing but the truth. Do not spare us and do not indulge yourself."

The twofold injunction did its work, and Lesbia did

neither of these things. Silence succeeded her account and Lucius's confirmation of it, and a summons to the children followed at once. The parents could brook no delay in hearing their version of the matter, and their support or denial of Lesbia's. They hoped for a refutation of it, hoped it too much to face the frailty of the chance.

Lesbia raised her hand.

"Stay, Maria. Do you know the questions you will ask, the answers you expect? We must not plan answers to our questions. That is not our part. The part of the questioner is to accept the replies."

"Could you really bear to hear them?" said Oliver.

"We can have neither questions nor answers until the people concerned are here," said Sir Roderick.

"People concerned!" said Juliet. "It seems such a callous way to refer to the young."

"They will have to face the tribunal of seven grown people. There is no help for it."

"Of course there is," said Oliver. "We can all do what we can. I withdraw from the tribunal, and so do Aunt Juliet and Grandpa."

"I am not part of it," said Maria. "I am simply their mother."

"And I am their father. But certain things are binding on me as that. They must face their ordeal. They cannot have their chance without it."

"Then I am the tribunal," said Lesbia. "I will not disclaim the part. It may be mine."

"So a thing can be said between a smile and a sigh," said Oliver.

"It was nearer to the sigh, Oliver," said Lesbia, coming nearer even to it.

"I may not withdraw," said Lucius. "My place is with Lesbia."

"Thank you, Lucius."

"I cannot bear the spectacle of wasted nobility," said Oliver. "I would so much rather not see it at all. Indeed, I would always rather be spared the sight. I only admire it when it is hidden."

"Do not be hard on us, Oliver," said Lesbia. "We have but a thankless part."

"When people are thanked too little, they ought to pause and think."

"And you think we have not done so, Oliver?"

Miss Petticott led the way into the room, unaware that the summons did not include herself, and advanced at once to Lesbia.

"How are you, Miss Firebrace? There is a closer bond than ever between us, now that we actually share a pupil."

"How do you do, Miss Petticott?" said Lesbia, simply returning the handshake.

Miss Petticott cast her eyes over her face. The children came forward as though hardly conscious what they did. The parents' eyes sought their faces, and Sir Roderick's fell.

"Tell the tale again, Lesbia, and we will see if the children corroborate it."

"No, I do not think I will 'tell the tale again', Roderick," said Lesbia, just moving her lips. "I did not know that I had told a tale. What I said, remains. It does not need repeating, certainly not corroboration."

"But the children did not hear it."

"No. We were able to spare them that. But they could have told it themselves. I hoped to hear they had done so."

"I wonder if you did. Your own account had been prepared, and one from them would have forestalled it. It would have rendered your effort meaningless."

"Yes, it had been prepared, Roderick. It told the truth in the fewest words, with the least possible hurt in them. I had given thought to it. It is the last thing I wish to deny. I should not approach the matter in a careless spirit, or claim to do so. It would seem to me a strange claim."

"Have you said 'how-do-you-do' to the guests?" said Maria to the children, in an empty tone.

"How do you do, Clemence? How do you do, Sefton?"
said Lesbia, shaking hands with them in turn.

No one else offered to do the same, and the children
approached no one. Everything seemed to be centred in
Lesbia, and Sir Roderick and Maria appeared to accept the
view. Sefton gave a glance at Lucius, who stood aloof.

"Now let the children tell the tale in their own words,"
said Sir Roderick, not shaken in his own conception.

"No, pray do not," said Oliver. "No one could bear it,
and naturally they could not. And we must not see people
as culprits, and then expect them to rise to the heights."

Lesbia looked at her nephew, and then gravely bowed
her head.

"Were you going just to say nothing about it, Clemence?" said Maria.

"Well, we knew the people from the schools were coming, and that it would be on the reports. It was no good to
say anything."

"So you talked about it to each other?"

"Yes, we did that."

Lesbia drew the reports from her bag, and held them in
her hand, as though rendering them available for anyone
concerned, and in a moment passed them smoothly to Miss
Petticott.

"Miss Petticott may see them, Maria?" she said, in
incidental question. "There are things that might interest
her. The one thing is not the whole."

Miss Petticott looked at them uncertainly, and Mr.
Firebrace intercepted them, put on his glasses and scruti-
nised them.

"It reminds me of my young days. How the old
generation passeth away, and the new generation cometh!"

"Did you cheat?" said Oliver.

"Why, yes, my boy. We could not have managed without it. Everything was in Latin and Greek, you know. And it
was not thought so much of in those days, not taken so hard.
And it was the masters we were outwitting, not each other."

"Did you do it, Oliver?" said Maria, at once.

"Maria, I wish I could tell you that I did. But I did not. There was no need. You see, I had no mother. But I have a word of comfort for you. I have met a downfall."

"What was your trouble?" said his father.

"I feel guilty in drawing attention from the children's trouble to my own. I made a conspicuous friendship."

"With a boy?"

"No, no, Father. You and Grandpa have your own knowledge of life; no doubt you have gained it; but there is no need to drag it in. Only with another master."

"The young man, Oliver Spode?" said Mr. Firebrace.

"It sounds like the Bible and goes on sounding like it. The only son of his mother, and she is a widow."

"Did your friendship attract attention?" said Sir Roderick.

"I think only that of Uncle Lucius."

"I was afraid it might do so," said the latter, "and lead to unfounded suggestions. I had no personal uneasiness."

"How much less well you think of other people than of yourself!" said Oliver. "I suppose that is a tribute to anyone."

"What did you mean by saying you had no mother?" said Maria. "What difference did that make?"

"Well, no one cared whether I was a success or not."

"So I am the culprit. I see that the guilt is mine, and I am glad to see it. You see it too, Oliver, and I see you are glad, though I do not know your reason."

"It is the same as yours. We are glad that no helpless person is cast for the part. We see that it is good."

Sefton threw himself into his mother's arms and broke into weeping. She held him close and looked at Lesbia over his head. Sir Roderick beckoned to Clemence, and drew her on to the sofa at his side.

"They are ours, Maria. They owe us life, and therefore we owe them everything. Their sins and sorrows are ours. Who else are the authors of them?"

Clemence leant against her father and sank into tears, and he kept his arm about her.

"So it is all true," said Juliet, "all that we have tried to disprove. A mother does love her erring children best, and it seems that a father does too, though no one has thought about it. We may be the first people to see an instance. And men do not have to hide their feelings, and mothers are not the last people to bring up their own children, and there is no hostility between fathers and sons, and home life is best. And keeping a school is a thing to be ashamed of. Not that people have ever thought it anything else, but their reasons were not the right ones. Schoolkeepers should be despised on quite different grounds, or anyhow on some extra ones. And cynicism has no place in life, though it will make conversation very difficult. No one will be able to be clever."

"I think someone will be able to be," said Lesbia, laying a hand on her sister's arm.

"How was it? Why was it?" said Maria. "Have I urged them too much, asked more of them than they could do? Were they forced to it to satisfy me? But they knew I would rather they did nothing than sink to this."

"But you were not prepared for them to do nothing," said Oliver.

"But had I any reason to be? Had I any ground for thinking of them in that way? Look at their heads; look at their faces. What would any mother have thought?"

"What you did, Maria," said Lesbia, gently. "And she would have been right in thinking it. Your children have good abilities, in some ways high ones. There was no reason for them to hide their talents in the earth, or for you to wish them to do so."

"Oh, I should have been so pleased, so proud. If only it had not been for this! Indeed, I was pleased and proud, when I heard of their first success."

"We went too far," said Sir Roderick, identifying himself with his wife. "That was our mistake. We urged them beyond their bounds, and they could not cross them of themselves. We forgot their lonely position; we forgot their childhood."

Maria was silent, facing the accusation in the only form it would be made.

"And so they looked to higher aid," said Juliet. "Well, it was lower aid, I suppose. They looked to aid and it failed them; and that was hard on them in a school, which is a place designed to give aid. But I am glad they gave Maria pleasure. They had their reward."

"They are getting it, poor children!" said Sir Roderick.

There was a pause.

"I am sorry, Miss Petticott," said Lesbia, turning and putting a hand on Miss Petticott's arm. "You will let me say it."

"It is a great shock and trouble to me, Miss Firebrace. I was quite unprepared. There has never been anything of the kind in all the years I have taught them. It is strange that a new environment should bring about such a change."

"It would be strange," said Lesbia, allowing the faint smile to reach her lips. "But a new environment does not cause essential change. It can only reveal or release something that is there. Or we will say something that has grown somehow out of the earlier experience."

"Shall we say that, Father?" said Oliver.

"The new environment supplied the conditions that led to the change," said Sir Roderick. "That and an undue pressure from home, which we acknowledge. The fact that the result was the same with them both, shows that it came from something outside."

"You do not allow for a possible likeness between them, arising from the same blood and the same upbringing?" said Lesbia. "How do you explain the fact that no other pupil in either school has done the same?"

"I do not explain it. It cannot be a fact."

"Neither can it," said Mr. Firebrace. "But do not lose hold on yourself, my boy."

"Actually, Roderick it is very rare," said Lesbia.

"What is the truth, Lucius?" said Sir Roderick, hardly attending to Mr. Firebrace's injunction.

"Well, 'rare' is scarcely the word in a general sense. But in a case of a sustained course like this, I am afraid it is."

"Poor little boy!" said Maria.

Her husband held Clemence closer to his side, in lieu of voicing a similar sentiment.

"It is clear that the schools exercised a disruptive influence."

"Honestly, Roderick, we considered seriously whether we could keep the children in them," said Lesbia.

"And came to the conclusion that you could. I have considered equally seriously, and come to the conclusion that I cannot."

"Why have so much honesty, my dear?" said Mr. Firebrace to his daughter. "It is not always the best policy. You must have found that."

"Oh, Roderick, Roderick," said Lesbia, shaking her head and seeming just to avoid amusement. "Will anything do for an excuse to indulge yourself?"

"This will do well enough. When I did the opposite thing, we see what came of it. And when two innocent children stumble and fall on the same path, it shows that it is too rough for them, and that it is wise to guide them to another."

"Then they are of weaker stuff than the other children."

"It has emerged that they are of different stuff."

"Roderick, it is not an occasion for pride."

"I was feeling that it was," said Juliet.

"I have felt it all the time," said Oliver.

There was a pause.

"You would not like them to live it down?" said Lesbia, just raising her eyes. "You have not that amount of respect —or we will say that kind of respect—for them?"

"Parents have too little respect for their children, just as the children have too much for the parents," said Sir Roderick, stating the belief as it came to him. "But I have a father's love for them, and that can be my guide. I could not have a better."

"And an ordinary human love for yourself, Roderick?"

"Well, that is to say I am an ordinary human being."

"But surely you would not say that," said Oliver.

Sir Roderick was silent, finding that his mood of the moment did prevent his doing so.

"So it is settled that Clemence is not to return to us, Maria?" said Lesbia, making a movement of rising from her seat. "Because, if so, I must telegraph that there is a vacancy."

"If you will draft the telegram, it will be taken for you," said Sir Roderick.

Lesbia disengaged her skirt from her chair, and went to the door, thanking Oliver for opening it. As though at a sign, Maria turned to her children, and as though at another, Juliet followed her sister, and was followed by her husband, father and nephew.

"It seems pitiless," said Oliver, as they gained the hall. "But they had better strike while the iron is hot, if I say what I mean. A scene in cold blood leads to the worst results, and as the blood always gets hot in the course of it, it leads to everything else as well."

The door opened and Miss Petticott broke into the hall, suddenly aware that her presence was preventing the family solitude.

"So you are like the rest of us," said Mr. Firebrace. "You can bear things better if you do not see them."

"I am in such distress, Mr. Firebrace, that I hardly know what I am doing," said Miss Petticott, smoothing her hair, as if she felt it ought to be dishevelled.

"Come along, my boy," said Mr. Firebrace to his grandson. "The children have their years to forget the scene, and the same cannot be said of me. So I will not concern myself with it."

"I shall not be myself until it is over," said Oliver. "It shows what a feeling heart can beat under a polished exterior."

"No one would be more ashamed of a rugged one," said

Lesbia, smiling at him in disregard of her own preoccupations.

"No one indeed. And it is natural for the better heart to result in the better exterior, though no one has thought of their going together. You are looking at the door, Aunt Lesbia. You are thinking what a door may hide. I wish I dared to think of it."

"The judges and the culprits are facing each other," said Lesbia, with a sigh.

"I dare to think of that. But the parents and children are doing so."

This was the case, and continued to be so after the door had closed. Clemence afterwards remembered the things that had passed through her mind in those moments. It was almost a relief when Maria spoke. The extreme moment had come, must soon be actually past.

"Now, Clemence, tell me it all from the beginning. We took your part before outsiders. We are your parents, and owe you our help in any kind of need. But we do not know how to face such a thing, hardly how to listen to it."

"I expect they wish that was the case," said Sir Roderick, tightening his arm round his daughter. "And I think we have done our listening. I do not expect that Lesbia left out anything."

"There was nothing more than she said," said Clemence.

"And surely it is enough," said her mother. "How did you come to do what you did? You had been taught the difference between right and wrong. You could not have thought there was any meaning in a false success. You could not have taken any satisfaction in it."

"We thought you would be pleased. We did not know you would ever come to know the truth."

"The truth! The thing I have taught you comes first in life! What mistake have I made? Would you have been better if you had had another mother?"

Maria seemed to hear her own words, and to be seeking an answer to them from herself.

"They would in a sense," said Sir Roderick. "They

would not have been urged to a point beyond their scope, and forced to things not natural to them. That is what it was. That was your—that was our mistake."

"But I thought they were children above the average, and would naturally go beyond the others."

"My dear, good wife, there you are again! We must accept what they do, not plan it ourselves beforehand. That is how the trouble came."

"We are above the average in many ways," said Clemence, with a pang for her mother's baffled, disappointed face. "Miss Firebrace said we were. That is how it all began. We did do better than the others, and then we tried to keep it up more than we could."

"If only you had been content to be true to yourselves! How proud I should have been! Even now I can't help being proud of what you did at first. But nothing counts but trustworthiness. Or nothing counts without it."

"Proud we cannot be, my pretty," said Sir Roderick, bringing another pang to his daughter's heart, and as he saw it, again tightening his hold. "We must be content without that. But there are better things that we can be. We can be loving and loyal enough for the feelings to hold through a test, and our children are not the people whom they should fail. We will let the dead past bury its dead, and go back to the old days and the old ways and the old happiness." Sir Roderick glanced at his children, saw the admiration in their eyes, and felt that he and they were at one.

"But is that making it too easy for them? Will it lead to their taking too light a view of it? Is it really indulging ourselves? God knows, I should like to make it easy. But is that where the danger lies?"

"We need not avoid self-indulgence at their expense. And we need not fear it has been easy. There was the effort and suspense through the term, and at the end the shock and shame. And heavy guns were brought to bear on them. Account was not taken of their helplessness."

At these words the children gave their mother her

answer. They broke into convulsive tears, and at the sound the group outside the room turned and vanished up the stairs. Lesbia alone held her ground, and in a moment moved towards the door.

"Well, I will be guided by you, Roderick," said Maria. "I suppose I often am, though I hardly realise it. I will leave the burdens on you and follow my own heart."

"You will not be wrong, my pretty. And so the trouble belongs to the past. We shall remember its cost, and the memory will do its work. We shall not talk of it again. It will be as if it had never been. And now I hear Lesbia coming, I can always recognise that noiseless step."

"Run up to the schoolroom, my dears," said Maria, in her ordinary tones. "We do not want her to see you in tears. After all, you are in your own home and have a right to happiness there. And you have a right to your mother's help in leaving a stumble behind. It is not the end of everything. Go up and settle back into the life that suits you, and lets you be what you are. It was breaking it that was the mistake; and the mistake was ours, not yours."

Sir Roderick looked at his wife in admiration of the qualities of motherhood. Lesbia passed the children with her eyes held from their faces, as though she divined their mother's wish; and a spasm of annoyance crossed the latter's face at her observance of it.

"Well, the telegram is sent, and the way is clear," said Lesbia, in an almost cordial tone, resuming her seat. "I shall be sorry not to see Clemence about the place. And I am sorry too, Roderick, for the pains and penalties of changing the plan. They must follow as the custom has it."

"Do you mean that we have to pay for next term, even though they do not return?"

"Yes, that is what I mean," said Lesbia, smiling. "And you make me feel I might have said it. Why not put a simple thing simply? The rule of a term's notice cannot be broken. Of course Clemence can take the term with us, if you prefer it."

"That would be a mistake, when she is going to leave you."

"Yes, I think it would. Yes, it would be a mistake," said Lesbia, her tone trailing away on a reflective note. "To return to variety in teaching and companionship, before resuming the routine of sameness. It would not be the right transition."

"And I suppose we owe a term's fees to Lucius too?"

"That is the position. But Lucius may be more corruptible. He may not observe the integrity of the law, as it exists between school and school. He may stoop to accepting the bribe of gratitude."

"I do not wish any favour done me."

"Then you owe him the fees. But I think in your place I should not object to it," said Lesbia, giving her little laugh. "And I think I detected the inclination in you, pending the withdrawal of the word, favour. Is not that so, Roderick?"

"The word, favour, was my own."

"A favour is what it would be," said Lesbia, gravely. "By the way, what does Clemence think of the change of plan? Does she herself wish it? It is heedless of us to pass over the person most concerned."

"I think she is too sad and ashamed to raise her voice in the matter," said Maria.

"Poor Clemence! A concern for her will always remain with me, Maria, as it does for any of my pupils. The term behind us will be the term when Clemence was with us, or will be until further terms have superimposed their impression. Oh, and one more thing—it is the very last, and we may allow ourselves to be glad of it—how about the responsibility for Miss Petticott? It is a heavy one."

"She does not shrink from it," said Sir Roderick. "The fact that the children came to grief when they left her, and had never done so before, is in its way an encouragement. It does not suggest that there is much wrong with her methods."

There was a pause.

"Are you speaking seriously, Roderick?"

"Yes. What is wrong with what I said?"

"What is education but a preparation for life?"

"A school is not life."

"Then what is it?"

"A little artificial corner of it, designed to turn out people to pattern, who are already made to it. I do not claim that mine are average children."

Lesbia appeared to give way to genuine amusement.

"Pride may go before a fall," she said. "But it may also continue after it. Well, I daresay that is a happy thing. And it does not do to be too cast down by our falls and failures. They may not be much more than mistakes."

"And we learn by our mistakes," said Sir Roderick. "So what would happen to us, if we did not make them?"

"My pride has not survived this," said Maria, wiping her eyes. "But now let us talk of something else. Wrong-doers are not the only people in the world."

"Well, if we all do wrong, I suppose they are," said her husband.

"These wrong-doers bore themselves well, considering how hard that was in their place," said Lesbia. "Yes, they did, Maria. We recognise it. They would have been able to build on that foundation, the foundation laid by themselves. But they are to have the hard part and not its recompense. That in itself may be a lesson."

"The hard part has been enough," said Sir Roderick. "They do not need anything more."

"No, it is not to be, Roderick," said Lesbia.

"I thought for the moment it was all going to start again."

"I do not think we, any of us, want that."

"Well, what news have you of yourselves and your affairs?"

"This has been one of our affairs," said Lesbia, simply. "And as for selves, I sometimes doubt whether I have one. It gets so merged in other people's."

"They survive in most of us," said Sir Roderick. "Mine has done so in me. Or enough to enable me to take my children into their home, and keep them there, whatever the cost."

"Well, we have counted that," said Lesbia.

"What will it be?" said Maria, coming out of an abstraction. "The school fees without the extras, I suppose?"

Lesbia almost gave another laugh.

"We were talking of the other kind of cost, or we thought we were."

"Well, you can answer my wife's question," said Sir Roderick, who seldom used this word of Maria with his first wife's family. "It is a simple one."

"So it is, Roderick. But I cannot answer it," said Lesbia, with a tremble in her voice as of imperfect self-recovery. "I do not remember at the moment."

"I do not see why we should not talk about fees, if they are taken."

"There is no reason why we should not. And we will do so, if you will. Only, as I have forgotten them, I am a rather unsatisfactory informant."

"You would remember them, if they were not rendered correctly."

"Should I? Would that be a reliable spur to the memory?"

"Well, something would have to be, if you were not to suffer."

"The discrepancy with the accounts would emerge when they were made up," said Lesbia, in an almost absent tone.

"Well, after all, what has happened?" said Sir Roderick, as though speaking under a goad. "Two children copy to get to the top of the class. What else do they suppose is their business at school? To stay at the bottom?"

"I think they were conscious that there was another purpose."

"It was the duty of the people in charge of them to see that they fulfilled it."

209

"No, no, Roderick, we are not going to start the matter again upon another basis. We could not prevent what we did not conceive to be possible. And we should not do better to pursue a policy of suspicion. And now I will say my last word, disclaiming any inclination to have *the* last one. May your arrangement for your children meet with every success. May it prove all that you hope for them."

"I wonder what they are doing now, poor children," said Maria.

"We have said enough to them, my pretty," said her husband.

Clemence and Sefton were sitting by the schoolroom fire in a silence they could not break. It seemed to press upon them as a cover for feelings that forbade words. Sefton was the first to struggle through it.

"Was that as bad as anything could be, Clemence? Or could there be anything worse? Father and Mother were kind. But did that make it any better?"

"Yes, of course it did. It is nonsense to say that that makes things worse. But I daresay it was worse than anything else will ever be."

"Then we are prepared for life, aren't we?" said Sefton, with wonder in his tone.

"No, we are shattered by it, before it comes."

Sefton almost gave a laugh.

"Father and Mother still seem to love us. We did not really know them."

"I expect they feel that about us," said Clemence. "Indeed I could see they did. And I would rather bear anything than see Father think that."

"It is strange that three places, that were really kind, should bring us to such misery. Because our home and both the schools are really gentle worlds."

"I suppose the thing to say is that we brought it on ourselves. But don't let us talk about it. We were new to everything, and did not know how to deal with it. That is all it was. The others were versed in things, and, of course, behaved accordingly. The people at school have not seen things as they are. I should not think they ever do. And Father and Mother had no one else to follow. I wonder they saw as much as they did."

"They seemed to know a good deal, and without being told. Shall we ever be happy again, quite happy as we used to be?"

"It will take some time. But we shall get nearer to it. Though perhaps we were hardly as happy as we think now. It will be difficult to judge, now that we have known something else."

"Will people ever speak about all this?"

"There will always be the risk. It will be the worst with Mother. Father will not do it, as he has said he will not. And we can deal with Miss Petticott. But we shall see the thoughts in people's minds."

"But we need not take any notice of them, if they are not spoken," said Sefton. "We can forget them. And it was really for Mother that we did it."

"We should not have done it, if it had not been for her. But that is not the same thing. She only wanted us to succeed in the real sense."

"But she would have had no happiness at all, if we had not done it. And she had a good deal, before it was found out. So it was not quite wasted."

"Of course it was. The pleasure was not as great as the trouble afterwards. We should have been content with what we could do."

"But she would not have been content, Clemence. The real thing is that she wants us to be cleverer than we are."

"Well, we all want other people to be better in some way. You see we want Mother to be. But pretence is no good. It cannot be kept up. If it could, perhaps it would be different."

"Will Mother begin to want us to be clever again?"

"Perhaps she will in the end. For a time she will be on her guard."

"It is strange that the people at the schools seemed to be kind about it, and yet let it be so bad."

"I don't think they were kind. No kind person would have told about it. They knew what that meant, or knew part of it. I could see they did. They were too stupid to know all of it, but stupidity is not kindness. I don't think a really kind person would ever be stupid."

"But people who teach in schools are supposed to be clever."

"They are only clever along their own line. And they are not so very clever on that. You can tell that, when you learn with them; there is not really so much difference. They did not even try to see the real truth. They just did what made them feel superior and powerful, and left us to suffer what we might. And you could see them taking a kind of satisfaction in it, especially Miss Firebrace. She is much the worst."

"I liked Miss James," said Sefton. "Wasn't there a matron at your school?"

"Miss Tuke. Yes, I liked her too. You could hardly be a matron unless you were nice. You are always doing things for other people, that don't make you thought any more of, yourself."

"It seems that the nicest people don't have the important places. Perhaps the others know how to get them for themselves."

"Well, my two, poor, tired little culprits!" said Maria's voice.

Clemence gave a start, and suffered a reaction of feeling that overcame her.

"Be silent, Aldom. Do not dare to say another word. And don't dare to do such a thing again. Don't you know better than to listen at doors and repeat what you were not meant to hear? You are a dishonourable, ill-mannered young man. This is the very last time. Do you understand? I see you do; so we need have no more words. I have said mine, and I wish to hear none from you. I have heard enough."

There was a pause.

"Well, she has come on," said Adela.

"As far as she needs to," said Aldom, examining his boot.

"Adela, you still like us?" said Sefton. "You will always feel the same?"

Clemence drew an audible breath and began to weep.

"There, there," said Adela, putting her arms about them. "I don't care what you did, if you don't do it any more. Miss Petticott will see it doesn't happen again. You want someone's eye on you, of course. The mistake was your going away from home. And they have lost you by complaining about you, as is quite right. If they can't manage their pupils, and look to the parents to do it, why take them from the parents at all? That is what I should like to know."

"I think that is what Father thought," said Clemence, in a steadier tone. "And I daresay it helped him to bring things to the pass."

"Oh, Roderick, Roderick, will anything serve your purpose?"

Aldom's voice, or rather Lesbia's, was faint.

"There isn't so much you can tell them now," said Adela. "They know it better than you do. And their kind of school is not yours. That is how it must strike them. They must wonder why you think you know about it. And you heard what Miss Clemence said. Well, it is a good thing the trouble came at once, as it had to come. And putting off would have made a harder reckoning."

"It did not exactly have to come," said Clemence. "It was not that everything was bad. There was another side."

"Oh, was there? And what was that?"

"Well, there were the girls. And Miss Tuke and Miss Chancellor were nice. And so was Miss Marathon in a way."

"Well, all those Misses! And now only Miss Petticott. It shows how much good they were."

"And there was Miss Laurence as well. And, of course, Miss Firebrace. And several other mistresses. And some more came by the day."

"Well, to think what she has seen! And her looking just the same. Well, she can only see it once. She knows about it now."

"And there were eighty girls, and most of them were taller than I am. You should have seen them going downstairs in their party clothes! All the dresses were as good as mine. And we never had the same person to teach us for more than an hour. And no one taught more than one or two things. Everything was done by specialists. That is how it is in these days."

"Well, I must say it does Miss Petticott credit," said Adela. "To take the place of all that. And no wonder you could not keep up with it!"

"You are contradicting yourself," said Clemence. "And I did keep up with a good ideal. And in some things I did better than the others did, only Mother wanted me to do too much. And there were nearly a hundred people at every meal. And the break-up party was a sight you would not believe, with all the girls and mistresses and guests."

"And what of Sefton's school?" said Adela.

"We had most of those things," said Sefton, with startled eyes on his sister. "But I don't think it was really the same. I should not like to go back to it."

"Of course it was different," said Clemence. "Yours was a school for younger boys. I don't suppose there was anything to learn, apart from books. Or, if there was, you did not see it. But there is not much that I don't know now. I know such a lot of unexpected things. Things that are said and not thought, and things that are thought and not said. And there are so many of both. I should never have known, if I had stayed at home, or never have known that I knew. That is another thing you learn, to know what you know."

"Well, one term has been enough," said Adela. "Or you might begin to know what you didn't know."

Clemence was approaching this stage when Miss Petticott returned. She at once broke off, and Adela looked at her and gave a laugh. Aldom withdrew without furtiveness or haste. Sefton looked at Miss Petticott in mute appeal, seeking some ground beneath his feet.

"Well, shall I read to you before you go to bed?" said the latter, keeping her eyes from Clemence, whose mood she divined. "We were in the middle of this book when you went away. Shall we go on from there, or begin at the beginning?"

"Begin at the beginning," said her pupils, feeling this would be the case with many things.

Maria and Sir Roderick, yielding to temptation, came up to the schoolroom and opened the door. Miss Petticott was reading in a fluent, distinct voice, now and then making a gesture in accordance with her words. On either side of her, sunk back in their upright chairs, were Clemence and Sefton, asleep.

"Poor little creatures!" said Maria. "It has all been too much for them."

"Worn out by things foreign to them," said Sir Roderick, taking the appearance of innocence as proof of it.

"Speak softly. Try not to wake them. They might be embarrassed by being discovered asleep."

Miss Petticott sat with her eyes rather wide, finding that this feeling resulted also from causing the state.

"I thought a little reading aloud might rest their nerves, Lady Shelley. And I seem to have been almost too successful."

"You were right, Miss Petticoat. Here is the proof. You understand what they need."

"And that comes from understanding them, Sir Roderick."

"I wish Lesbia could see them now," said Maria, as though the sight must in some way confute the former's position. "They should all be coming downstairs at any moment. I have a good mind to call them in."

"The sight would convey nothing to her, my dear. She is blunter than the run of women."

Maria was listening for sounds on the stairs, and tiptoed to the door with a beckoning movement.

"Come and look, all of you," she said, as though further words were needless.

The group hushed their steps at the sight of her raised hand.

"And no one will ever call me 'Mother'," said Juliet.

"I would I were alone," said Oliver, "so that I could weep."

"Cannot someone take them to bed?" said Mr. Firebrace. "Are there no women about their business?"

"I am glad, Roderick, that they are in their own home," said Lesbia, just shaking her head. "Whatever their general need, that is their need now. You and I are at one."

Sefton opened his eyes.

"Good-night, Mother dear," he said, and smiled at Maria and closed them.

"Lucius, must you be silent?" said Juliet. "My feelings are too deep for words, but I don't think yours can be."

"Lesbia's word will do for me."

"We must be careful not to see them as martyrs," said Maria, in a tone of repressing any rising pride.

"Well, that is better than seeing them as evil-doers," said Sir Roderick, as if this were the last of possible views. "Good-night, Miss Petticoat. Good-night, good-night. Thank you for letting us intrude on your domain."

"Cannot you even say it once, Miss Petticott?" said Leslia, smiling.

"Good-night, Sir Roderick," said Miss Petticott, accompanying the group to the door in her character of hostess.

Sefton opened his eyes again and found they met his sister's.

"Were you awake when they were here?"

"Not at first. I did not hear them come in. Then I heard their voices."

"We could not be really asleep in these chairs. But they would not know."

"Did you say what you said to Mother, on purpose?"

"Yes, in a way. My eyes were open and I had to say something. And that sounded as if I were partly asleep."

"Well, shall we ever make any progress with this book?" said Miss Petticott, her voice betraying that she had waited for this dialogue to end. "I do not think we will make our third attempt to-night. And we shall have plenty more opportunities. I will tell them to bring your supper. And then you will go to bed."

When the children came out of the room with this purpose, a shape that was almost a shadow, moved across their path, and a sound that was hardly a voice, came on their ears.

"Clemence, there is a word I have to say to you, a word I want to say. No, do not start and shrink, my child; there is no need; I am here to tell you there is none. There will be no further word from me on this that is between us, to you or your father or your mother or anyone that is yours. I am your guest in this house, and need not be anything more. Good-night, my child."

"Good-night, Miss Firebrace."

Sefton crept after his sister and put his hand in hers.

"That is the last thing we had to dread."

"We have had too many things to keep count of them. I hope I shall not grow up like that, boastful and self-satisfied and proud of being it. Why should she be complacent about doing no harm to us, when we have done none to her? But I would do it now, if I could. I would break up her school and throw her out to beg her bread, except that Father might have to support her."

"But we have really conquered her, haven't we? Father does not like her so much, and she has not had things as she meant to. She really helped Father to take us away from school. If they had not told about us, we should still be there. It fits in like things in a book. And we can rest now for the first time for months. There is nothing more on our minds. And we have Miss Petticott and Adela, and Aldom too. And Father and Mother will soon be the same. I think Father is now."

Sir Roderick's voice on the stairs supported this view.

"Well, we made the right choice in Miss Petticoat. We were not wrong there. Our mistake was in letting other people supersede her. Poor Miss Petticoat! It was a shabby return. We must do what we can to atone."

"What is this in my hand?" said Maria, leaning against the balusters and moving something before his eyes.

"I do not know. A bundle of something."

"A bundle of what?"

"Money notes. What a number! What is their meaning, my dear?"

"Money is something else in another form. What would you like this to be? I will tell you what it is. The land cut out of the place."

"It is the very sum. But my dear, good wife! What is its source?"

"That is my affair. Women have their ways and means. I was not an empty-handed woman, and I have been working up to this. I thought the moment to bestow it was when you were out of heart. Well, does this neutralise the troubles?"

"It does indeed," said Sir Roderick, with simple truth. "It makes an occasion of rejoicing out of one of sorrow."

"Well, it helps the sorrow to fall into place. And it will show Lesbia that our lives are our own."

Sir Roderick was intent on his own line. He entered the drawing-room and walked straight up to his elder son.

"Well, Oliver, what do you say to this? It does as much for you as for me. It is bound up with your future. The price of our lost farmland! It is Maria's gift."

"But it is the price of so much else," said Oliver, as he handled the notes.

"It is, indeed. That is the measure of our debt. The place is whole again, the place I have lived to serve, that I betrayed when I was helpless. It went hard with me to do it. It is whole again, and I am again a whole man."

Silence followed these words and was broken by Lesbia.

"I suppose these things to which we give our hearts, do take on a sort of human guise, and stand with human creatures in our sight. Their fate takes on the same significance, or perhaps I should say a similar one."

"We do indeed congratulate you, Roderick," said Lucius.

"I congratulate myself too much for that to be necessary."

"That is a good thing," said Juliet. "Then it does not matter about Lesbia."

"Do I fail in what was expected of me? Was the transition from the human sphere to the material rather much? Then let me fulfil my part. Roderick, I offer you my felicitations from my heart. It is true that I was troubled by human problems, that I am still troubled by them."

"They have vanished," stated Sir Roderick. "They are swallowed up in joy. Anything else would be ingratitude."

"Have they vanished?" said Lesbia, just contracting her brows.

"Yes, dear. You heard," said Juliet.

"Roderick waves his wand, does whatever is the proper thing, and troubles are no more! But a wand in the form of a packet of notes is a new idea."

"No, dear. Things in a fairy sphere always take on some different guise. I think the difference is generally greater than this."

"A fairy sphere," said Lesbia, half under her breath. "This hard, unhappy human world."

"I wish you would stop these innuendoes about the children and their stumble," said Sir Roderick. "Why do you not use open and honest words? You cannot expect young creatures to steer straight, with such an example."

Lesbia put back her head.

"Oh, Roderick, Roderick!" she said, contracting her eyes towards him in tearful mirth.

"Let us talk about Maria," said Oliver. "It is she who waves the wand. Her powers are mysterious and great."

"Yes, hers is the fairy world," said Lesbia. "I hope the rain of gold and precious stones will not change into one of toads and snakes, in the approved way."

"You mean it would be approved by you," said Sir Roderick.

"No, Roderick, I do not mean that. I mean what I said, if I may still mean it, if your words do not imply that the change has already taken place."

"The gold is to turn into the farm," said Juliet. "Are we rejoicing enough about that?"

"I am doing so," said Sir Roderick. "And it is a pure and personal joy, and that is the one that counts."

"I have always wondered what was wrong with joys," said Oliver. "And of course that is it. They do not count. Now I do wish people would sometimes talk about me. I have had a downfall as much as the children, and no one takes any interest in it. I shall begin to think you believe I really had one."

"I suppose school must be a naughty place," said Maria. "There is no help for it."

"So it is as easy as that to lose one's character. Some things do turn out to be true."

"Well, we have got away from it," said Sir Roderick. "And after this paying instead of notice, we shall leave it behind. I suppose we do not go on paying for ever."

"What ground have you for supposing that, Roderick?" said Lesbia, in a quiet tone.

"Well, you said it would be for a term."

"Then I do not know where you got the idea of paying for ever."

"From making you an allowance, and always doing it," said Sir Roderick, in a burst of irritation to himself, or rather inaudibly to Lesbia; and then glancing to see if Juliet had felt what he said, and perceiving that she had, and smiling.

"I have always thought it would be undignified to quarrel with parents," said the latter, keeping her eyes from him. "But it seems to bring out all the innate dignity in us."

"The farm is mine; the children are mine; the future is mine," said Sir Roderick.

"Roderick, is it simply an occasion for rejoicing?" said Lesbia, just uttering the words.

"I find it so, and I am going to rejoice. We have had enough lamentation and great weeping over nothing."

"Yes, we made it as little as we could. We drew veils where we could, glossed over what we could, gave the benefit of every doubt. But the main thing remains, inescapable, itself. We do not accept the word, 'nothing'."

"The word is mine, not yours," said Sir Roderick, allowing his eyes to wander. "Well, Aldom, we can give you a piece of news. We shall be able to buy the farm from your mother."

There was a pause.

"You will, Sir Roderick?"

"Your mother will rejoice to hear it."

"Well, Sir Roderick, she *was* thinking of selling it."

"I thought she was anxious to do so."

"Well, she thought she might, Sir Roderick, if it turned out to be to her advantage."

"I thought she wanted to set up a shop in the village."

"She has spoken about it, Sir Roderick. It seemed that it might be a change. Only when you have done a thing for a good many years, it seems you might as well go on with it."

"Has your mother changed her mind?"

"Well, not to say that, Sir Roderick. It is only that things look different, the more you think about them. And when you have led a life for so long, it cannot be gainsaid."

"She has never made up her mind, I suppose. I got a wrong impression."

"Well, a shop in the village would suit her, and suit her health. She finds the farm life rough-and-ready, with her being withdrawn and reserved."

"She must be past the age for heavy work."

"Well, Sir Roderick, it is contrived to spare her. And she shows no sign of her years, as she has herself remarked. The words have passed her lips."

"And what is your view of the matter?"

"Well, I sometimes feel that I have the easy life, and she the hard one, which is not your choice when you have been a good son. Though neither her work nor mine is of the kind that is ever done. And she might miss the country life, if she were to leave it."

"You would be nearer to each other, if she were in the village."

"Yes, Sir Roderick, though distance is soon covered. And the shop suits our requirements, though the rooms are what we see as dark and small. It might have been made for us, as we say. And so the matter goes on. And we often say we may as well continue as we are."

"Perhaps your mother will come and see me."

"Well, Sir Roderick, it is the quiet season. And if you are going to leave a place, why go on putting your strength into it when you have put in enough? It is like throwing good money after bad."

"Dear, dear, people should be educated," said Lesbia, as Aldom left them. "Roderick and I must be one of mind at last."

"Oh, the question of education does not fill the whole of my horizon."

"It ought to have its place in it," said Lesbia, just shaking her head, as she rose and passed from the room. "No, do not be afraid; I have said all I have to say."

"We do not often have a chance of doing that," said Sir Roderick. "But I do not grudge it to Lesbia. She has so much more to grudge to me."

CHAPTER VI

"Something normal is going to happen to me to-day," said Oliver.

"Do not normal things usually happen?" said Maria.

"Surely you have noticed they do not. It is easy to see I have no mother."

"Well, what is to happen?"

"Thank you for trying to fill the place. I do like swift compunction. Well, the friend I made at the school is coming to see me. It may be an odd way to make a friend, but otherwise the incident is ordinary. He is returning to the school early, and coming to see me on his way."

"Well, he is welcome," said Sir Roderick.

"That shows how you see the occasion. What a thing to say about a guest! It shows that the shock and effort of having him might have been too much."

"That could hardly occur to any of us," said Lesbia, "when we are housed and sustained without sign of either."

"I have been grateful for the echo of my own home life," said Mr. Firebrace.

"I have felt uneasy," said Juliet. "I have not the generosity that can accept. It seems to give someone else the superior place. I believe it does."

"The young man, Oliver Spode, the only son of his mother, and she a widow," said Mr. Firebrace, in a rapid undertone. "To say the truth, my thoughts have run on that young man. I think he may owe me his name, as Oliver does. The name has stirred my memories. His mother is an old friend of mine, unless I mistake. And I do not see why I do so."

"Someone you have not seen for years, or wanted to see, and would not have thought of by yourself," said Oliver.

"That is what an old friend is. I would not ask an old friend to my home. This friend is new enough to be made a stranger of, and what could be nicer for him, or become us better? It is dreadful to do things on the ground of having known some one for so long."

"His mother and I were hardly such ships in the night. We served a purpose for each other. It was after your grandmother died, when you were young. I came to this house, feeling alone and homeless, though I was given a home. That is the truest homelessness."

"How can you be so absurd, Grandpa? The truest homelessness is not to be given one."

"Well, I was glad of a friend who wanted something from me, whom I could know on terms of give-and-take."

"It was on terms of give, wasn't it?" said Sir Roderick. "I remember the matter now. You made over some money to the lady; a Miss Spode; yes, that was the name. She must have been in some sort of trouble. In one sort anyhow."

"You made it easy for me. And I did not know then that for you it was not so. I had the poor man's ignorance. It was a Mrs. Spode, whose husband died a little later. We came together and went apart. As the boy says, we name that an old friendship."

"You were a friend in need," said Juliet. "That would lead to going apart. When the need is ended, both sides want a different sort of friend. And one sees the reasons."

"A sense of obligation seems a hard thing to carry," said Lesbia. "I have always found the benefit worth it. I have not that sort of pride. When gratitude has been the payment I could make, I have made it willingly. Not that I have felt the other side was so much richer for it."

"But you yourself were richer," said her father. "You had paid your debt."

"Of course she had not," said Oliver.

"I shall like to see this young man and send my word to his mother," said Mr. Firebrace, moving to a desk. "There is a trinket that I will send to her, an old jewel that I have by me, an old earring that has lain idle through the years. I gave her its fellow the last time I saw her. It was a parting token. This one can be a greeting."

"Oh, Spode has sold that earring," said Oliver. "He showed it to me and said it was unique, but I knew I had seen one like it. Of course it was the one I played with as a child. He took it to a shop near the school, that deals in such things. Someone came in while he was there, and said she had a duplicate of it, and the man said the pair would fetch a price, and it worked out well. It must really be a stock design. Spode was very pleased, as his mother was in debt, and if the earring had not got her out of it, he might have had to do so. It sounds as if she is still the person she was."

"How soon will he be coming?" said Maria.

"By the afternoon train. He will not be here yet."

"He is right that the earring is unique," said Mr. Firebrace, searching in the desk. "The one supposed to be a duplicate cannot be the same. This one of mine is its mate. They were made for my family, to a special design and of rare stones, but, of course, in the fashion of the day. One might be found that could be used to make a pair. So she still lets the money slip through her hands. She never kept a hold on it. I will send this earring to take the place of the other. One does as well as two. They are too large to wear as the fashion goes, and it can be made to hang on a chain. That is its natural destiny."

"But that is a thing that is never done," said Oliver. "Spode told me about it. It had not been done through all those years."

"Well, it can be done now. It will awaken memories and start the train of thought, and probably will be done. But I cannot find the thing at the moment; I do not put my hand on it. It was in this drawer in its case, and neither is there. And no one knows of this drawer but you and me. The secret drawer we call it."

"I know of it," said Sir Roderick, "and so do Maria and Aldom. We all call it that."

"It seems kind of us," said Oliver.

"But no one uses it or thinks of it, except that some things of Maria's are there. The desk is hers and she gives me the use of it. What should I have, if she did not give it to me? The drawer is supposed to ensure absolute safety."

"Of which we may all avail ourselves," said Sir Roderick.

"But I hope only in a certain way. Has any of you put the earring to some use? You knew I had none for it."

"What purpose could it serve?" said Maria. "No one could wear one earring. It is a useless thing, unless it is made into something else. And, as Oliver says, that is a thing that is never done."

"Then Aldom must come into our minds. There is no help for it. I hope no murkiness is brewing."

"Aldom has not touched it," said Maria, "if that is what you mean."

"Well, it has gone, and the case with it, and it cannot have taken up its bed and walked."

"Aldom is as honest as you or I, as anyone else in the house."

"Then let him say an honest word to us. He may have taken it for some lawful purpose, let us say to clean it. That can be our cover and his. I do not suggest there is any black stain on him, but people are not as white as snow."

"Of course you suggest it, if you broach the matter. The question would be an insult."

"Well, I ask you all to consider. Did anyone take it to use in any way, any time in the last score of years?"

"Neither Maria nor I wear earrings," said Lesbia, "and neither Juliet nor anyone else could wear a single one."

"I suppose Aldom does not wear them either. But the thing has found some escape. So no one had any purpose for it? Anyone may have had one. I have found one for it myself."

"You are the most likely person to have disturbed it," said Sir Roderick. "When did you see it last?"

"But I am not the actual person. I saw it last in Oliver's hands, when he was a child."

"That was probably the means of its escape."

"No, I locked it up when he put away childish things. To him it was one of those."

"Earrings always seem of those to me," said Lesbia. "As far as I am concerned, it could remain locked up for ever. But I remember my mother's wearing these, if I am thinking of the right ones."

"It is a long time to depend on your memory, sir," said Sir Roderick.

"It may be failing, but not as much as that."

"I am going to fetch my glasses," said Juliet. "I want to feel that nothing can escape me."

"I did not know you wore them," said her father.

"I did not mean you to know. It is a thing we are ashamed of without any reason. They make us look older and plainer and suggest mortal decay. And I should almost have thought those were reasons."

"Well, the intended recipient does not know of her misfortune," said Lesbia, "and need never know."

"It is not nothing to me, my dear," said her father. "I remember, as you do, your mother's wearing the earrings. My not touching this one for so long did not mean that I did not keep it safe. It should have been the safer."

"You remember that, and you were going to give it away!" said Oliver. "And you gave one away all that time ago, when the memory was fresher! I am quite ashamed of you, Grandpa. I wonder you confess it."

"I saw nothing against the simple truth. Things are of no use to the dead, and may do what they can for the living."

"They seem to be of use to them for some while after they are dead. They are always kept intact at first."

"I do not gain much from mementoes. And it is no good to manufacture sentiment."

"I think you ought to manufacture a little. Indeed you seemed to be doing so."

"Why did you not give the earrings to your daughters?" said Sir Roderick.

"I do not know. I wish I had. It would have saved this trouble."

"It would have given pleasure to your own family," said Juliet, as she returned. "And you felt you had done enough for them. The pleasure of people we have not seen for many years seems really worth while. Perhaps we want to make up to them."

"I fear it escaped from the desk in Oliver's childhood," said Lesbia, "and has remained at large. And it must have got a taste for liberty by this time."

"I wonder why it is a jest to all of you," said her father.

"Your purpose for it was a sudden one, and will soon pass," said Sir Roderick.

"Might the children know anything?" said Lesbia. "If it was ever about the house, they may have come on it."

"I will not have them asked," said Maria. "Why should they be the target for anyone's chance suspicions?"

"They could not be for mine, as I had none. Neither the word nor what it carries comes from me."

"No one can be asked about it. No one should have taken it, and therefore no one has done so."

"And no one who had taken it, would admit it," said Sir Roderick. "The person who would do the one thing, would not do the other. There is no use in questions of that kind; I never know why people ask them."

"They want to clear up a mystery and cannot believe that people will not help them," said Oliver. "They want the truth and are vexed that they do not have it. And, of course, it is vexing."

"So it is, my boy," said Mr. Firebrace.

"Is that it?" said Juliet, pointing to the floor. "There in that crevice between the boards, a sort of gleam! It seems to come and go. There it is again, a sudden spark!"

Oliver followed the direction of her eyes, picked up the earring and laid it on the desk. His grandfather took it in his hand.

"Well, will that ever be explained?"

"It will, in many ways and many times," said Lesbia. "I am trying to think of the first."

"It will not be by me. But I make no protest, as I have no proof."

"But that is when protest is useful," said Oliver. "You would not need them both."

"It may have lain there for years," said Sir Roderick.

"Someone would have seen it," said Mr. Firebrace, "as someone saw it today."

"Perhaps some dust was swept away, and left it exposed," said Lucius.

"It was certainly exposed, my boy. The more so, that it was without its case."

"Grandpa, you have a dark, sad mind," said Oliver.

"He cannot take his eyes off the earring," said Lesbia. "When he did not look at it for twenty-five years or more!"

"It would be a wonder if I could. This is not the earring that was lost. It is the other, that I gave away all that time ago. I know it by a mark on the back."

"You have confused the two," said Sir Roderick. "It would be an easy thing to do."

"Too easy. I have not done it. Even though I am an old man, with a mind already confused."

"The thing has its own reminders and sets off your imagination."

"Thank you, my boy, for seeing that I know what you do."

"Grandpa, please do not frighten me," said Oliver.

"It is very highly polished," said Lucius.

"Fancy speaking so little for so long and then saying that!" said Juliet.

"It is on the point," said her father. "It has not lain there for years. That is what he meant."

"Did he? I am proud of him. How inferior women are!"

"Do you think you took it out yourself, sir, and forgot about it?" said Sir Roderick.

"I have no doubt that you do. So that can be your solution."

"You may have put the open case somewhere, with the earring in it. Think along that line and see if it stirs your memory."

"It does so, and shows me I have touched neither."

"If the case should turn up, it would support that view," said Sir Roderick, looking round as if in hope.

"Well, there may have been some oversight, my boy. Perhaps it will appear."

"Well, now the earring can go out on its journey," said Juliet.

"It has come on one," said her father, balancing it on his hand. "I have a feeling that it should rest now."

"You assign it a human personality," said Sir Roderick. "That would lead you into all kinds of ways."

"In which case it could lead me out of them."

"We think of earrings as a pair," said Lucius. "The sight of one would suggest the other. They would hardly give a separate impression."

"I knew them apart. That is the simple truth," said Mr. Firebrace.

"Almost too simple to be believed," said Lesbia. "Well, there must be mysteries in life."

"I do not know why, my dear. Secrets are not the same thing."

"Pray do not be so sinister, Grandpa," said Oliver. "And before me, whom you knew as a helpless child."

"It is ungrateful to say there are no mysteries," said Juliet, "when we have such a good one, and are making the most of it. Maria, you are pale. I have noticed it all day. The household has been too much, and you are fidgeted by these problems. Why not go and rest, and miss Oliver's friend? You can see him on another day."

"Yes, do, my pretty," said Sir Roderick. "You are not yourself. We have hardly heard your voice. I wondered what the difference was. Go and rest and take a weight off my mind."

Maria left the room. Sir Roderick threw off the weight. Mr. Firebrace handled the earring. Juliet walked to the window. Oliver and Lucius looked at the crevice in the floor, where the earring had lain.

"Come, sir," said Sir Roderick, "admit you have made a mistake. Admit it to yourself, if to nobody else. There is no need to be prodigal with the confession. One earring was marked; the other was not. You thought of them together and confused the pair. It is not such a great matter. There is no need to make too much of it."

"And the other earring may have acquired a mark," said Lesbia. "Metal can be scratched, or anyhow this metal can be."

Her father held the earring to the light, turned it and looked at the back, seemed to be trying to accept the account, seemed to be tired and to wish to end the matter.

"Well, a mark might come, I suppose. What has been done can be done again. And I do not remember its shape."

"And the earring had been on the floor," said Oliver, "wedged into that crevice between the boards. It may have got rubbed against the broken oak. The polish on it suggests it."

"Well, you suggest it, my boy. And the idea does as well as any other. I do not think much of any of them, but I have no proof, even for myself. I am old; the earring was between the boards; metal may be marked; the case may be about somewhere; it is all true. We will say that the earring was dead and is alive again, and was lost and is found."

"So we will," said Oliver. "I wish I had said it."

"Mr. Spode!"said Aldom at the door.

"Well, Mr. Spode, this is a great pleasure," said Sir Roderick, as though glad to address himself to another matter. "We give you our first welcome, and hope it will not be the last."

"There cannot be many, good as you are. I am leaving the school this term. I could not remain without your son. I could not do what I once did."

"This is not good hearing, Spode," said Lucius.

"So Oliver has been an upsetting influence," said Juliet. "We might have known what would come of employing a relation."

"What a way to talk, when I obliged you for a term! Why have you returned so early, Spode?"

"The other masters are not there. Miss James and I are by ourselves."

"There are two good reasons, but surely there is another."

"My mother and I are estranged."

"Why, that is not good hearing either," said Mr. Firebrace. "I remember your mother. She is an old friend of mine. I am interested to meet her son, and to have news of her. But your news is not of the best."

"It means nothing, sir. It is only that difference is not a basis for companionship. That is an error. And she chooses her words to wound me. She stoops to that."

"What are her words?" said Oliver. "I always like to hear them."

"You have heard these before. That I am afraid to hunt. I am glad they give someone pleasure. They give me none."

"Well, that is not true. I am sure," said Sir Roderick, heartily.

"It is true," said his guest. "There lies the meanness of saying it."

"You do not understand Spode, Father," said Oliver. "It cannot be done all at once."

Sir Roderick did not question this.

"Your son and I are good friends because we are cast in the same mould. The soul of Spode was knit unto the soul of Shelley."

"You are certainly alike. You might be taken for brothers."

"And my mother and I might be strangers. Anyhow when we pass each other without speaking."

"I am sure that does not often happen."

"Never until the latter half of the holidays. Then it does."

"Do you call each other 'Oliver'?" said Sir Roderick, looking from one young man to the other.

"We call each other Shelley and Spode, as is necessary in a school. It is a hard and hardly judging world."

"That is why our intercourse was suspect in it," said Oliver. "Suspicion must flourish in a school. There is so much ground for it."

"I shall be sorry to lose you, Spode," said Lucius. "It will not be easy to fill your place."

"I fear it may not, sir, with my being a just man."

"We shall miss you both," said Juliet. "The two tall, ponderous figures will no longer pace arm-in-arm along the corridors."

"They would not have done that anyhow," said Oliver. "Uncle Lucius had forbidden it. They say it is nice to be missed, but I never understand how one knows about it. I wish I had known that the passages were corridors, before it was too late."

"So your brother will return alone?" said Mr. Spode.

"He is not returning either. The experiment for both of us has failed."

"Oh, that is how it has turned out."

"How what has turned out?" said Sir Roderick at once.

"The trouble," said Mr. Spode, on a deeper note.

"Yes, it was a great and sad trouble to us all, and to the poor little boy as well."

"It must have been to him."

"We tried to make it a light one."

"And you did not succeed. You attempted the impossible. But the attempt should be honoured."

233

"Perhaps it was a case where failure was greater than success," said Oliver. "I had not ever met one."

"Success would have been greater," said Mr. Spode. "Success is very great. We were right about it when we were young, as we were about so many things. Not that we are not right about more now."

"What did you think of the boy and the trouble and all of it?" said Sir Roderick, as if the words broke from him.

"You could not repress the question," said Oliver. "It would come out. Why do we talk as if questions should not do that? What else should happen to them? And if they did not, the answers would not come out either."

"And answers to questions always contain some truth," said Mr. Spode.

"So they do," said Oliver. "People are so cruel."

"Do you see your way to answering this question?" said Sir Roderick, seeming to control his voice.

"I thought badly of the trouble," said Mr. Spode. "I do think ill of such things. But the boy only tried to command success, when he should have done more, deserved it. He may have thought people would not think it was more. He may, indeed, have noticed it. I pitied the boy, and it was pity with equal feeling in it. It was the kind I give myself. I am often in need of it."

"Would you advise me to keep him at home?"

"Roderick, ought you to ask advice from our masters, when you have taken your son from the school?" said Juliet.

"I am asking the advice of Oliver's friend. And he will be leaving himself at the end of the term."

"I love to give advice," said Mr. Spode. "It makes me feel so much at home. I advise you to keep him where memories are shortest. That would probably be at school. But the matter is in your hands."

"I understand you. I will see that the thing is forgotten."

"My father takes advice without resenting it," said Oliver. "You can cast your bread upon the waters, and see it return on the same day."

"The seed falls upon good ground and brings forth fruit," said Lesbia, half to herself. "Sixty and an hundred-fold."

"No wonder Shelley does not apologise for his home," said Mr. Spode.

"Do most people do that?" said Lesbia.

"Everyone but your nephew."

"How do you know of our relationship?"

"He has told me about his home life," said Mr. Spode, with a note of reproach.

"I expect the apology for home comes from a sort of pride in it."

"No, it comes from a sort of shame. The simplicity of life is inescapable."

"The two feelings probably have the same source."

"They have opposite sources. Life is as simple as that."

"Do you apologise for your home?"

"I owe it to myself. Apology is called for."

"You despise yourself, and yet you find yourself doing it?"

"I do not despise myself. It is my home that I despise."

"I daresay there is not as much reason as you think," said Sir Roderick.

"I know the reasons. It is economical and comfortless, and my mother says the things that——"

"That are not always said," said Sir Roderick, on an understanding note.

"That people's parents say," said Mr. Spode.

"Well, those are not such terrible things."

"No, they are not. One would not apologise for those."

"I hope you can go round the place with my son. It is to be his home for life."

"If I may send a telegram to my mother."

"Of course, if it will ease her mind."

"It will ease mine. The manner of our parting weighs on it."

"If you will dictate the telegram, it will go at once."

"I would rather write it, as it is a message from the heart."

"You will retract every word you said?" said Oliver.

"I said no words. That is what I retract. But those minutes will never come again."

Sir Roderick put writing materials on the desk, and Mr. Spode sat down. As he rose he suddenly exclaimed.

"Why, there is my earring!"

"One like it. I knew it was," said Oliver.

"So it is a stock pattern. My mother will never believe it."

"And she will be right," said Mr. Firebrace, coming to the desk. "The one that was matched with yours could not have been the same. As you say, this one is yours, or rather it is hers. Take it to her from me as my message from the past. I gave her the other all those years ago, and this one was to have made the pair. But it can take its place."

"I think she deserves this one, if she has the other," said Lesbia. "The separation was a mistake."

"She has not the other," said Mr. Spode. "But she always gets more than she deserves. That is a tribute to her."

Aldom entered to take the telegram and spoke to his master as he passed.

"My mother has come to see you about the farm, Sir Roderick. I have shown her into the library."

"Oh, yes, Aldom. I will go to her at once. I am sorry to leave you, Mr. Spode. I was not the object of your visit, but you make us feel you came to see us all. I hope you will be here when I return. We will shake hands, in case I am not so fortunate."

"I should hardly have known your father was a parent, Shelley," said Mr. Spode.

"No, he has not been a father to me. And you make me feel I should be glad. You take a load of bitterness from my heart. The old, sad burden is rolling away."

"I have never had a mother."

"And I have not been a son. I have only just realised it."

"You have been a good stepson and a kind nephew," said Lesbia. "We cannot all fulfil ourselves in the deeper relations of life."

"Thank you, Aunt Lesbia. I have heard there is good in everyone."

"I do not think your father would change you, Oliver."

"Only for Sefton. He wishes that Sefton could inherit the place."

"A thing that Maria does not wish," said Juliet. "How Maria is a person by herself! I think we take it too much for granted."

"It is the best way to take it," said Oliver. "Of course I am attached to Maria. I say that, to show I did not mean anything disparaging. Or rather in case I did."

"I have never heard you express affection for Maria before," said Lesbia.

"Well, it is not my habit to disparage her."

Sir Roderick went into the library, and a small, thin woman rose to meet him, and lifted a face that was Aldom's, apart from the eyes. He suddenly saw, with a rise and fall of his heart, whose eyes Aldom's were.

"Elizabeth!" he said.

The small, even voice, though having no likeness to Aldom's, recalled Aldom himself.

"It is a good many years, what some would call a great many. We have had the farm, but you have never known the truth. It was best, and I had given my word. My husband bought it with the money you gave me, though we often said we might have put it to a better use. The boy has had his name, and has never known. And the same may be said of others, as it may of you. But if we move to the village, encounter will be natural. So I have come myself, instead of leaving it to the men, as women do."

"You are well, Elizabeth? Things have gone fairly with you? Your life has been a success?"

"Well, words may be easily used. I lost my husband and

those have hardly been the terms. But my son is good, and has kept his place, and it is to his credit not to have wanted a change. I was not aware, when he took it, in whose house it was, and then it seemed no good to speak. It seemed the time was past, and silence was the best safeguard. And you have never known, with my keeping on the farm. Indeed it has not been often that I could get away."

"So the boy has been here—your son. He has had his home under my roof."

"It is where he has earned his bread. It has often seemed strange, as I have said to myself, but it does not do to pursue things in your heart. It does not take you any further."

"I have done my best for him, though I have not known. I trust he has been happy in my house."

"Well, the years go by, and we have never made a change. And when a thing has gone on, it seems as if it might as well go on doing so."

"Your son is very like you, Elizabeth."

"Yes, though there must be the other aspects. But it does not do to dwell on those. Or I always say, what is the good of giving your word? But it might be thought there might be some difference made, as it is a thing by itself, as it is no good to deny. It is not as if you had much to spare, as is well known not to be the case. It is a wonder you can go on here, as we all know."

"I will add what I can to the price, and be glad to do so. It can only be a small increase for the reasons you give."

"You are what you always were, as we look to find people. The change is in what strikes the eye. Of course, the years must do their part."

"There must be changes in us all," said Sir Roderick, keeping his eyes from the face that seemed so much the simple orginal of Aldom's, that he hardly believed in his own past. "And we must hope that some of it is gain."

"Well, silence can now supervene, Sir Roderick, except for the word when we encounter, that would naturally pass," said Mrs. Aldom, using the normal address for the first time, and rising with such a complete assumption of her future manner that Sir Roderick saw Aldom's dramatic talent related to its source. "And I am sure, if the farm proves what you wish, we do not grudge any improvement."

Sir Roderick saw her out of the house and returned through the hall. As he did so, three figures came towards him, walking abreast on their way to the door. He paused and drew back, his eyes upon them, his sudden thought in his face.

"Goodbye, my boy, goodbye," said Mr. Firebrace, grasping the guest's hand with a feeling that seemed to transcend the occasion. "You will carry my gift to your mother with the word from me. I shall picture her receiving both."

He rested his eyes on the closing door, as though it shut off some vista from his sight. Sir Roderick moved towards the library, picked up a scarf of his wife's that lay on the threshold and beckoned the older man within.

"I must say a word to you, sir. It cannot be left unsaid. It would be, if I had the choice."

"Well, what is it, my boy. You are not afraid. So why talk as if you were?"

"The three of you walking together," said Sir Roderick, with the feeling that he was carried forward on a flood of common experience. "That look you all have; that heavy, swinging movement; the ridge beneath the eyes, and the way the lids fall over them; even the shape of the hands. If it suggested anything, it could only be one thing."

The pause seemed too inevitable to carry any uneasiness. As he waited, Sir Roderick glanced through the door, saw Oliver and Aldom crossing the hall, and Sefton leaving the hiding-place where he had caught a glimpse of Mr. Spode; and felt the current that bore him rise and swell. Mr. Firebrace's voice recalled him.

"Did it suggest it to anyone?"

"As far as I know, only to me. But it would be wise not

to repeat the risk. You should not encourage the visits. The danger is not only for yourself."

"You mean it might spread to her and to him. I see there is the chance."

"I remember the matter, as I said. It was all those years ago, the right number of years; the young man is of that age. You were in trouble about the woman and needed money for her. It was a thing I understood, as I had the same need. It was to help her with some debts, you said. So it was also to pay your own. I sold the farm to meet the claims on us both. So she has lived as a widow; the son does not know; it is possible that no one knows. Anyhow no one can tell her that he does."

"So I can tell you nothing. You have told it all to me. It is a good deal to see and sum up. It shows someone else might do it. You are not such an astute man. I cannot deny it; I will not condone it; I do not know that I regret it. My heart has been stirred today."

"Well, let this meeting be the first and last. Let it stand by itself. It will hold the better place."

"The first and the last. My hail and farewell," said Mr. Firebrace to himself, and also to Sir Roderick. "My 'ave atque vale'. Well, we will leave it so. I have sent my message, sent my token across the years, seen—well, that is enough, I will be content."

"We must serve the past and present as we can," said Sir Roderick, catching the note.

"There is a truth that I see. The closer tie of blood counts less than the feelings that the years have fed. The one does not threaten the other. The place that is filled, remains."

"It is the hidden thing that does not flourish," said Sir Roderick. "Nothing can grow without the light. We can only tend it as we·can, leaving it safe in the dark. And although 'out of sight' may not mean 'out of mind', this talk must be as if it had not been. We must trust each other."

"You speak wisely, my boy. You speak well. You might speak from experience."

"We should be able to use our imagination," said Sir Roderick, suggesting another source of success. "I am sorry for you and also glad. And I might be sorry for many, and sorry without gladness. In future our lips are closed. We are not women, that we cannot seal them."

"No, we are both men," said Mr. Firebrace.

"Will you leave this scarf in Maria's room? I picked it up in the hall. I am remaining here to write to the bailiff. I am increasing the price I am giving for Aldom's farm. His mother seemed to think it fair, as they have put work into it."

"And also got their living out of it. The two things fit with each other. But fulfil your obligations. You know what they are."

Mr. Firebrace left the room, leaving Sir Roderick uncertain if he also knew, with a suspicion that he had always known. He put it from his mind and sat down to express himself on paper, a thing not among his gifts. It never struck him that he could write the word he spoke.

Mr. Firebrace carried the scarf upstairs and met Maria on her way to recover it. She took it as if she hardly saw him, and entered the drawing-room, where Juliet was sitting alone.

"Well, Maria, the guest has gone and the house is itself again. I forget I am a guest myself. I expect that is paying you the truest compliment, a thing that always has a selfish sound. I hope you have had a sleep?"

"Yes, but it has made me restless. I think a sleep in the day often does that."

"Other things that happen in the day may do it. Things quite different from sleep. I am going to talk of some of them. My reason is that a question will always pursue you, if it is not answered. Will you sit down and hear me?"

"I would rather stand."

"I daresay you would. I expect you would choose to

pace the room. But your attention will soon be arrested."

"I may not listen."

"I will take the risk. Just let me begin at the beginning. A young man went into a shop to sell an earring. Now do not be too much arrested, Maria. If you are in my hands you are safe in them. There is no need to describe the young man. Someone else came in while he was there, and said she had an earring like it. There is no need to describe her either."

"How do you know it was me?"

"No one else knows. No one else need ever know."

"I went into the shop for something on the day when I visited Sefton. The young man was there with the earring, and the jeweller said the pair would have great value. I meant to tell your father, and suggest that he should send his own."

"And then you sent it yourself. Of course second thoughts are best. And the pair of earrings was put in the window for sale. I saw them and was reminded of some of my mother's, and bought them at the price. You know I have money to spare. The man had the case that originally held them. It was wrapped in one of your large, grey envelopes and directed in your hand. I thought you had sold them for my father, and assumed they must be the actual ones I remembered. I forgot the matter until today, when it was brought to my mind. The truth was clear to me in time to prevent my betraying it."

"You told me to go and rest."

"You could not meet Mr. Spode. And I could not have him meet you. You had to have some reason for going."

"But what of the earring on the floor? Were there three? Was one of them a different one?"

"That is what we are to think. The one that was sent to the shop. It is what my father thinks, though he clearly has other thoughts. But there were only the original two."

"Then how did it get on the floor?"

"Well, who saw it there?" said Juliet.

"Oh, you put it there! You brought it back when you went out of the room on some pretext. And you put it between the boards, when you moved those rugs. I thought you were restless; I remember wishing I had as little reason to be. No wonder the earring was polished, when it had so lately come from the shop. And you would not have noticed that one of them was marked. And you did not think of the case. What a clear and complicated tale! So you brought the earrings here."

"To wear them. I thought it would please my father. I supposed he had sold them from necessity, and would be glad to see them rescued."

"It is true that I am in your hands, Juliet."

"I never know why people say that, when someone knows something to their disadvantage. Anything she said, could be denied, and she would get great discredit. I would never risk my fair name just to blot somebody else's, however nice it would be. And why should I want to blot yours? It would put you in a pathetic position, and I dislike feeling pity."

"Well, anyhow you know what to think of me."

"I don't feel I know much more than before. Might not many people do what you did? To take something that someone did not want, to give someone something that he did—was it so bad? It sounds as if it was almost right?"

"You cannot think the same of me."

"Not the same; I do think differently. But I don't know that I think any less; I am not quite sure. I rather like your anxiety to serve Roderick to be stronger than your respect for yourself. Self-respect is too common a thing to rouse my feeling; people have so much. You may have acted rather nobly. I do not mean that Shakespeare would have thought so; he took the accepted views; but I am inclined to think so myself. And I don't mean that all crime is noble. I am not a modern person."

"You are making it easy for me, Juliet."

"Well, it would be unkind to do anything else."

"You would not have done such a thing yourself."

"I wonder if I should. I always wonder if I should withstand temptation. I never seem able to meet any. I should like to be put to the test. I am so interested in myself."

"I am not," said Maria, with a sigh. "I have never met a drearier subject. And I reproached those poor children for doing as I had done, when they did it for my sake!"

"As you did it for Roderick's. There must be a strain of pure nobility in you."

"It is a thing we must hide and be ashamed of."

"Well, that does happen to nobility. People are always disconcerted when it is found out. I suppose they feel it makes their ordinary life so inexplicable. Not that that is true in your case."

"You are trying to comfort me, Juliet."

"Well, my dear, you seem to need comfort."

"Suppose something of the kind happened in your family?"

"Well, people are known to be harsh judges of their own families."

"You and Lesbia are upright people," said Maria. "I never feel so sure about your father. I do not feel I know him, though he has lived in my house longer than I have. You do not mind my saying that?"

"That is what people say, when they know it is not the truth. But I do not mind very much."

"Of course I am not without affection for him."

"I wonder if you know how unusual you are, Maria?"

"Do you feel you know so much about him yourself?"

"I have come to know more lately."

"In the last few months?"

"In the last few hours," said Juliet, throwing her eyes over Maria's face. "It was seeing him with Oliver's friend."

"It did show him in a new light. He was really almost fatherly. The three men made quite an impressive group, and he seemed to fit in as the head of it. If they were related, we should remark on the family likeness. It shows how types can repeat. I suppose I owe your father money for the earring. Though not any more than if I had not been found out. How confused our minds are!"

"Yours certainly is. Of course you did owe it, but you do not now. The earring on the floor was mine, and he gave it away as his own. The score has been paid."

"So it is to you that I owe the money."

"Yes, but I forgive you the debt."

"What will you do with one earring?"

"Keep it in case some use for it arises. I can hardly believe it will not fulfil some need."

"Suppose you showed it to them all! They would think it was a stock pattern indeed."

"I shall not show it to them. They might not think only that. Indeed, too much thought would be involved. It is a subject that always entails a good deal."

"I wonder if Roderick is worthy of what I did for him."

"If he is not, it is the better to have done it. If he is, it is no more than you ought to have done. And we do feel it was a little more?"

"I do not mean I am proud of it. I should not like to tell him the truth. But I daresay he has not told me everything about himself."

"Well, we all keep some things to ourselves, those little, mean things that cause us more shame than big ones, though we do not know why. Not that we do not really know."

"The big ones cause us shame," said Maria with a sigh.

"I do not believe you commit the small ones. And that is almost unique. Though this thing is not a big one of course. You have simply committed one small thing."

"I am grateful to you from my heart, Juliet. If the earring had not been found, the quest and cry would have continued. And what should I have done, if the cloud had fallen on Aldom?"

"Left him under it, as you did when it did fall on him. What else could be done? And protested your own trust in him, and probably protested a thought too much. You almost did that today. It put me on the track and prepared my mind for the truth."

"Other people are not as alert as you are."

"Oh, no, they are not," said Juliet.

"Your father does not suspect me. It makes me feel I have sailed under false colours."

"We could not sail under our true ones. It would mean sailing under too many."

"Was your sister, Mary, like you, Juliet?"

"A little. More than Lesbia is. And we were greater friends. And my father loved her the most of the three. Of course, she was the best."

"Why 'of course'? Because she is dead?"

"Yes," said Juliet.

"I wish I had known her, though it is an odd thing to say."

"I wish she had known you. And I do not think it is odd."

"Well, my pretty, you had your rest," said Sir Roderick, leading in his household. "You had a sleep and feel the better for it. I feel rather fatigued myself. It has been an exhausting day."

"I have been wondering," said Maria, with an impulse to hasten into talk, "if the children might ask their friends at school to spend a day here at some time. They seem to have liked some of them. And there is no need for them to disappear from sight, as if they had been expelled."

"No need at all," said Lesbia, "as that was not the case."

"You would allow your girls to come?"

"But by all means, Maria. I have advocated companionship for Clemence, and half a loaf is better than no bread. And I hold no brief for all work and no play."

"And you would let the boys come, Lucius?"

"Yes, if someone may bring them."

"Of course. But it had better not be Oliver's friend. Now he has been here as a guest, I would rather have someone else in the other character."

246

"Miss James will be the right person."

"I may also send a mistress, Maria?" said Lesbia. "The ewe lambs do not go out unshepherded from the fold."

"If you will not come yourself."

"I will come with pleasure, if it does not preclude the mistress. I have no experience in daily superintendence. It is outside my sphere."

"Will you come, Juliet?"

"No, I am afraid I should superintend, and appear to disadvantage. I do forget myself so easily. It might seem to be within my sphere, when honestly it is not. And the boys will be happier without Lucius or me."

"And the girls will not without Lesbia?" said Sir Roderick.

The faint smile came to Lesbia's lips without her summoning it.

"I do not know, Roderick. I do not concern myself with the matter. That is the best way to be free of them, and have them free of me."

"Perhaps that nice woman, Miss Chancellor, will come," said Maria. "We met at the station and had a talk. We should meet as friends. And she seemed to be fond of Clemence."

"She was fond of Clemence, Maria. It is probable that she would like to come. Her duties will be in abeyance. I will make the suggestion."

"Cannot you just tell her to come, as her time is yours?" said Sir Roderick.

"Why, no, Roderick," said Lesbia, slightly raising her brows. "And her time is her own. I do not know whom you are thinking of."

Sir Roderick did not tell her.

"Of course we do not mean there is any chance of Clemence's returning to the school. Maria is not making any move towards that."

"I should hope not, indeed," said Lesbia, laughing, 'after all we have been through on the score. It would be a sinister threat."

"Would you refuse to take her now, if I wanted to send her?" said Maria.

"Yes, I think so, Maria," said Lesbia, in an incidental manner. "I do not care for uncertain pupils. They have an unsettling influence."

"And it would not be the right policy to encourage that," said Sir Roderick.

"It is fairer to the parents not to do so."

"Would you also repudiate Sefton, Lucius?"

"You can say you would, Lucius," said Juliet, "as there is no chance of your having the choice."

"No, I think I should just accept him in the ordinary way."

"Both courses have their own dignity," said Oliver. "But I think the second has more."

"I do not make sacrifices to dignity," said Lesbia.

"How will you entertain the guests, Maria?" said Oliver.

"They will see the children, and have good things to eat, and wander about the place. That will be enough for them. They are not grown-up. You appear to be amused."

"I am," said her stepson.

"Will the girls expect anything more, Lesbia?"

"They will be glad to do as you say, Maria, and will think it kind to ask them," said Lesbia, in a faintly recitative tone.

"Well, the day will come and go," said Sir Roderick.

"It will come," said his son. "And in the end it will go, though Clemence and Sefton will find themselves in some doubt about it. And with them it will remain."

CHAPTER VII

"WELL, CLEMENCE, IF we are not to see you at school, we must be content to see you in your home," said Miss Chancellor, as she entered the Shelleys' hall. "Not that that is not an ungracious way of referring to your invitation. We are most pleased to come, and thank you very much for thinking of us. Are we blocking your path, Miss Firebrace?"

Lesbia gave Clemence a smile as she passed, and followed Aldom to the drawing-room.

"It is nice of you to want us here, Clemence," said Verity glancing round the hall.

"I was so upset when you did not come back," said Gwendolen. "I felt that our lives had gone apart, and that to you it meant nothing."

"We were all disappointed not to see you, Clemence," said Maud. "And it came as such a complete surprise. There had been no hint or suggestion of it."

"Why did you suddenly decide to leave?" said Esther.

"Esther has not lost her abruptness," said Miss Chancellor.

"I cannot help thinking it was a pity, Clemence," said Maud. "Of course I know nothing about it, and have no right to form an opinion."

"Only to express one," said Verity.

"But you had settled down and got over the uncertain period," went on Maud, without looking at Verity. "It seems a waste of the initiation stage, of which the point is that it leads to something further."

"We must hope it will do so," said Miss Chancellor. "We can build upon foundations anywhere, if they are well and truly laid. Not that a term was not a short time in which to lay them; which amounts to saying the same thing as Maud."

"Who teaches you now, Clemence?" said Verity.

"Miss Petticott and my brother's tutor, who taught us before."

"And taught you well, if I remember," said Miss Chancellor, with a note of having relegated Clemence to the past. "Miss Tuke, you have not greeted your former charge. It is remiss of you when she is also your hostess."

"Poor Miss Tuke was ill in the train," said Gwendolen, as though this explained the omission.

"Yes, Clemence, I was quite poorly," said Miss Tuke, finding her tongue in this accustomed sphere. "And I felt quite a novice in attending to myself."

"Would you like to lie down?" said Clemence.

"Dear, dear, no indeed. I should think I was somebody else."

"And that would not do," said Miss Chancellor, "when we are all dependent on your being yourself."

"Shall I ask Adela to come to you?"

"No, no, I should have nothing to say to Adela, whoever she may be. But thank you, Clemence, my dear. I see you would do the right things in illness."

"Such as fetching someone else to deal with it."

"Well, that might be the right thing," said Miss Chancellor, "as you are without experience in such matters. But Adela is baulked of her patient this time. Miss Tuke will have none of her."

"Didn't you wear that dress in the evenings at school sometimes?" said Esther.

"Yes, I believe I did. Or one something like it."

"Did you have two dresses made almost alike?" said Gwendolen, looking at it with attention.

"It has been altered, hasn't it?" said Esther.

"Yes, I think it has. Oh, yes, that is it," said Clemence, looking down at the dress and giving it a careless pull.

"And you do not care whether it has or not," said Miss

Chancellor. "You will never cure Clemence of her indifference to such things, Esther. You may as well relinquish the effort."

"She might have taken more trouble for our visit," said Verity. "We have all made the most of our resources."

Clemence sent her eyes over the figures before her and gave a faint frown, as though perplexed by the account.

"I cannot help laughing at your expression, Clemence," said Miss Chancellor, proving what she said.

"Don't you think Miss Chancellor's dress is nice, Clemence?" said Gwendolen.

"Confess now, Clemence. You had no idea whether it was nice or not, and no wish to form one."

"Don't you like Miss Tuke's new dress?" said Esther, at the same moment.

"Oh, my dress; well, I have to wear something. If I did not, what a saving it would be of time and trouble! It is other people's dresses that are my province, and an interesting one I find it. I am pleased with Esther's dress. Are not you, Miss Chancellor?"

"I could not have it made in the way I wanted; it would have cost too much," said Esther, in the space of a second.

"Why, what change did you want, Esther?" said Miss Chancellor, surveying the dress.

"I wanted the embroidery carried down the front. It looks so scanty as it is."

"Well, I do not know that I agree with you. Esther. It is very nice and simple and finished. And suitable for any occasion, when it might easily have been too much."

"But it has to do for other occasions."

"And so it should. But it is a good rule to keep one's dressing a little down," said Miss Chancellor, holding her eyes from her own garments. "Better a little under-dressed than a little over-dressed is a sound motto."

"Do you still learn Greek, Clemence?" and Verity, tapping her foot on the flags of the hall.

"Yes, with Sefton's tutor, as I did before."

"And with considerable success, if I remember, Clemence," said Miss Chancellor.

"And are you as clever as you used to be?" said Gwendolen.

"She can hardly have altered in this time, Gwendolen. Indeed I hope she is cleverer, as she is in the developing stage."

"Are we all in that? I don't think I get any different."

"Yes, I think you do, Gwendolen. At your own pace, and in your own way. We must not expect you to be anyone but yourself."

"I think you ought to expect a little more of me than that, Miss Chancellor. It sounds as if you had given me up. Of course we have no one really clever, now that Clemence is gone."

"Perhaps we might make an exception of Verity, Gwendolen," said Maud, "if we are to be open in our discussion, which is a breach of convention, of course."

"I am not prepared to be drawn into a comparison of the respective gifts of Verity and Clemence," said Miss Chancellor.

"What is this about Verity and Clemence and their gifts?" said Maria, coming from the drawing-room, and throwing an arm about her daughter, as she surveyed the guests. "I know which one is Clemence. So now which is Verity?"

"We do not meet quite as strangers, Lady Shelley," said Miss Chancellor, shaking hands. "We had a talk at the railway station at the end of last term. I do not know if you remember."

"Of course I do. Why should my memory be poorer than yours? I was glad to meet the mistress of Clemence's form. And now I am glad to meet a friend of us both."

"We did not know then that we were to lose Clemence."

"Why did she desert us, Lady Shelley?" said Gwendolen.

"She was the cleverest of any of us. Things are quite

different without her," said Esther, attracting Maria's eyes by her sudden utterance.

"We thought she would tread the thorny path of learning at our side," said Verity.

"And that to her it would not be thorny," said Maud.

"How kind you all are! Clemence could find many pretty things to say about you. So fresh and nice as you all look," said Maria, taking the arm of the nearest and leading the way to the drawing-room. "I cannot feel much pride in the little ragamuffin herself. She ought to have profited more by your example. Her father is waiting to meet you; he has been looking forward to the day."

"Let me introduce Miss Tuke, Lady Shelley," said Miss Chancellor.

"Oh, kind Miss Tuke! I know her well by name," said Maria, putting her other arm through the latter's, and continuing suitably to talk of her in the third person, as she had not looked at her face. "She was so good to Clemence when she was ill. I do not know Clemence's reason for keeping you in the hall."

This did not matter, as the girls knew and understood it, an instinct to postpone the meeting of family and friends.

"Now here you all are! This is kindness indeed," said Sir Roderick, sending his eyes over the girls in open appraisement. "Now come and sit down and talk to me. I am not going to waste this opportunity."

The girls obeyed him with an ease and success that suggested a regard for effect. Miss Chancellor rested her eyes on them. Lesbia did not do so. Clemence leaned back in her chair, already pale with her experience.

"Now you two should have things in common," said Maria, with a hand on the shoulders of Miss Chancellor and Miss Petticott. "You must be initiates in many of the same mysteries."

"We have Clemence in common, Lady Shelley, and that is a foundation you share with us," said Miss Chancellor, who inclined to her hostess's company. "Or rather that we share with you."

"And you share it too," said Maria, transferring a hand to Miss Tuke. "Though I do not know why we should choose that particular foundation."

Miss Petticott and Miss Tuke looked at each other, suddenly exchanged a handshake and fell into fluent talk. Maria turned to Miss Chancellor and discussed education with lively interest, and the latter gave of her best and had her reward. Sir Roderick's talk with the girls resolved itself into a discussion on equal terms with Maud, and the others transferred their attention to Clemence.

"I feel as if I had always lived here," said Gwendolen. "I suppose anyone who had, would always have done it. It feels as if things had always been the same."

"Even the clothes," murmured Verity.

"Yes, Clemence, both your dress and your mother's are those you wore on the day you came to school," said Esther, in a tone of interest. "We saw your mother from the window."

"Are they?" said Clemence, idly.

"Don't you remember?" said Verity.

"I daresay I should, if I threw my thoughts back over all that time."

"The Petticoat!" said Verity, with her covert smile, indicating the bearer of this nickname.

"Yes, but do not let her hear you call her that."

"Would she mind what we do?"

"I daresay not. But she might not like me to have told you."

"What is there to like about it?" said Gwendolen. "Verity, why are you not on your proper behaviour as a guest?"

"I suppose because Maud's back is turned," said Verity, locking her hands behind her head, and then glancing at Miss Chancellor and withdrawing them.

"What a lot Miss Tuke and Miss Petticott have to say to

each other!" said Esther. "Miss Tuke does not generally open her mouth."

"They look rather alike," said Verity. "No, I do not mean alike; rather as if they were somehow in the same sort of world."

"Well, I daresay they are," said Clemence. "Miss Petticott is not a qualified person like your mistresses. We have Sefton's tutor to teach us their sort of subjects."

"Where is your brother, Clemence?" said Gwendolen.

"He will be coming in presently, when his friends are here."

"Is he having friends too, today?"

"Yes, from his school. They are coming by a later train. He left the school at the end of the term, as I did."

"Did he leave for any particular reason?" said Esther.

"No, just as I did," said Clemence, hurrying her words. "He was supposed not to look so well, or to have been over-worked or something."

"If there had been ten of you, would you all have left?" said Verity. "I suppose some of you would have reached the leaving age."

"Oh, the powers that be, settled it between them. I do not know much about it. My parents seem to like home education best."

"They may be afraid of your becoming unfitted for home life," said Esther. "That would have happened soon enough. If you were not relations of Miss Firebrace, you would have had to give a term's notice. I mean, you would have had to pay the fees for the term."

"We did have to. I heard it being talked about. My father and mother were not very pleased about it."

"I should think not," said Gwendolen. "Mine would not have been pleased at all. I should have been made to feel quite guilty."

"Did you not have to feel guilty, Clemence?" said Esther.

"It was nothing to do with me. School customs are not my fault."

255

"Why did you not come back for the one term?" said Verity.

"Oh, I don't know. It was not even suggested."

"So your parents wasted a term's fees to indulge their inclinations," said Gwendolen, while three pairs of eyes passed over Clemence's clothes. "I wish mine had as much to spare, and would spend it so easily."

"People spend on such different things," said Esther.

"Which life do you really prefer, Clemence?" said Verity.

"It is a good thing that Maud cannot hear, so that we can show our true natures," said Gwendolen. "She would be so ashamed of us, and so would Miss Chancellor. I should be ashamed of myself, if I were capable of such a feeling."

"Really, Gwendolen, I think you do yourself an injustice," said Verity, in idle imitation of Miss Chancellor.

"I have seen no sign in you of such insensitiveness," said Esther, in the same manner.

"Well, which life do you prefer, Clemence?" said Verity.

"Oh, home on the whole, I suppose. But there were things I liked about school; the changes in teaching and the different people as companions. Home life does incline to be rather the same."

"You have no affection for us, as we have for you," said Gwendolen. "I shall give way when we get home, because we never won your heart."

"You continually promise us a sight of you in tears, Gwendolen, and the promise is never realised," said Clemence, taking up the mimicry. "Not that we wish it to be."

"Yes, imitation of everyone is the thing at school now," said Verity. "You left just in time to escape it."

"I shall hate home life when I have nothing else," said Esther.

"Esther, are you thinking what you are saying?" said Verity, changing her voice the next moment to her own. "How old is your brother, Clemence?"

"He is eleven, three years younger than I am."

"And will his friends be—are his friends of his own age?"

"I suppose so. About that age. I had not thought about it," said Clemence, her face changing as she thought about it now. There was a pause.

"Why did you ask us all on the same day?" said Esther.

"Oh, I do not know. It was planned in that way. I did not have much to do with it. It was thought we might like to see our friends, and then it was just arranged. Perhaps we said we should like to. I don't remember."

"I wish my chance words were attended to like that," said Esther. "You must have to be careful what you say."

"But I could not suggest that the age of Sefton's friends should be altered," said Clemence, in a rising tone. "It would have been no good to drop a hint like that."

"I don't mind what age they are," said Esther. "What difference does it make to us?"

"None, unless you talk to them. And that you need not do. Indeed, I don't suppose you will have the chance. They will keep together."

"They will awaken my maternal instincts," said Gwendolen.

"We can let them do that," said Verity. "And that will solve any problems."

"I did not know it presented any problems, just to have some boys about," said Clemence. "I am too used to Sefton to worry about his age. I don't suppose he troubles about mine. We have all been that age ourselves."

"Clemence is more of a child since she settled down at home," said Verity, resting her eyes on her hostess. "She is more as she was when she first came to school."

"Well, I daresay that is natural," said Clemence. "We are all children up to a point in our own homes. I expect it is the same with all of you. And we shall have plenty of time to be grown-up."

"If I were not a child with my parents, they would be more unloving towards me," said Gwendolen.

"I don't know that my family is so fond of my winning infancy," said Verity, lifting her shoulders. "They don't mind my being myself. If we outnumber the boys, our maternal impulses may overwhelm them. Perhaps we had better suppress them."

The girls appeared to have no difficulty in doing this when Sefton entered with his friends. They regarded the latter without expression, and gave no sign of distinguishing one from another. Maria saw the position and did not introduce them. Maud moved away from Sir Roderick, as if she had taken enough of his attention, and he gave the boys the welcome he would have given to any guests; and having seen Miss James attracted by some hidden force to Miss Tuke and Miss Petticott, sat down among them and talked with serious interest, asking for accounts of their school life and giving recollections of his own. He obtained light on Sefton without betraying his purpose or without knowing that he did so; and if Bacon gave him what help he could, was no less the gainer, that he was unaware of it. Any jests he made were well received, partly because the boys were amused by them, and partly because they involved no rallying of themselves. When luncheon was announced, he guided them to places that kept them together, and put Sefton at the head of the board, on the ground that he was the host.

"Then Clemence is the hostess and should sit at the other end," said Maria, rising and preparing to undo the arrangements, without thought of an alternative scheme.

"No, no, my pretty, she is well enough. Leave her among her friends."

The girls exchanged glances at this description of Maria, and then looked again at the latter, as though to reconsider their impression.

"You should not call me that before strangers, Roderick. They cannot fit the words to a weatherbeaten woman like me."

"I call you what you are to me, my dear."

The luncheon was based on youthful ideas of luxury. Sir Roderick saw that the boys could eat without any sense of eyes upon them; Miss Petticott that the girls did much the same; Maria saw to nothing with an unconscious inattentiveness that did its part. Oliver entered the room as everything was under way.

"I could not resist being late, Maria. I wanted to enter at a moment when every eye would be upon me."

"You should not be so conscious of yourself."

"I did not think I was. I wanted other people to be conscious of me. I thought that was being conscious of them."

The girls looked at Oliver and then at Clemence.

"It is my grown-up brother. He will behave in his own way."

"How are you, Aunt Lesbia?" said Oliver, going to greet his aunt.

Lesbia raised her face for his salute, keeping her eyes from the girls, whose expression perhaps did not invite scrutiny.

"How do you do, Miss James?" said Oliver, moving round the table. "I hope you find you cannot fill my place."

"That is just how I should put it, Mr. Shelley. The place is formally filled, but it seems to lack the one thing needful."

"How does your brother know Miss James, Clemence?" said Verity. "I thought she was the matron at your younger brother's school."

"So she is. He taught music there last term by way of an experiment. He soon gave it up, of course."

"Was it a sort of joke?" said Gwendolen.

"Yes, and the humour of it soon palled."

"My sister is betraying my confidence," said Oliver, playing into Clemence's hands. "Have you given up your music, Holland?"

"No, sir. I learn with the new master."

"Then he does what I could not do."

"I mean I have lessons with him."

"You should say what you mean. How the school-master's touch returns! Is the school different without my brother and me?"

"No, it is the same," said Bacon. "Of course we wish Sefton was there."

"And not that I was?"

"Well, that does not make so much difference. Except to the boys who learn music—who have music lessons," said Bacon, correcting himself without change of tone.

"Do you still eat potted meat, Sturgeon?"

"No, I never take it now."

"When it was the thing that raised your life to the heights?"

"He did not like the heights," said Bacon. "They are not always congenial to people."

"And you yourself still go from strength to strength?"

"Yes, he does," said Holland.

"He is still a leader of men?"

"Yes," said Bacon, grinning.

"Did the good fairies preside at his birth?" said Sir Roderick, looking at Bacon.

"Yes, they gave him a great brain," said Holland, "and that large head to keep it in, and give it room to grow."

"And how did the rest of you come?" said Maria, using the past tense to bring Sefton into the lists.

"Shelley came next, and the rest of us nowhere."

"And no one near to Bacon?"

"Well, Shelley came up to him in brains, but not in other things."

"My little son!" said Maria.

"Shelley looks as if he did not like the description," said Holland.

"Though it cannot be called incorrect," said Bacon.

"You are in an advantageous position, sir," said Sir Roderick to Mr. Firebrace, who sat opposite the girls.

"That is so, my boy; and as I am too old to be of account, I avail myself of it."

"Who is the old gentleman, Clemence?" said Verity.

"Oh, some sort of relation, who lives in the house."

"Isn't he your grandfather?" said Esther. "Your brother called him that."

"He is Oliver's grandfather, not mine."

"How can he be? You must have the same."

"Oh, I can't keep on expounding it all. If you were interested, you would not need so much explanation."

"My husband married twice," said Maria, in a clear, cordial tone, smiling at her daughter's guests. "I am his second wife. Mr. Firebrace is the father of the first, and so Oliver's grandfather and not my children's."

"Oh, I see," said Verity. "It is like a lesson."

"Not at all, Verity," said Miss Chancellor. "I hope your lessons are not often as simple as that. I cannot understand your difficulty. You are not usually so easily perplexed."

"These family trees are complicated," said Sir Roderick, with a note of sympathy. "They are only clear on paper."

"Then I am right that they are like a lesson, Sir Roderick."

"Then remember that lessons should be mastered as quickly and thoroughly as possible, Verity."

"You should not be so harsh, Miss Chancellor, when we are having a day's pleasure," said Gwendolen.

"You need not give your intelligence a rest, Gwendolen. That is a misuse of a holiday too often made."

"I wish Miss Chancellor would take a holiday," said Esther, in a murmur audible to Sir Roderick, who controlled a smile, and to Lesbia, who kept her eyes down and did not do so.

"I think it is dignified of me to have my particular grandfather," said Oliver. "It is not everyone who can keep his own forbear in the house. Do you not agree with me, Miss Gwendolen?"

Gwendolen was taken aback and made a conscious response.

"I don't think it was dignified to be music master in a school, Mr. Shelley."

"And why not, Gwendolen?" said Miss Chancellor.

"Well, he must have watched five-finger exercises and heard all kinds of strumming. It was an extraordinary choice."

"I did not dislike the idea," said Oliver. "It reminded me of a picture in the Academy. The Music Master. Myself resting my head on my hand and my eyes on the keyboard. And a boy pupil seemed to be a change from a girl, and to have a certain pathos."

"And had he any?" said Sir Roderick.

"Well, not of the kind I thought."

"You might as well say my position was undignified, Gwendolen," said Miss Chancellor.

Sir Roderick raised his eyes.

"She was talking of a man teacher and a boys' school," said Oliver. "The opposite situation. She thought it suggested poverty and the common task."

"Well, no one could apply the term, 'undignified', to such things as those."

"Isn't it dreadful that people can?" said Oliver.

There was some laughter, in which Miss Chancellor joined a moment later.

"I should be proud if I could teach anything," said Maria.

"Yes, that is my view, Lady Shelley."

"Now I am going to desert the boys for the girls," said Sir Roderick, rising and gathering up the implements at his place.

Aldom came to his aid; other changes of position were involved; and as the stir subsided Maud's voice was heard.

"In using the word, 'dignified', we should be clear if we are using it in its true sense. Dignity is not synonymous with prosperity."

"Quite right, quite right," said Sir Roderick.

"Does it tend to rise out of it?" said Oliver. "Of course I hope it does not."

"Are you going to take up any work when you leave

school?" said Maria to Maud, unconscious of the sequence of her thought.

"Well, Lady Shelley, that would be my choice in a way. But there will be other claims upon me."

"Home claims save women from a great deal," said Sir Roderick.

"And deprive them of as much in some cases," said Miss Chancellor. "I am afraid in a good many."

"Well, that may sometimes be so. But what do they deprive them of, now? Incessant work and a daily grind that ages them before their time. What is there to be said for it?"

Miss Chancellor's amusement was so easy that it suggested no prospect of a serious reply.

"Roderick, if you had been a little less foolish, you might have been rewarded differently," said Maria.

"By that flash of the eyes that carries terror with it," said Gwendolen. "Miss Chancellor would not do for a picture in the Academy."

"That would have been a reward indeed," said Sir Roderick, just bowing towards Miss Chancellor.

"Well, really, Sir Roderick, you are the last person to make a target of people's eyes," said Miss Chancellor, looking through her glasses at her host. "You have, without exception, the bluest pair it has been my lot to meet."

"I have never seen such blue ones either," said Esther to her companions. "And the butler's are just the same. They come suddenly open in just the same way."

"It may be a mark of the local stock," said Maud. "The same characteristics do appear in the same place. In some counties the tendency is marked."

"My husband is not used to compliments on his appearance," said Maria, as Sir Roderick's eyes fell.

"We ought to talk about the girls' eyes, though we might find ourselves confronted by a row of lashes."

"Well, if you give warning like that, Sir Roderick," said Miss Chancellor, looking full at him, as one who had not received it, "I do not know what you would expect."

"What colour are your eyes, Miss James?" said Sir Roderick, as the result of looking round the table to see that everyone had full attention.

"Hazel, Sir Roderick, what ever that may be. Or that is what I have been brought up to believe. I am never quite sure what the colour is, or whether it is the colour of my eyes or not. And I have never concerned myself much about it."

"Hazel," said Sir Roderick, after leaning forward with an air of concerning himself more.

"No one has dared to tell me that my eyes are green," said Maria, overestimating the general courage, as no one knew they were.

"Green is a most unusual colour, Lady Shelley," said Miss Chancellor. "Not that I think it is a fair description."

"What colour are your eyes, Miss Tuke?" said Sir Roderick, seeing, or rather feeling, an alertness in Miss Tuke's bearing.

"Blue-grey or grey-blue, Sir Roderick. It does not much matter which, and anyhow it cannot be determined."

Miss Tuke was wrong.

"Grey-blue," said Sir Roderick, after leaning forward again.

"Now the boys' eyes, Father," said Oliver.

"What are they?" said Sir Roderick, as if this hardly mattered.

"They are different colours," said Bacon, as though he did not think it did.

"You have a noble pair, my boy," said Sir Roderick, as he saw this.

"All the better to see with."

"And is the noble head the better to think with?"

"Well most people do not think much."

"Would you put me among them?"

"Well," said Bacon, after looking into his face, "I don't think it matters with everyone."

"Do you envy this great man?" said Sir Roderick, to the other boys.

"No," said Holland. "I only want to be a nice, ordinary person."

"I don't especially want to be ordinary," said Sturgeon. "I don't see any good in it. I am rather sorry that I am."

"I should not call Sturgeon ordinary, Sir Roderick," said Miss James, from across the table. "I do not think the word gives him."

"Well, you must know, Miss James. Your word carries weight."

"Well, I have many opportunities of observing the boys, and it leads to forming an unconscious estimate of them."

"Where would you put my boy?" said Sir Roderick, in a tone so easy that he hardly seemed to utter the words.

"Well, there is no need to say he was not ordinary, Sir Roderick, as no one thought he was."

Maria's face flushed, and she seemed to hold herself from moving forward.

"Where would Miss Tuke put my girl?" she said, her tone seeming to echo the easiness of her husband's.

"My work is to look after them, Lady Shelley, and with such a number I find it enough. I do not see their work and play. All I can say of Clemence is that I miss her so much that I could cry when I go into her dormitory."

"Why did you snatch her from us, Lady Shelley?" said Gwendolen.

"Perhaps for that very reason, that I cried when I went into her dormitory. I hope it was not too much because of that. I thought the life at home would suit her better, kind and clever as you all are."

"It may suit her health better," said Miss Chancellor, looking at Clemence. "She was paler and thinner as the term went on, sorry as I am to admit it. My hopes of taking her back with us are fading. I confess I was not quite without them."

"I did not know we had a traitor in the camp," said Lesbia.

"Oh, you are the person I ought to have asked about her standing, Miss Chancellor."

"It is not my habit to talk of the girls to their faces, Lady Shelley. I remember how I disliked it when I was a child. But this hardly comes under the head of what can be termed personal remarks. I will say what Miss James said of your son, that there is no need to say she is not ordinary, as no one thought she was."

Maria drew a breath and turned her eyes on her husband, as though calling his attention to a vindication of herself.

"What was my standing among the masters?" said Oliver. "I do not like it to be thought that no one wants to know. I am sensitive about my position in my family."

"We are dependent upon you, Miss James," said his father.

"Well, Sir Roderick, I can only refer to the humorous and original atmosphere that was diffused through the school in Mr. Shelley's time with us. I cannot say anything more intimate, as I was not thrown with him."

"Cannot you say a word against the new man?" said Oliver.

"I am not criticising him, Mr. Shelley. He does his work and takes his part in the common life, and that is as much as can be said for most of us. I do not imply any disparagement. There would be no occasion."

"I think we will have coffee in the drawing-room," said Maria, rising.

"You cannot give your mind to the talk about me," said Oliver. "How I am alone amongst many!"

Miss Chancellor followed Maria with an air of ease, and Miss James and Miss Tuke with observation and reproduction of it. The girls appeared accustomed to the ceremony, and the boys to be surprised by it.

"Do you always have coffee with your parents, Shelley?" said Holland.

"No, it is only because you are here."

"Do you, Clemence?" said Verity, in her idle tone.

"Well, I do sometimes, but I am older than Sefton," said Clemence, looking to see if her family was in earshot, and seeing only Oliver, who appeared not to hear.

"Are we to see Adela?" said Verity, with her veiled smile. "We have seen Aldom."

"That suggestion should surely have come from Clemence," said Maud.

"You can come upstairs, if you like. She will be in the schoolroom. Mother, we are going upstairs to see Adela."

"Yes, do, my dear. She will be very pleased. But do not exaggerate the entertainment. Bring your friends down when they have had enough."

The girls linked arms and mounted the staircase, the guests noting its shallowness and breadth, the hostess relieved that no eyes were upon them. She had not reckoned with this transference of school customs to her home. Adela rose at their entrance, set chairs for them, and stood in silence.

"Is this the schoolroom, Clemence?" said Esther, in a tone of lively interest.

"Yes. It used to be the nursery. It still looks rather like that."

"Of course your brother is only eleven," said Verity, in smiling quotation.

"The room has grown of itself and never had anything done to it," said Gwendolen. "It somehow makes me feel homesick."

"I used to want it sometimes, when I was at school," said Clemence.

"We have heard so much about you, Adela," said Maud, her tone suggesting that it was time for such a speech.

"Thank you, miss. No doubt your name is familiar."

"We grudge you your companion," said Gwendolen. "I believe you used your influence to wean her from us."

"Well, miss, I do not take the view that her own home is not the place for her. I do not disguise the opinion."

"I think you ought to," said Verity. "It savours of mean triumph."

"Well, triumph it may be in a sense, miss. But meanness does not come into it, it not being in my nature."

"You have looked after Miss Clemence all her life," said Maud. "You have more claim to her than we have."

"Well, miss, claim is not the word, as I am aware. But a bond remains."

"Do you help her to choose her clothes?" said Esther.

"Well, miss, she has not reached the stage of interest, as you have no doubt observed. But the time for that is to come."

"I was thinking of the dress she had at Christmas."

"It would not do to think of the other things," said Clemence.

"You go further than you know, Miss Clemence," said Adela, on a severe note.

"Why don't you come back to school, Clemence, with a lot of nice things?" said Esther.

"The prospect is not in my line. Neither one part of it nor the other."

"There are other things at school than wearing pretty clothes," said Adela. "When Miss Clemence came home, my heart ached to see her."

"But she is clever at her books, Adela," said Maud.

"Clever at her books," murmured Verity, in mockery of Maud's adaptation of herself.

"She can be that at home miss, as she always had been. It did not come from leaving it."

"What a lovely view!" said Esther, going to the window. "We should like to see the park, Clemence."

"Esther, that suggestion should have come from Clemence," said Verity, in the tones of Maud.

"I will have Miss Clemence ready in a moment, miss."

Clemence stood to be dressed, as though used to doing nothing for herself, regardful of Adela's conception of a girl attended by her maid, but feeling that the clothes modified it to one of a child and a nurse. Then she accepted the arms of her companions and descended the stairs. They walked with linked arms about the park, now and then catching a glimpse of the boys, but showing no wish to advance on it. Clemence held herself uneasily, fearful of eyes at the windows. The gulf between the words of school and home, the ignorance in each of the other, made her wonder she had ever thought she could live between them. Exhaustion was superseding excitement, and she found herself longing for the end of the day.

"I suppose you know every inch of this park, Clemence?" said Verity.

"Well, all the separate parts of it. It is different at different times of the year. It is best in spring and autumn."

"I think I like the country in the winter best," said Maud.

"I wonder how often that is true," said Verity. "It sounds a thing worth saying for the sake of saying it."

"It is true in my case, Verity, or I should not have said it."

"What time is really the best, Clemence?" said Esther.

"I think, myself, the spring. Then it changes every day. In the winter it is always the same."

"You are a happy creature, Clemence," said Gwendolen, causing Clemence a sense of surprise. "The house and the park, and your father and brother, and your mother and Miss Petticott. It must be perfect, mustn't it, Maud?"

"Well, talking of perfection, Gwendolen, I should say that the last item, if I may use such a word, is the dubious one. The sameness in the education is perhaps the weak point."

"Of course you may not use the word. Miss Petticott is not an item."

"That was surely unworthy of you, Maud," said Verity.

"Never mind, Maud," said Esther. "There are times when self-approval must be enough."

"I did not know that such a feeling came into the matter, Esther."

"I must stop you all and fasten my coat," said Gwendolen. "Adela does not take as much care of me as she does of Clemence."

"Clemence must have found it odd, when she came to school, to do things for herself," said Esther.

"Well, she has soon forgotten again," said Verity.

"Oh, Adela does not always fuss over me like that. She was making an impression on guests. And it does not make much difference, with my kind of dressing."

"Why do you have a special kind?" said Esther.

"Oh, I do not know. I did not know I had until I went to school. I think it is a sort of family custom."

"You knew you had those, when you came to school," said Esther.

"The shabbiness of a duchess!" said Verity. "I will not emulate it until I become one."

"Clemence made no such implication," said Maud.

"It is odd to see Miss Firebrace in the house," said Esther. "I wonder how she likes not being deferred to by everyone."

"I should always just defer to her," said Gwendolen.

"That is what I did this time," said Clemence. "It was easier not to change."

"And the difference in your age and position does give a certain basis to the relation," said Maud. "Though an assumption of general deference might be the danger of a situation like hers."

"Was there any mention of what happened at school, Clemence?" said Esther, with more than her usual suddenness.

"Oh, it was in the atmosphere at first. But it soon passed off. School is only school, after all. And I suppose that was what was felt."

"I should hardly have thought that implication was in place, Clemence," said Maud. "About your father I cannot say, as we talked of other things, but your mother seemed interested in education, and anxious for your success."

"Oh, yes, she has a serious mind in her way. In a sense she is ambitious for us, though it is difficult to know what she wants. She does not seem to know, herself. She had Miss Firebrace thrust upon her as a ready-made relation, and that did not prejudice her in favour of what she represents. She has made every effort to get over the bias, and with a good deal of success; she does not show it, as you say. But one term of school for us was enough for her. It was easy to see that."

"It sounds as if an afternoon with Miss Chancellor might make it all too much," said Verity.

"Oh, I think she likes talking to Miss Chancellor. That easy, obvious intellectualism is just the thing. Not that it would be, if she had had different opportunities, because it would not."

"You never used to strike that disparaging note about Miss Chancellor at school, Clemence," said Maud. "And as you have not seen her since you left, it can hardly have much foundation."

"It is seeing her suddenly with people outside the school. It seems to show her as she is."

"Do we all stand exposed in this merciless light?" said Verity.

"Well, I had not seen you in it before. But then neither had you seen me with my family. We all know more about each other now. These things are the same on both sides."

"I am frightened," said Gwendolen. "Clemence has a hidden self."

"Which would you put higher as an educationist, Clemence, Miss Petticott or Miss Chancellor?" said Maud, in an even tone.

"Oh, the dear old Petticoat! I do not compare her with other people. She is just herself."

"We honour you for the sentiment," said Verity.

"Maud, are you honouring Clemence?" said Gwendolen.

"I am a most appreciative guest, Gwendolen. But this is

a matter by itself. You made a great advance when you came under Miss Chancellor, Clemence. Are you taking that into account?"

"Yes, but not too much. It was more than I should have made, if I had not had the foundation. That rather points to something in Miss Petticott."

"When things are pointed to, ought we to see them?" said Verity.

"No, of course not. Not in Miss Petticott's case. None of you would see anything about her at first. No ordinary person would."

"I can't help my own nature," said Gwendolen, giggling. "I find I like Maud to be called ordinary. I wish I were a better girl."

"I have no objection to being included in that category, Gwendolen."

"Oh, nonsense, everyone has," said Verity. "How Clemence does despise us all! No wonder she wanted to leave the school. I wonder she asked us here today. I suppose she imagined that her better nature would triumph."

"I do think you want a good deal of appreciation of yourselves and the school."

"I like a little for myself," said Gwendolen. "And I somehow feel I am having it. I think Clemence is one of those good hostesses who attend to the wants of their guests without seeming to do so."

"Did your father mind what happened to you at school, Clemence?" said Esther.

"Oh, he seemed to think it was a natural thing. He said it always happened when he was a boy. He seemed to see it as quite ordinary."

"I know who your grandfather is," said Gwendolen. "I mean the man who is not your grandfather. I am not too stupid to understand. And I was beginning to think I was."

"I was beginning to think you all were," said Clemence.

"Does your mother mind his living here?" said Esther.

"Well, I do not suppose she would choose it. She has

272

been very good about it. I think my father is grateful to her."

"She must like having his gratitude," said Gwendolen. "I think it would be an ample reward. He was an angel with us, and with the boys, and with the matrons, and a different sort of angel with each. How nice the other matron is! I like matrons much better than other people."

Miss Petticott's figure was seen advancing across the grass.

"Now it is sad to interrupt your walk and talk, but tea has to be early because of the trains."

The girls turned at once, attached Miss Petticott to their line with an ease than ranked her with the matrons, and proceeded towards the house; and she accompanied them with a springy step that was the result of the latter's companionship.

"It is pleasant to eat for so much of the day," said Gwendolen, as they came to the table. "At school we have such long breaks from food."

"Well, really, Gwendolen, what impression will you give?" said Miss Chancellor, who herself gave one of unwittingly finding herself where she was.

"I hope you did not catch cold in the park," said Maria. "I saw you from the window and wished you would run about. Perhaps you kept each other warm."

"We always go about linked up like that, Lady Shelley," said Gwendolen, "even at school, where the staircase is not wide enough to allow of it. I do not know how we manage."

"I have never quite solved the problem, Gwendolen," said Miss Chancellor.

"I wondered how it was done, when I first got to school," said Clemence. "I was at the end of the line and wondered what would happen to me. But nothing did."

"Clemence despises the school ways," said Verity, causing Maria to turn fond eyes on her daughter. "She has asked us here today with contempt in her heart."

"You should not speak true words in jest," said Esther.

"Verity is rather speaking untrue words in earnest," said Maud. "And that she clearly should not do."

"I wish I had taught in a girls' school instead of a boys'," said Oliver. "It would have done much more for me."

"Why do you not try the experiment?" said Miss Chancellor. "You could come to us as a visiting master."

"If I could not be at prayers, and jostle people in the passage, and hear housemaids sing on the stairs, I should not count it."

"I am afraid you could not fulfil that programme at our school, Mr. Shelley."

"Well, naturally, I was not thinking of any other."

"Suppose all these were my grandchildren." said Mr. Firebrace, looking round. "I might have had as many."

"Then I am sure Maria would let you have them all here," said Oliver. "But do not speak to wound me, Grandpa. I have tried to be enough for you."

"Would you like to have me for a grandfather, my dear?" said Mr. Firebrace to Gwendolen.

"Well, I don't much like having people for grandfathers. I have two for them, and they say I am brought up in the modern way."

"They ought to be ashamed of themselves."

"It is me they are ashamed of, and it is embarrassing to cause shame. I do not mind feeling it. One has to get used to that."

"These are three good boys, Miss James," said Oliver. "I think I remember them."

"You remember Sturgeon," said Bacon, "because you asked him about the potted meat."

"I remembered the potted meat, and wondered what reminded me of it, and found it was Sturgeon. Do you remember the potted meat, Miss James?"

"No, it is the kind of thing one forgets, Mr. Shelley."

"And you remember Holland," said Bacon, "because you asked him about his music."

"And I remember you. You are the boy who tends upwards. How I have proved my social memory! It is a thing one should always possess. I think I am really at the mercy of it."

"Do you all enjoy your school life?" said Maria, to the girls.

"It is not the life that I mind, as much as the advantages," said Gwendolen. "I do find those a great strain."

"I enjoy it to the full, Lady Shelley, and do so consciously," said Maud. "I realise that it will not last for ever."

"I wish I could," said Verity. "Some things seem never to come true. I envy Maud her simple faith."

"Do you think I am depriving Clemence of something she ought to have?"

"I expect you are," said Gwendolen. "People ought to have advantages. They are like plain, wholesome food, and not too much excitement. It is the duty of parents to attend to it."

"What do you think, Miss Chancellor, if I have not asked you before? Anyhow I ask you again."

"Well, Gwendolen and I are not often of one mind. I usually find myself correcting her views. But this time I am of her opinion, though I should not express it quite in her way."

"Do you think I am thinking of myself and not of Clemence?"

"No one who knows you even as well as I do, could think that, Lady Shelley. Thinking of yourself has not played a large part in your life."

"I am thinking of Clemence and of myself as well," said Sir Roderick. "Why should not we both be considered? Answer me that, Miss Chancellor. I mean, do you not see it as a reasonable view?"

"In the matter of education the young person claims the thought, Sir Roderick. Her future is involved, as the older person's is not."

"But my present is involved, and there is nothing else for

me. And Clemence does not want to leave her father."

"I shall break down in the train," said Gwendolen, "because it is all so sad."

"Well, it is no good to think that life can always be as we would choose it, Gwendolen."

"Talking of trains," said Maria, rising, "I fear the moment has come to consider them. I could not face Miss Firebrace if you missed yours."

"Does not Aunt Lesbia conduct her own party?" said Oliver.

"I am going later, Oliver," said Lesbia, holding her eyes from this group.

"I should be reluctant to encounter her myself, Lady Shelley, at the head of a line of bestranded charges," said Miss Chancellor. "Now we all want to thank you for quite a memorable day."

"I have liked everything better than anything else," said Gwendolen. "I have not considered anyone but myself, and I have not eaten a single wholesome thing."

"Thank you so much for a day of so many pleasures," said Maud, suggesting that other tastes had been met.

"If school life were often like this," said Verity, "we should not long for it to be over."

"One of its advantages is its opportunities for making friends," said Miss Chancellor. "To-day has been an illustration of it."

"Why do you not come to the school functions with your mother, Clemence?" said Esther, awkwardly keeping her eyes from Maria. "Then we should see you both."

"I have a message from Miss Laurence for you, Clemence," said Miss Chancellor, slightly lowering her tones. "Quite a deep little message, that I hope you will carry with you into your life. She says she will think of you as rising on stepping-stones, of which one may perhaps be said to be laid by herself. Will you remember that, and let me tell her that you will?"

"Yes," said Clemence, seeing through Miss Chancellor's

276

eyes a living thread spring up in the mesh of her future.

"Why, this is not a member of the party, is it?" said Sir Roderick, failing to recognise Miss Tuke in her outdoor clothes. "Why, yes, of course, the matron; that is the most important work of all. Now do not catch cold, Miss Tuke; we want you to take care of yourself as well as other people." He adjusted Miss Tuke's coat and fastened the collar.

"Good-bye," said Holland, to the girls.

"Good-bye," said the latter, smiling at him and then at each other.

"Good-bye," said the other boys on a compliant note.

Sefton said nothing, feeling that Clemence's brother must say more, if he spoke at all, and the girls kept their eyes from him with something of the same feeling.

Clemence and her parents stood on the steps. Oliver mounted the box of the carriage as escort. The six guests were accommodated inside, by dint of a sacrifice of Miss Tuke, which by her own account she found congenial. As the girls waited on the platform with Oliver, they made some terse remarks in distinct tones, and Miss Chancellor responded in a similar manner. When the train moved out of the station, a different note was struck.

"Which do you like better, Miss Chancellor, Sir Roderick or Lady Shelley?"

"Well, Gwendolen, comparisons are odious, and I think may really be so in the case of two people whom we can like so well. I think I should class Lady Shelley as the higher type; but Sir Roderick has his own charm; and that is a thing that goes far with many people, perhaps further with some than with me. I think we need not decide between them.

"I wondered why I liked him better," said Gwendolen. "Of course it was because he was a lower type. That would be my reason."

"What do you think of Sir Roderick's way of calling Lady Shelley 'my pretty', Miss Chancellor? Do you think it is a fortunate one?"

"Well, Esther, as I have implied, I should not be inclined to criticise people of that quality. I think it suggests his own point of view, and does so with the ease and openness that would be expected of him, and might not be possible in anyone of another calibre. The matter is between themselves, and may be left so."

"But those are the matters we do not want to leave," said Gwendolen. "It is easy to know about the others."

"Do you suppose Lady Shelley minds, Miss Chancellor?"

"No, Verity, I think she is too large a woman to mind any superficial incongruity in a term used as this one is. I am sure we need not trouble about her inconvenience, as she suffers none."

"Would you like her position, Miss Chancellor? How would you feel about being a second wife?"

"Well, Verity, my own feeling is that I should not like it," said Miss Chancellor, settling her glasses to look straight at her questioner. "I admit that, if I were to marry, I should look for the experience in its fullest form. But that is my own point of view. There is no reason why Lady Shelley and I should be copies of each other."

"Anyhow their Maker saw none," murmured Esther. "And I daresay Lady Shelley feels with him."

"I daresay she does, Esther," said Miss Chancellor, in a pleasant tone, as the train slackened and left Esther's voice clear. "Indeed, I hope she does, as she has chosen to fulfil herself so differently. No one hopes more than I do, that her life seems to her as full as it can be. If fuller than mine, then be it so. I am the last person to grudge her the conviction, or indeed the reality. Do you not feel with me, Miss Tuke?"

"Certainly, Miss Chancellor," said Miss Tuke, not sounding quite sure of her ground.

"The two lives offer and ask such different things," said Maud. "They do not meet on any point. It is not a very fruitful theme for comparison."

278

"It was Lady Shelley's being a second wife that we wanted to talk about," said Gwendolen. "I think that theme would have been fruitful, full of prying and gossip and a naughty sort of pity."

"Well, really, Gwendolen, after your pleasant day! I am quite ashamed of you."

"But you said you would never be a second wife yourself, Miss Chancellor."

"I am not aware that I said quite that. But as I have no thought at the moment of being a wife at all, the matter may be outside my sphere."

"Have you had many proposals, Miss Chancellor?"

"Really, Gwendolen, the effect of excitement on you is not very happy."

"But I did not ask you how many proposals you had had. I asked if you had had many. That is quite different."

"I see your distinction, Gwendolen. But as at your age you cannot have had any, you need not concern yourself with the subject."

"Is Miss Chancellor embarrassed by really having had many proposals, or by having had none?" said Esther, again unfortunate in the moment of her speech.

"Esther, I find myself laughing before I know," said Miss Chancellor, not in time to check a peal, and speaking with a light in her eyes. "You had better talk to each other and not to me, as I seem to set your thoughts running on romantic lines. Holidays in the term are not to be recommended."

"Oh, please recommend them, Miss Chancellor; please do not say that to Miss Firebrace."

"Well, do not let us hear your voice so often, Gwendolen. That will be the best way to ensure the result."

"I will not open my mouth again. Miss Chancellor, do you think Sir Roderick would often think of his first marriage?"

"The elder son must think of it," said Esther.

"I cannot give an opinion, Gwendolen. I am not such an

authority on romantic matters as you seem to think."

"Did you notice the view from the dining-room windows, Miss Chancellor?" said Maud, in the tone of a rescuer. "It reminded me of an old picture."

"A Constable, Maud, though not a very early one. I hoped it would strike you in that way. Did anyone else think of it?"

"I saw it as a view, but not as a Constable," said Esther. "And, after all, it was not one."

"It struck me as belonging to his later period," said Verity.

"Why did you not tell me, Miss Chancellor?" said Gwendolen. "I did not know about a Constable; I believe I thought it was some sort of policeman. And I am willing to learn."

"Now I am going to forget you all for a time," said Miss Chancellor, closing her eyes to ensure this prospect, "and lose myself, as the expression goes. And I should advise you all to do the same. I see Miss Tuke has set us the example."

There was silence until Miss Chancellor had followed it.

"Is pleasure really exhausting?" said Gwendolen.

"I do not know," said Esther. "I have never had enough of it to judge. Miss Chancellor was quite excited by the idea of having had many proposals. I suppose it shows she has not had one."

"Well, I think the idea is exciting," said Gwendolen.

"I think you deduce a good deal from very slight premises, Esther," said Maud.

"Straws show which way the wind blows," said Verity.

"I should advise you to modify your voices. People are apt to be awakened suddenly in a train. It is not a homogeneous method of travelling. Indeed, it is a good rule to say behind people's backs what you would say to their faces."

"We cannot judge of it," said Verity, "as it is not a rule."

"It certainly has a good many exceptions."

"It is no good to think it consists of anything else," said Esther. "Do you think Clemence is happy in her home? I was not quite sure."

"I see no reason why she should not be," said Maud. "She certainly looks better than she did at school, anyhow at the last."

"She was involved in a good deal of trouble then. I wonder if she ever thinks of it."

"You saw that she should do so to-day, Esther, the day on which we were accepting her hospitality. I confess I was sorry about it. Was it a gracious way of responding to her kindness, to bring up the one thing known to her disadvantage?"

"Our being there was bound to remind her of it," said Verity.

"But should not that have been enough? It was a thing to regret, not to bring further home."

"I hope it will not prevent her asking us again," said Gwendolen, as the train drew in to the station. "How gloomy it is to get home after a holiday!"

"It is gloomy to get to school," said Esther.

"It is gloomy to see how spoilt people can be by one day's pleasure," said Miss Chancellor, rising in the mood of awaking, and ushering the girls to the door. "There are your gloves, Esther. Gwendolen, do you intend to walk to school without a hat? I do not know why Miss Tuke should wait on you all. Thank you, Maud."

"I wish we could have a cab," said Gwendolen.

"Miss Tuke cannot wish it," said Verity. "It would be smaller than the Shelley carriage, and more than one person would have to sit on the top of her."

"Why on Miss Tuke rather than on anyone else?" said Miss Chancellor. "It does not do to depend on the unselfishness of one person. And, Gwendolen, too much reliance on luxury is not a sign of quality or breeding, and would not be so considered."

"It is only a sign of weariness, Miss Chancellor. I mean

it is a sign of healthy tiredness. Pleasure does not do me any harm. I shall work all the better tomorrow for it. I always like lessons when we are not supposed to have prepared for them."

"I hope that forecast will come true, Gwendolen. And I admit that pleasure has its exhausting side, like anything else. I ought to know, as I have enjoyed the day as much as you have. But I am not like you in preferring to come to work without preparation. I look forward to my share of it, as well as to yours, with a certain misgiving."

"I wish we could live at Clemence's home, while we are not welcome in our own," said Esther. "I don't mean that she would like to have us, but I believe Lady Shelley would."

This was hardly a correct estimate of Maria's feeling, as she showed on her return from speeding her daughter's guests.

"How exhausting half-grown creatures are!" she said, smiling at the boys as creatures wholly ungrown. "You do not know whether they are going to talk as women or children; and it is always one or the other, and never the thing they are. But they are all very nice, Clemence, my dear. And how much they seem to like you! You went a long way in the time. People cannot say now that you have no friends. Which of them do you like the best?"

"Well, I was only with them for one term," said Clemence, while Lesbia smiled to herself over the fleeting experience. "And we were always together, so that it was difficult to know them separately. I think perhaps Gwendolen, though she was not as clever as the others, or was supposed not to be."

"The happy one who was going to cry in the train?" said Sir Roderick. "I suppose she is up and down."

"I like the tall one," said Holland.

"Verity. She is a handsome girl," said Maria. "But how advanced for her age! She seems to be missing her childhood."

"The one in the grey dress seemed an interesting type," said Miss Petticott. "I was struck by her conversation. Maud I think was the name."

"She was struck by it herself," said Bacon. "I thought at first she was a mistress."

"Did you think they were all mistresses?" said Sir Roderick to Sturgeon.

"No. Two of them I knew were not."

"They did not worry you much," said Maria. "I suppose they found you too young."

"They did not find us anything," said Bacon, grinning. "They took no steps to do so."

"You did not manage much of an approach yourselves," said Sir Roderick.

"It was not for us to make the advance," said Holland.

"Did you admire them?"

"No," said Bacon.

"I did," said Holland.

"And so did I," said his host. "As pretty a group as could be wanted by man or boy. I cannot imagine Lesbia lording it over them. I mean, I cannot picture you ordering them here and there and everywhere, Lesbia."

"Is that what I did, Clemence?" said Lesbia, hardly moving her head.

"No," said Clemence, smiling. "You believed in self-government."

"You rascal! You saw the whole thing with a twinkle in your eye," said Sir Roderick, feeling that this disposed of any idea of his daughter's losing by the change in her life.

"Clemence has a keen sense of humour," said Miss Petticott. "I confess I kept on thinking of things she had told me, while her guests were here. I hope I did not betray myself."

Lesbia's eyes rested on Miss Petticott.

"No, no, Miss Petticoat. You talked to the two who did not matter," said Sir Roderick. "Who did not mind, I should say. And here is Miss James still with us. She would always be kind, I am sure. I hope she need not leave us just yet. Would you like to look after girls instead of boys, Miss James?"

"Well, boys are my speciality, Sir Roderick. We matrons are specialists as much as anyone else. And the matron in a boys' school has a rather unique position. Her being the only woman on the staff throws her into several kinds of prominence. In a girls' school she tends to become a mere character for attending on people."

"Is Miss Tuke that? I thought she was nice," said Bacon.

"And so she was," said Miss James. "You are quite right to think so, and to say what you think. She may be in danger of becoming rather too nice. That is what I meant."

"I should have thought you might be too," said Bacon.

"Oh, ah, Miss James, you are given away," said Sir Roderick. "You are betrayed by the hand that fed you, by one of those whom your hand has fed. I do not doubt that he is right. There is more give than take in your life, I am sure."

"Well, that position may have its own privileges, Sir Roderick. Indeed, it may itself constitute a privilege. And my life, as I have said, includes those of another kind."

"I am sure of it, Miss James. And quite right too. It would be very wrong if it did not. I hope Miss Tuke has a fair deal, I am sure."

"I did not mean to imply that she had not, Sir Roderick. Unfairness did not come into my mind. I was only making a sort of generalisation, a thing that perhaps one should not do, as it may result in a false impression."

"We are too ready to deduce the particular from the general."

"Exactly, Sir Roderick. Those would be my very words."

"But they were not," murmured Bacon.

"You make me feel that Sefton must be dull without you

all," said Maria. "Do you think his life is a dreary one?"

"No," said Sturgeon, seeing it as consisting of days like the present one. "But it could not always be a holiday."

"Every day at home would be a half-holiday at school," said Sefton.

"The hours at school are too long," said his father.

"Yes, they are," said Bacon.

"You would learn more in shorter ones. Or you would learn as much."

"No, we should learn less. But we should like it better. People do not so much like to learn."

"I cannot think how your parents can part with you all," said Maria.

"It is for our good," said Holland. "They have to make the sacrifice."

"And you are grateful to them?"

"Yes," said three voices on a dutiful note.

"And are they grateful to you for being such good boys?"

"No," said Bacon, opening his eyes.

"You do not have much trouble, do you, Miss James?" said Sir Roderick. "And the credit for that is largely yours, I am sure."

"Well, things are not always quite as the moment may suggest. There are two sides to every picture, and more than that to the nature of boys."

"And if anyone knows all sides of it, you do."

"Well, I have got to the stage when they seem to repeat themselves, and that probably shows that my knowledge is pretty complete."

"What would you all do without Miss James?" said Sir Roderick, with a faint note of reproach.

"Even the masters could not do without her," said Sturgeon.

"Do you think I am wrong to take Sefton away from school, Miss James?" said Maria.

"Yes, in the sense of mistaken, Lady Shelley."

"My wife acts first, and asks advice afterwards," said

285

Sir Roderick. "What she wants is support of her own opinion, and she cannot always have it."

"I am afraid I am rather an uncompromising person to face with a straight question, Sir Roderick. I am likely to give a straight answer. I think that shows more respect for the person who asks it. People are apt to say the right thing, to feel they can do nothing, and may as well present themselves in a welcome light. But I do not claim to be a person who oils the wheels of the world. It might be better if I were; I make no claim."

"Does she make none?" said Bacon.

"Ah, you are a brave girl, my dear," said Mr. Firebrace, in an automatic manner.

The boys met each other's eyes.

"She cannot help what the old man said," said Bacon.

There was a sound of people's entering the house, and Oliver came into the room accompanied by Mr. Spode.

"Why, Mr. Spode, this is a pleasure indeed," said Sir Roderick. "We hardly felt we could hope for it."

"Why, my boy, my boy," said Mr. Firebrace, rising and advancing with outstretched hands.

"I have come to conduct our party home. Cassidy felt that Miss James should have an escort. It came to him after she had gone."

"Well, her companions are young to be seen in that light," said Sir Roderick.

"The dusk is gathering," said Mr. Spode on his deeper note.

"Well, I am not sorry to see you, Mr. Spode. I will not claim to be," said Miss James, rising as she voiced her welcome. "As you say, it is getting dusk, and reminding us that our pleasant day is at an end. And very young people are not more manageable after excitement."

Mr. Spode almost glanced at the young people involved.

"You have not met my wife," said Sir Roderick. "She was not with us the last time you were here. I am glad for you to know each other."

"Why, we already do that," said Mr. Spode, advancing to Maria. "We met in that jeweller's shop behind the school. I remember it as if it were yesterday. I was selling an earring, and you were to provide one like it. They made a pair, and the transaction was a great success. And I was given another here to take the place of the first. So they all came from this house. You must have had a collection of them. My mother was grateful for the earring, sir. She told me to say, if I saw you, that she would never part with it. And that means a great deal from her, as it is her nature to part with things."

"I hope she will put it to any use she likes," said Mr. Firebrace.

"Did you have it adapted, before you gave it to her?" said Oliver.

"No," said Mr. Spode. "That is a thing that is never done."

"Sit down and have some tea, Mr. Spode," said Maria, in her usual tones, keeping her eyes on the guest. "We will have it fresh in a moment. I hope you are not in a hurry to leave us."

"Mr. Spode will have to—I am afraid our train is due in half an hour," said Miss James. "I expect he had his tea before he came."

"It was doled out to me at an early hour."

"It sounds as if it might be supplemented," said Sir Roderick, "I hope there is time for that."

"Was it not enough?" said Miss James. "Not that I should broach our domestic problems here. But I expect you had a little tray to yourself."

"That is what it was. And solitude is not completely satisfying, though I find it so up to a point. But you are right that we should go."

"Well, we must bow to necessity," said Sir Roderick. "We will depend on better fortune another time."

"We might well have it," murmured Oliver.

"Your cap, Sturgeon," said Mr. Spode.

"On my head, sir," said Sturgeon, putting up his hand.

Mr. Spode did not contradict him, and he snatched off the cap.

"Now, boys," said Miss James.

"Thank you very much," said Bacon, shaking hands with Maria.

"Thank you very much for our happy day," said Holland.

"Thank you," said Sturgeon, looking down and twirling the cap.

"I should like to kiss you all," said Maria, on a faintly reckless note.

Mr. Spode looked surprised, but glanced at the boys, as if they were available for any purpose of hers.

"But I suppose I must not."

"No," said Bacon. "But thank you very much for it all."

"I don't mind," murmured Sturgeon, and flushed as Maria did not hear, and his companions did.

"Thank you once again," said Holland.

Miss James was handed into the carriage. Mr. Spode settled himself at her side, as though his obligations ended here. Miss James leaned across him and directed the boys to seats. As the carriage followed the curve of the drive, Juliet came from some bushes and hurried into the house.

"I am here in time to conduct the scene. I did not know Mr. Spode was coming. Lucius sent him as an afterthought, and I was not in time to prevent it. I caught the quick train and got the guard to stop it for me. I got out of the cab at the gates and waited in the bushes until they had gone. I hope the scene has not broken. I have told you enough, for you to give it all your minds."

There was a pause.

"Yes, do what you can for us, my dear," said Mr. Firebrace. "We do need some help."

"Come and join us at the fire, my pretty," said Sir Roderick to his wife.

"So you are worthy of the name of a man, Roderick,"

said Juliet. "I thought you would be, but one can never be quite sure. As there is no problem for you, there is none for anyone; for Maria least of all. How much do you know, and how much do you want to be told? There must be the questions, and the answers can be quick and complete. The whole truth can be revealed."

The questions came uncertainly, Mr. Firebrace's the most direct and full. Juliet answered them simply, without explanation or comment. Sir Roderick kept his eyes down, now and then raising them openly to his wife. He was the only person who asked none.

"I had heard of a woman's power of sacrifice," said Oliver, "but I had not met an example of it. I had come to wonder if it existed. And Maria, of all people, to sacrifice her principles! Perhaps it is an instance of the supreme sacrifice. I had heard of that too."

"My dear, good wife!" said Sir Roderick.

"This is what I hoped," said Juliet. "My anxiety was simply lest Maria should not have enough praise. The danger seemed to be that people might be grudging with it. But you are all on my own level, the especial level I had arranged for the situation. We are all on it together, and of course Maria as well."

Maria covered her face and broke into weeping.

"Come, come, my dear," said Mr. Firebrace, "it is not so much. You had not enough money to pay for the farm, though you had thought and saved to get it. The trinket was serving no purpose, and served that one of yours. You were doing no harm to anyone, and good to your husband. That is how you saw it. And a woman does not see the abstract principles behind."

"Of course she does," said Maria, without lifting her head. "She sees them as much as a man, and often acts on them more. I knew I was doing a dishonest thing. I simply yielded to temptation. I meant at first to tell you of the earring in the shop, and suggest that you should send your own. What I did was an afterthought."

"What a light thing it sounds!" said Oliver. "And that is what it is, of course."

"I reproached my poor children for their innocent deception. I was indeed the person to blame them!"

"Children are always reproached for doing what we do ourselves. What else could they be reproached for? They must have some bringing-up, and that consists of reproach. A term as a schoolmaster shows you that. And without it they would yield too much to their instincts. You see we yield enough, as it is. I do not mean Maria, of course. She yielded to just the right extent."

Sir Roderick took one of his wife's hands from her face, and held it in his. His face was dark and set, and might have belied his action, if she had seen it. But he knew that she did not see.

"Aunt Juliet is the heroine of the story," said Oliver. "If it were written, it would bear her name. She is the only person who has lost anything. But I gather she has one earring left. Who would have thought one pair would go so far? No wonder Spode thought we had a collection. You would think the pair bred."

"The earrings are the chief sufferers," said Lesbia, speaking for the first time. "They have lost the name of being unique, when they have every right to it."

"It is a trivial sort of a tale," said Mr. Firebrace.

"What a shallow word!" said his grandson. "When the facts are trivial, and it is itself rooted in the depths. It is the sort of thing that is a test, and you have failed."

"Of course we ought to pay the debt to Juliet," said Maria. "But she would not consent."

"I think we may leave Juliet in her place," said Sir Roderick. "It carries its reward."

"Father, I never thought to hear you say a mean thing."

"But we seem to get things out of the position," said Maria.

"And so we do," said her stepson. "Everything has its

bright side. Why should this be an exception, though I should almost have thought it might be? Father has the farm. You have the honour of giving it to him, and many other kinds of honour. Aunt Juliet has her own kind. Spode has an earring for his mother. I have had interest and excitement; it is dreadful, but I have had them; and Grandpa has too. The children will have understanding. I do not know what Aunt Lesbia has had."

"I have had a shock, Oliver," said Lesbia, with quiet distinctness. "And I do not think I am paying any less tribute to Maria than the rest of you, when I say that."

"I think you are," said Oliver.

"So, Miss Petticoat, you have been in the room all the time?" said Sir Roderick.

"Well, Sir Roderick, I did not know what to do. I was following the children upstairs, when Mrs. Cassidy arrived; and I paused to say the conventional things, and found myself involved in the group before I knew. I could not escape without attracting attention, and it seemed better to avoid that. No one seemed to notice me, and I hoped I was such a familiar figure, that I should not be noticed any more than the furniture———"

There was silence, as it was realised that this had largely been the case.

"Oh, come, Miss Petticoat, you are more to us than that," said Sir Roderick. "And as regards discretion, we can rely on you as much—you will not betray us any more than . . . than as you say."

"Need you ask, Sir Roderick? Am I a stranger to you?"

"Of course she is not," murmured Juliet. "She has told him what she is."

"And he seemed to follow her," said Oliver.

"Do you feel you can remain with me, Miss Petticott?" said Maria.

"Do not hurt me, Lady Shelley. What do I know of your mutual lives, or of your claims upon each other?"

"That is a wise word," said Mr. Firebrace. "After all

I have taken here, anything that is mine is theirs."

"He gave what was his to Spode," murmured Oliver. "But it is nice to give it twice, so ungrudging. How the best is being brought out of everyone! Generally it only comes out of one person, as it did out of Maria."

"Miss Petticott knows better," said Maria. "And I am glad she does. If she did not, I could not leave the children in her hands."

"Poor Miss Petticott! A middle course is so unrewarding. Or anyhow so unrewarded."

"I do not ask reward, Mr. Shelley."

"But you have it, Miss Petticoat," said Sir Roderick, in a rather loud tone. "In our trust and affection and the other things worth having."

"Father, do think what you are saying," said Oliver. "We shall not know where to look."

"I wish Lucius was here," said Juliet. "We could depend so upon his silence."

"It would be no good to us," said her nephew. "Silence never does what has to be done. It would not show that we think nothing of the matter. It is not true that it is golden."

Sir Roderick looked at his son with the expression that was almost of gratitude. He had not wished for his silence.

"There is almost too much of this generosity," said Maria, with a break in her voice. "It would mean more, if there were less. All this care to avoid looking at the truth only means it cannot be faced."

"But it can be," said her stepson. "It has to be, to be grasped at all. I have never met a matter that called for closer attention."

"There, there, my pretty, we have been clumsy, have we?" said Sir Roderick.

"You may have, Father. It is a thing I could not be. It is a quality that Maria likes, and I do see her point of view."

"She does not want a too tactful and easy smoothing over of things. She is too honest to want anything but honesty in other people."

"Honest!" said Maria.

"We never get honesty by itself," said Juliet. "It is inseparable from other things, and the last ones to be coupled with it. Do not insist upon it, Maria. It would show us in such a bad light, and we have been so careful to present ourselves in a good one."

"Yes, care has been taken," said Lesbia.

"By you as well, Aunt Lesbia."

"No, I do not think so, Oliver. I think I have appeared in an unconsidered one."

"I am not going to pose as an authority upon honesty," said Maria.

"Or to pose at all, my pretty. It is not in you. I know how you have wanted to make a clean breast of it all."

"Have you really, Maria?" said Oliver. "I should so like to know."

"Of course I have not. I could easily have done it. I meant the truth to remain hidden."

"Easily have done it! No, no, no," said Mr. Firebrace.

"Well, most truth does remain so," said Oliver. "Think what would happen if it did not."

"I do want to think," said Juliet. "I have often thought."

"We know in one case," said Maria.

"There, there, my dear. Your nerves are all on edge," said Sir Roderick. "And I do not wonder."

"Ought you not to wonder, Father? You are losing the thread of things. I am in rather a carping mood. It is because I was accused of clumsiness."

"It seems to me a mild accusation," said Maria. "What could I be accused of? I have been accused of clumsiness all my life, and never been the worse."

"Not by me, my pretty, not by me," said Sir Roderick.

"Anyone who finds you so in any deep matter must be a poor judge, Lady Shelley," said Miss Petticott.

"And it is a disgrace to excel in anything on the surface," said Juliet.

"When people are sound at bottom," said Mr.

Firebrace, "who cares for so much smoothness on the top?"

"Now they have all accused Maria of clumsiness," said Lesbia to Juliet, hardly moving her lips. "And, as she says, she is none the worse. I wonder if she is better."

"My children will not know what I have done," said Maria. "And they had to face my knowing what they had. How the heavier burdens fall on the helpless!"

"People who are not helpless would avoid them," said Oliver.

"I actually did not think of my own stumble, when we were dealing with theirs. I gave the money to Roderick on that very day. I was as dishonest with myself as I was with other people."

"Then clearly they have no cause to complain," said Juliet. "That is a very rare equality."

"You are upset, Maria, and hardly know what you say," said her husband. "And I am sure you have every reason."

"Of course she has not," said Juliet. "She has so little reason, that I am going to give her more trouble and stay for the night."

"I also should like to stay with you, Maria," said Lesbia.

"Well, that is good news," said Sir Roderick. "It will help us through what might have been an awkward evening. I mean it will be good for Maria to have your company, as she has been out of heart."

"I wish Father would say what he means," said Oliver.

"Does Lucius know you are here, my dear?" said Mr. Firebrace to Juliet.

"Yes, I told him I was coming. He did not ask for reasons. If he ever does, he can have one."

"There is to be a secret between husband and wife," said Lesbia.

"There is none between my wife and me," said Sir Roderick. "And I do not thank Mr. Spode for it. I do not call this thing a secret. Maria did not want the left hand to know what the right hand was doing, did not want me to know how much she had done for me."

"Of course it is not a secret," said Juliet. "No one would count it."

"I did not see Miss Petticoat go," said Sir Roderick.

"I think I felt she was gone," said Juliet. "We know that we do not see her. She has explained."

"A nice woman," said Sir Roderick. "Sound at heart. I was glad there were some people on her own level here for her to-day."

"I had forgotten it was a festal occasion," said Oliver. "Somehow nothing reminds me of it."

"We ought to compare her to Miss Chancellor," said Maria. "She manages the children's education. The people she talked to were the matrons."

"And none the worse for that," said Sir Roderick. "Any more than the other one was the better for what she was. Of all the people here today, she was the one I was not quite sure of. I am a judge of people in my way."

Lesbia rested her eyes on him with uncertain lips, as though he might not be this in other people's.

"This hopeless trouble of mine has prevented our discussion of everything," said Maria.

"Postponed it," said her husband. "It will last us for several days. There were eleven guests without Spode. I counted them."

"You are so thorough, Father," said Oliver.

"I did not have to do that, as I had arranged for them all," said Maria.

"That gave you an advantage," said Lesbia. "I did have to."

"How did you manage it without looking at them?" said Oliver.

"It was only at the girls that she did not look," said Sir Sir Roderick. "And she knew the number of those."

"People certainly looked at me," said Lesbia, laughing. "I wonder I did not get counted twice."

"Those dear little boys!" said Maria. "I only just kept from embracing them."

"Grandpa kept from embracing several people," said Oliver. "I saw him keeping from it."

"And that was a dear child with the round face."

"Gwendolen," said Lesbia, easily. "We have had her with us for years. It has been interesting to see her go from stage to stage."

"She seemed so fond of Clemence. I wonder if Clemence would really be better with friends about her."

"This day has put us back for months," said Oliver. "I knew it would."

"Not if you hold to your advance," said Lesbia. "Do not let it go."

"She is better at home," said Sir Roderick. "The life amongst numbers is too much for her. She was pale and tired at the end of today. I noticed it. If anyone understands her, I do."

"Miss Chancellor and Miss Petticott hardly exchanged a word," said Maria. "I do not know how that happened. They were the natural pair to come together."

"Ah, Miss Petticott knew better," said Sir Roderick. "She knew where she was safe. Trust a woman's instinct. And you were talking to Miss Chancellor, or she was to you. Someone had to talk to the housekeepers. Miss Petticoat threw herself into the breach, and enjoyed her day. And I was glad for her to have a change."

"It seems that a man's instinct would have done as well," said Oliver.

"You put her on the housekeepers' level," said Maria. "And she should rank with the mistresses, if she is in her place."

"Well, we have settled that," said Lesbia. "We will not throw doubt on it."

"If Miss Chancellor is a mistress, I rank her above them," said Sir Roderick.

"I know what you mean," said his wife. "But you know what I mean too."

"You are right, my boy. The day has put us back," said Mr. Firebrace.

"Do not let it, my dear. Keep a hand on yourself," said Sir Roderick, with some urgency. "We cannot keep on going backwards and forwards. Our family life is settled. Let it be."

"It is good advice, Maria," said Lesbia.

"We behave as if nothing had happened," said Maria. "But I know what must be in your minds."

"Forget it, my pretty. You will soon get used to the feeling."

"It had gone from my mind," said Juliet, "and left a sense of blank. And I mean a real blank with nothing in it. But it seemed such a stimulating thing, and it is fading away."

"Yielding to temptation seems so natural, that I was hardly stimulated," said Oliver.

"There, my pretty!" said Sir Roderick.

"Are there any cases of resisting it?" said Juliet. "We never hear about them, but it does not seem there can be none."

"We all withstand it all the time," said Sir Roderick.

"Well, we cannot be expected to admit that," said his son.

"We are people who are not assailed by it," said Lesbia with a smile.

"I yielded to the first real one I ever had," said Maria.

"And I suppose it hardly matters if we yield to the others," said Juliet. "That is just living day by day."

"Are we to discuss now the difference between the real ones and the others?" said Maria, on a weary note.

"Well, it would be your fault if we did," said Oliver. "And Aunt Juliet and I may be going to."

"I will take you away, Maria," said Sir Roderick. "You have borne enough. We will go away together and leave them to discuss what they must."

"They are entitled to the opportunity. And they must be ready to make the most of it. They have restrained themselves long enough."

"And if anyone is grateful to them, I am," said Sir Roderick.

"Well, we the survivors," said Oliver.

"And from what a sad, little wreck!" said Mr. Firebrace. "And the rock we struck was the young man, Spode."

"Do we think more or less of Maria?" said Juliet. "That is the interesting thing."

"We will not say we have never liked her so well," said Oliver. "That means we like people in humility and self-abasement. It is sad that it should be so common."

"Well, well, it was a woman's slip," said Mr. Firebrace. "I grudge no woman a trinket."

"No, that is true, Grandpa. You tend to be lavish with them."

"How much are we attached to Maria?" said Juliet. "I hated the idea of her being exposed."

"So did I," said Oliver. "I really admired myself for hating it so much."

"You will keep your tongue still, my boy," said Mr. Firebrace. "Your stepmother has a right to it."

"This is the first time you have given Maria that name. Is it a mark of respect at this time?"

"Well, if it is, there is no harm in it."

"I do look up to you, Grandpa. Ought I to make an effort to call her 'Mother'?"

"Can it be that you have never liked her so well, Father?" said Lesbia.

"It is himself he has never liked so well," said Oliver. "And I am sure I do not wonder."

"I wonder if we really see it as a joke," said Lesbia. "If we do not, is there any reason to pretend to?"

"If it is not a joke, there is no advantage in talking about it," said her nephew. "Understanding and pity will not give us any pleasure. They have given us none."

"They only show that we can imagine ourselves doing the same thing," said Juliet.

"Can you imagine it?" said Oliver.

"I am not sure. But I cannot imagine Maria."

"So you have never liked yourself so well either."

"Well, do you not think I am being very likeable?"

"Do you wish we could hear the talk between Roderick and Maria?" said Lesbia. "I think we do not wish it."

"If the matter is not a joke, why should we?" said Oliver. "It might become even less of a joke, and that would not do."

"I believe I could imagine that," said Juliet. "If I did not keep a hand on myself, I believe I should."

Juliet's imagination would not have served her well. As the husband and wife reached the library, Maria turned to the door.

"There is a fire in here, Roderick. There is something I want to say to you. I had better say it on this day when everything is being said. Then there will be an end of it. I feel now that I shall not always keep it to myself."

"No more confession, is there? If so, leave it unsaid. I do not want to know any more about you. I know you well enough."

"I have not made any confession. My sin simply found me out. Oliver would say you should pay more attention. But other people's sin may do the same. I am not the culprit this time."

"The poor children again? Something transpired with this invasion from the schools? I knew we should regret it."

"This trouble is not theirs. There is a father to a family as well as a mother and children."

"Well, why speak in riddles, my dear? It does not help."

"My mind is not clear about my reasons for telling you. I want to be certain of them, before I speak. It is not that I want you to be on my level as a wrong-doer, though that may come into it; and it may not be such a bad thing to have that equality between us. I think it is that I do not want to have any secret from you, even that I know something to your discredit. You said there were no secrets between us, and when this is told, there will not be, on my side. Further than that I cannot know."

"There is not much you have not known about me, Maria."

"There may be only this one thing. As I say, I cannot know. Now I am going to speak, Roderick; I am going to speak, my husband. You remember the day when the ear-ring was missed, and all that perplexity ensued. I went away to rest because I was tired, and also for the reason that we know."

"Yes, I know. How should I not? But nothing else happened on that day, or happened to you."

"Something happened to us both, Roderick. I was too tired to climb the stairs, and I rested in this room, on the sofa behind those bookcases. And I was awakened by voices, yours and Mrs. Aldom's. Need I say any more?"

"Why have you said as much? What is the good?"

"Only what I have told you. But I felt I must say it, because some day it would be said, and possibly when harm would be done. To-day it will equalise things between us, and do no more."

"I picked up your scarf in the hall. Near the door of this room. In a book that would have been a clue. But I am not a man in a book. I am one on a man's level, as I need not tell you. There is nothing in your stumble that puts you on it, my pretty, that brings you down to it."

"You have had to remember that I am a woman. Well, now I must remember that you are a man. It might be better for us both to remember that we are both human beings, liable to human error. Being a man and being a woman seem to lead along the same way."

Sir Roderick laughed.

"I seem to be talking like Oliver. And I would rather be myself."

"I would rather you were too, though the boy does well

in his way. Well I have little to say to you. I was a widower; I had been a married man; it was a simple emotion; it was before you came into my life. There is really no more to say."

Maria did not dispute this. Her next words were not her stepson's but her own.

"Are you giving Aldom's mother enough for the farm? It is not a case for driving a matter hard. There are things to take into account."

"I am giving all I can afford. And giving too much would carry its own danger."

"Giving a little more would carry none."

"I am doing that. She did not fail to ask it," said Sir Roderick, telling his wife that his romance was of the past. "And I discharged my obligations all those years ago. I had almost forgotten it."

"And Mrs. Aldom had quite done so. I wonder what else has been forgotten."

"You are better, my dear. You are more yourself. This burden is off your mind. You no longer feel the sword hanging over you."

"And neither do you. You must have felt it, since that day. What is your feeling for Aldom now? Has it altered since you knew?"

"It has and it has not," said Sir Roderick, speaking easily to cover feeling more complex than his wife supposed, and perhaps less deep. "It is difficult to change a feeling that is the growth of years. It keeps raising its head. And I must not show any difference."

"It is strange to think that you have—that there are three of them in the house."

"I have had the thought and put it from me. It is a thing that must be done."

"I had always noticed the eyes. But I did not think anything of it. We do see likenesses between people. And those very blue eyes are not uncommon about here."

"One of the girls said something of the kind. I heard them talking. She noticed the eyes too."

"I did feel at first that Aldom should go," said Maria, answering the implication. "But I found myself forgetting it. As you say, an old feeling returns."

"He has not less right to be here than he has always had."

"But surely less reason, in his present character."

"He can be here in no other."

"I hope we are doing right, Roderick. If we are doing wrong, we must go on doing it. After all, we are used to it."

"Maria, we cannot continue to have talks like this. People are about everywhere. Houses hear and see. Could I say a word in my own library without being heard? We hardly know that this one is not finding someone's ear. Miss Petticoat was present at the revelation today. This first talk must be the last. Have you anything more to say?"

"Only a little more. But more would occur to me as I said it. So perhaps it is better not said. We know the truth about each other, and know there was no excuse for it. And that must be enough."

"Well, we must leave it there," said Sir Roderick, "though I think it is rather too much. Magnets are about on all sides to draw our secrets."

"To think what the children inherit! It will be hard to train them when we feel we should expect so little."

"They seem already to have come into their heritage," said Sir Roderick, with a reckless laugh.

"And I do not know how we shall meet Miss Petticott."

"That also has happened. Though I do not think it should have. It makes me like her less."

"Something would soon have done that. You were probably unconsciously waiting for it. She did not know what the scene was to be. And when she did, she would have been riveted to the spot. She is only human, though that causes you surprise. We do like people less when they know the worst about us. Their attitude is not so flattering. But she is not to blame. We must not think of parting with her."

"We cannot think of it. She will not fail us, while we do not fail her. But loyalty is a tender plant, not an everlasting one."

"How much we know about virtue, when we practise it so little! Well, people get used to anything, though it would not often be to things like this. We will go upstairs and talk to her and the children. They will expect to discuss their day, and the ice must be broken."

Miss Petticott was reading aloud to her pupils, a scene that recalled another, and Maria fulfilled her resolve to be simply herself.

"Not asleep this time?" she said, her brows contracting in uncertain recollection.

"Why, no, Lady Shelley. We have had too exciting a day. I am sure I have," said Miss Petticott, flushing as she realised where her words might lead. "It has been nothing but pleasure from beginning to end, as someone said in a book. And the end was as good as the beginning, which can rarely be said. The interest did not flag; it gathered as the moments passed—"

"And how did the host and hostess enjoy it?"

"Very much," said Clemence, "and so did they all. When you have been at school, you know what a change it is. Sometimes it seemed as if the term would never end."

"Dear, dear, we did make a mistake," said Sir Roderick.

"And the boys enjoyed it too," said Sefton. "More than anything this term. We played at brigands in the park. Bacon was the chief. And, of course, they liked the things to eat."

"And what did they think of your home?"

"We had told them about it. None of them has a home so near."

"I am glad you had a pleasant day, Miss Petticoat," said Sir Roderick.

"Very, Sir Roderick. I quite feel I have made friends. Miss James and Miss Tuke are extremely nice women. Miss Chancellor struck me as a slightly forbidding figure, but Lady Shelley acted as a bulwark and I basely sheltered behind it. So of her I am not qualified to speak."

"A straightforward, professional woman," said Maria. "I had not met one before, and was quite well entertained. I daresay she might become monotonous, if you saw her day by day."

"She is certainly one of those people who are always themselves," said Clemence.

"And that is not always such a compliment as it sounds," said Miss Petticott. "Clemence has found that out."

"What did you think of the girls, Miss Petticoat?"

"Well, Sir Roderick, I found myself feeling rather sorry for them. Nice, good-looking, well-cared for girls, but somehow with some lack about them. The lack that comes from a life lived too much on one line. Little conventions have too much meaning; little things loom too large. After all, the difference between their clothes and Clemence's does not argue any difference in the soul within. I do not care to see young girls too conventionally dressed, myself. Of course, the lack can be put right, but it is hardly the object of education to create hiatuses to be filled later. It should be a preparation for life, not an interlude before it begins."

"I thought Clemence was a favourite of Miss Chancellor's," said Maria.

"Well, perhaps I was. And I think Gwendolen was too."

"I have the same favourites," said Sir Roderick, "though I should not have expected it. That was a nice little girl, quite untouched by all that Miss Petticoat said."

"She has been at school for years," said Clemence. "It must have done its worst for her."

"Or done its best," said Maria. "We must be fair."

"I don't think it does anything for her. She does not seem to take any notice of it."

"That is the explanation," said Roderick. "She keeps herself apart. The others are sunk in the slough up to the neck. Miss Petticoat is right."

"Really, Sir Roderick, your powers of observation! We shall be afraid to meet you."

"We are all sunk in a slough of some kind," said Maria.

"No, no, my pretty, you are not fair to yourself. Things are not as bad as that. We all do some little things—have something on the debit side."

"Clemence is in spirits," said Maria, looking at her daughter. "Is it the result of a day with her friends?"

"A sense of duty well done, Lady Shelley," said Miss Petticott.

"Which is it, Clemence?"

"Well, I am glad it was all a success. But I don't think I want it again just yet."

"I should hope not, as it has to happen in the term," said Miss Petticott.

"You do not wish you were back at school?" said Maria.

"I don't think it is a good thing to live in two places," said Clemence, with a note of truth. "And, of course, you must have your home."

"You would not like to have the best of both worlds?"

"I don't think you do have it. You can't have the best of home in a few months. And the long terms do not seem the best of school. They are the worst of it."

Sir Roderick and Miss Petticott laughed.

"You would never find another term so long," said Maria.

"Do not confuse their minds, Maria. They are quite clear. Come and befog your own with your charity accounts. It will not rest while they are on it."

"Can I be of any help, Lady Shelley?"

"Well, if it were not at the end of a long day, Miss Petticott, and you were not tired out and only fit for bed ——" Maria hesitated to ignore these circumstances.

"A fig Miss Petticoat cares for any of that," said Sir Roderick, prepared to support the disregard.

"Tired out and fit for fiddlesticks, Lady Shelley! I have had a day of pleasure. It is you who have had the duties, you and poor Clemence here. Those accounts have been on my mind. I have had a sense that they were accumulating."

"You will soon have evidence of it," said Sir Roderick. "The library table is like a haystack, except that it has no shape."

"Well, it will not be so for long, Sir Roderick," said Miss Petticott, leading the way from the room with a firm step.

Sefton looked at his sister, as the door closed.

"We never seem to be alone until the end of the day. We always talk about things when we are tired. But I think we know about them."

"It may be the best time to see them. It is no good for the morning to bring fresh hope. There is not enough reason for it."

"You said we could not live in two places, and that seems to be the whole thing. Places do not understand each other."

"And some places could never be understood. Homes are one of them. To think there are thousands of them, all over the world! The girls did not understand this one, even when they saw it. And I don't suppose the boys did either."

"We did not really want them to. It is somehow a thing we could not bear. And yet there is not anything really to be ashamed of."

"There are things they would be ashamed of; and that would make us ashamed. Little things that do not matter, but that they would think mattered. You can't help seeing them with their eyes. And they all seem to see them with the same ones."

"And then we are ashamed of being ashamed. We should not like Father and Mother to know."

"It is really the people at school we are ashamed of, or should be, if we cared for them enough. I don't think people can often make friendships at school that last for their lives. The friendships would end when school ended.

It would be as it was with us today. And people are not often with people they knew at school. They are with people they have known later, and that is what you would expect."

"I think I could have a friendship with Bacon, if we knew each other better. I don't think that would end."

"That may be partly what it is. We did not have time to get far. But I don't think the friendships would go on, even if they were real at the time."

"But they would do for the time. And that is what matters then. It is a pity we went to school, if we were not going to stay. It would have been better not to know about it."

"Of course it is a pity. No one is in any doubt. Now we think Mother is odd and shabby; and Father is simple; and Miss Petticott is on the level of the matrons; and none of them is different from what they were. And they see us as children who would get things by cheating, if they could. They do not think of us in the same way. And that is hardly an enrichment of our family life."

Sefton laughed and his sister continued.

"And we think Aldom is an awkward little manservant, and should be ashamed of his acting before the schools, though we used to be proud of it. We know he wanted to act today, and let him be disappointed. The girls would laugh at his village ideas. They laugh at so much and are ashamed of so much, and yet they are not so much in themselves; they do not even know so very much. It is only that they know it in a way that makes it count."

"The boys are not as bad as they are."

"Those boys are too young. Older boys would not be different. You will find it when you go to a larger school."

"But that will not be for years."

"No, for years things will be the same. And there are three hundred and sixty-five days in every year. We shall get used to Miss Petticott; we are getting used to her now. We shall stop being surprised at her ordinariness, and go

307

back to trying less, and that will have its bright side. The schools will get further behind, and be just a thing to be remembered. We shall not even talk about them, as no one will know what we mean. I hardly think the people from them will come here again. Mother did not suggest it, though I could see it came into her mind. She will not say what may not be the truth. And it is no use to know people whom you are not to go on knowing. It is only feeling ashamed, and then having to be grateful; and the two things do not fit, and neither is any good——" Clemence started as the door opened, but relaxed on perceiving Oliver.

"I have come to ask how you are, after what you have been through. It seemed heartless to let you go to bed without a word of human kindness. The same blood flows in our veins."

"We are just as usual. Perhaps we are rather tired."

"You have a brave heart, Clemence."

"Why should there be anything wrong with us?"

"Things might have been too much for you. Something might have snapped."

Clemence and Sefton smiled.

"You will find what is graven on your hearts. You will never face a greater demand. You have never faced one as great."

The children raised their eyes.

"Except on the day of your exposure. I was speaking of the normal range of life. And that had the advantage of not being regarded as a festive occasion."

"It had no others," said Clemence.

"Did the girls admire you for having me for a brother?"

"Yes, I think they did. You are different from most brothers."

"The boys did not seem to," said Sefton. "You had been a master at their school. They don't admire anyone who is that."

"The girls thought it was a joke," said Clemence.

"Didn't you tell them it was?" said Sefton.

"It was a wise and brave word," said Oliver. "Did they think Maria's dress was a joke, or did they know it was worn in earnest?"

"It was the one she wore on the day she took me to school."

"Further words would add nothing. But yours was not the same?"

"Yes," said Clemence, almost smiling. "And it had been altered."

"And we wonder if you ought to return! Things had to happen to prevent it."

"Well, they happened," said Clemence. "And the same dress might be packed. It would be."

"So we stop at nothing," said Oliver. "And you could only do the same."

"Are other people as ashamed as we are?" said Sefton.

"If they wear the same clothes, and if their mothers wear the same ones, and order economical households. Those are grounds for shame."

"I suppose it is really false shame."

"That is what it is called. It is shame in its strongest form."

"The economy did not show much today," said Clemence.

"No, Maria is hospitable. But she has not the right kind of pride, not the kind that is really the wrong kind. We could never rely on her. We can only hide our heads at home. Homes cause the shame, but they also provide a hiding-place for it, and we have to take one thing with another."

"You would hardly think homes would be so fair," said Clemence.

"No, we see the claim they have on us. And anyhow they impose it. You see life whole, Clemence. I leave you with a heavy heart, but with an easy mind."

"I suppose the same words would apply to us," said his sister, as the door closed.

"Well, anyhow, we have nothing to dread now," said Sefton. "Everything seems to be over."

"That is what it is. There is nothing left. Nothing good, nothing bad, nothing to dread, nothing to hope for. Nothing."

"Really, Clemence, that is a needlessly negative view to take of life," said Miss Chancellor's voice at the door. "I think you might manage to be a little more on the positive side."

"Oh, we still have Aldom!" said Sefton. "He will always be here. He almost seems to be given back to us."

"He heard the talk downstairs. He knows as much as we do now. He may soon know more. Things in his mind seem to grow."

Maria and Miss Petticott, coming upstairs, heard sounds of laughter and paused.

"What is it?" said Maria.

"Relief, Lady Shelley. Relief that the aftermath of school is over, and home life stretches before them in happiness and peace. That is what it is."